Policy-Making for Education Reform in Developing Countries

Contexts and Processes, Volume 1

James H. Williams
William K. Cummings

SCARECROWEDUCATION
Lanham, Maryland • Toronto • Oxford
2005

Published in the United States of America
by ScarecrowEducation
An imprint of The Rowman & Littlefield Publishing Group, Inc.
4501 Forbes Boulevard, Suite 200, Lanham, Maryland 20706
www.scaroweducation.com

PO Box 317
Oxford
OX2 9RU, UK

British Library Cataloguing in Publication Information Available

Library of Congress Cataloging-in-Publication Data

Williams, James H. (James Howard), 1952–
    Policy-making for education reform in developing countries : contexts
and processes / James H. Williams, William K. Cummings.
       v.   cm.
    Includes bibliographical references and index.
    ISBN 1-57886-201-9 (pbk. : alk. paper)
    1. Education—Developing countries.   2. Educational change—
Developing countries.   I. Cummings, William K. II. Title.
    LC2605.W54   2005
    379.172′4—dc22   2004022658

∞ ™ The paper used in this publication meets the minimum requirements of
American National Standard for Information Sciences—Permanence of Paper
for Printed Library Materials, ANSI/NISO Z39.48-1992. Manufactured in the
United States of America.

Contents

Tables and Figures

TABLES

FIGURES

Preface

This book began, like many, with the decision to write the book we wanted to use in our graduate teaching, but which we could not find in the bookstores or on Amazon.com. We wanted a book that not only taught techniques of education policy-making but was also fully aware of limitations and alternative strategies. The limitations we saw include a focus on the ministry as exclusive decision maker, on technical solutions without provision for broader participation, on context-free strategies for education reform, and on unproblematized use of appealing, but power-laden, concepts. We sought a book that viewed the processes of reform as a critical set of variables along with the contents of reform, and one that considered implementation, institutionalization, and organizational learning in the process of planning. Ideally, such a book would provide options rather than prescriptions for change, including both bottom-up and top-down strategies.

We also wanted a book that acknowledged the profound lack of knowledge and control that decision makers have over education and the reform process. As practitioners and academics, we would argue that we have a good idea of the inputs and conditions that characterize effective learning environments. What we do not know with precision is how to create those conditions on a system-wide basis. Many of us believe that training teachers to use student-centered teaching is an important strategy for improving education. But is the use of student-centered teaching sufficient to improve learning outcomes? Likely not. And if learning does not improve as a result, was the time and money spent on training teachers a waste? Surely not in the short run. But when? Our knowledge base is insufficiently developed to tell us with any certainty what package of inputs and conditions will effectively and consistently produce learning at a system level. Given this lack of knowledge, it behooves us to adopt, in our teaching and our text, a stance of learning as opposed to knowing. And so we wanted a book that faithfully represents both what is known and not known, so that we might focus research on what needs to be learned.

We also sought a book organized around the truism that policy makers, even with perfect knowledge, cannot achieve reform on their own. A ministry can provide necessary inputs, for example, and can establish incentives and support for effective teaching, but its reach into the classroom is limited. It can lead the horse to water, as the saying goes, but cannot make it drink. Actors outside the central ministry, teachers, and school directors in particular must be enabled to act professionally, a process that requires cooperation and professional engagement on the part of teachers and is hindered by coercion, undue centralization, and the wrong kind of planning. Yet while planners would be well advised not to assume the engagement of teachers, they can investigate the perspectives of teachers toward particular initiatives and anticipate likely reactions, or involve them in planning.

We began to see the change process much like curriculum change. Policies and plans *developed through formal planning processes* are somewhat akin to the "intended curriculum." The policies and plans *as understood and put into practice by local educators* correspond to the "implemented curriculum." The policies and plans *as actually institutionalized in local and national education systems* (as well as the capacity to identify and respond to ongoing system needs) correspond to the "acquired curriculum." This capacity might be understood as a system's aptitude. A system's aptitude is dependent on technical capacity, leadership, sufficient resources, favorable political and organizational environments, and a certain amount of social capital. A system needs people who want to do good things, and requires conditions that encourage and support them in doing those good things well. The task of reform is to improve both the quality of institutionalized policies and plans and the capacity of the system to develop, implement, and institutionalize appropriate policies and plans on an ongoing basis. Such a mission, of course, represents a substantially enlarged charge, an order of magnitude greater than the development, implementation, and evaluation of single policies.

Doing so requires attention to the processes of change, their underlying theories, and the contexts in which change is to be implemented and institutionalized, as well as the content of reform. Just as improving learning achievement requires influencing the acquired as well as implemented and intended curricula, effective policies require understanding the system well enough to improve not just the intended reform, but also to influence implemented and institutionalized reforms. Reform can be understood as a systemic learning process. And learning always takes place by particular people in relationships in a particular context. All implementation, to borrow a turn of phrase, is local. And so we need a book that recognizes individuals, relationships, context, and institutions.

A word about terminology. We use the word *policy* broadly, to refer to intentional efforts on the part of education authorities, and other education actors, to improve education systems. Policy includes a normative dimension—a vision of what the system should be like, or at least how the system can be better in some way. Policy also includes a positive dimension, that is, a dimension informed by evidence. This book is organized around conventional stages of the policy formation and implementation process. We agree with Haddad et al. that good policies should be judged on the basis of desirability, affordability, and feasibility. We feel, however, that policy-making for reform must do more than formulate good policies. Policy-making must both anticipate implementation and work toward institutionalization of good practice. The entire process of policy-making we identify as reform, the process of working toward institutionalization of good policy—establishment of appropriate process, diagnosis of problems, policy formulation, implementation, monitoring, evaluation, and organizational learning. However, because education ministries and their policies play an important, albeit not determinative, role, it is impossible, in our view, to plan reform. Though, one can, and would, we hope, plan *for* reform.

Thus we return to individuals, relationships, and institutions. The book is intended to help individuals learn to build stronger policy-making institutions. While intended for instructional use, the book does not take a prescriptive how-to-make-policy approach. Instead it seeks to deepen policy makers' awareness of options and approaches they may wish to undertake in their particular contexts.

Introduction: Orienting Concepts

We walk a fine line between optimism and pessimism. As optimists, we are ever hopeful that new policies will improve education systems. As pessimists, we see the failure of many of the poorest systems even to maintain advances of the past. On the positive side, more children are participating in formal schooling than ever before. On the negative side though, in over half of the countries of the developing world, public resources for the support of education have declined as a proportion of gross national product (GNP) and national budgets, threatening to undermine quality and to reverse earlier advances in promoting access. A substantial number of countries in the world are not on target to reach the Education for All (EFA) goals set at Dakar in 2000.

The relative fate of education systems is often portrayed as unpredictable and even tragic, a function of the carnivorous global economy or unfortunate developments in national politics. Certainly, globalization and the economic dependence of poor nations complicate, perhaps even prevent, development in some contexts. Nonetheless, over the past decades, a number of countries have withstood the odds and significantly improved their education systems. In contrast, another, somewhat larger group of countries have witnessed, for various reasons, a corresponding decline.

We argue that education reform is best fostered by an approach that locates good policy in a larger process:

Reform = Context + Process + Policy & Planning + Implementation + Evaluation + Institutionalization & Organizational Learning

This chapter clarifies the argument by defining these components and illustrating their importance. The chapters in part I of the book provide background, discussing the contexts of reform and aspects of process. Part II reviews practical tools and options for translating these components into a reform program. This part is organized according to conventional stages of policy formation, implementation, and evaluation, even as we point out the limitations of a "hard stages" model.

CONTEXT FOR REFORM

At the outset, it is useful to touch on some of the trends affecting our understanding of the policy-making and reform processes. While not necessarily desirable, inevitable, or even true in all countries, these trends nonetheless provide a backdrop against which current strategies for education reform are considered.

Increased Salience of the Global Economy

A globalizing economy means an increasing interrelatedness among local, national, and international economies. Some individuals, groups, and nations are able to take advantage of the new opportunities and grow rich. Others become more dependent on economic forces and decisions beyond their control. Technological developments hasten the process of globalization by increasing the potential interconnectedness of local peoples with others around the globe. As a partial result, there is a weakening of the primacy of the state. For better or for worse, the state finds more difficulty playing a significant role in decisions affecting its people, as well as controlling information to present its vision as the only one. At the same time, many of the decisions affecting citizens are beyond the control of the state or the people affected. With the failure of the centrally planned economies, there is a waning belief in the efficacy of planning and a correspondingly greater use of market mechanisms. The gap grows wider between the wealthy and the poor. Decades of development have not delivered many countries from poverty. Liberal/neoliberal policies are ascendant.

Increased Civil Conflict

Competition between superpowers during the Cold War overshadowed much of the world's local conflict. With the end of the Cold War, however, the 1990s have seen a tremendous increase in civil conflict. Of 108 violent outbreaks between 1989 and 1998, 92 were conducted intrastate, that is, civil war (Colletta & Cullen, 2000). More than interstate warfare, civil conflict particularly affects civilians, often children. It displaces populations, who because of the internal nature of the conflict do not have recourse to the normal protections afforded refugees. Increasing numbers of children and youth are, in some parts of the world, involved in conflict, either as victims and/or as combatants or support. Civil conflict harms education at many levels, from community and school to system. Unlike interstate wars, civil conflict reduces social cohesion and weakens society's capacities to care for its members and its resilience.

Increasing Human Development

At the same time, human development has made remarkable strides forward. Among the great accomplishments of the latter twentieth century are advances in global health, mass education of the world's children, global movements toward self-determination and human rights (however fitfully), and advances in information technology. Despite setbacks with HIV/AIDS and other infectious diseases, such as malaria, the twentieth century saw substantial increases in life expectancy. Many diseases can now be prevented or cured. Fewer children die in infancy than ever before. Population growth rates are stabilizing in most countries.

In 1945, approximately two of five children in the world enrolled in primary school as compared with four out of five children in 2000 (Benavot & Riddle, 1988). Education has shifted from a training ground for the elite, and an expensive consumption item for the rest of the population, to a universal right and primary obligation of government. School enrollment has become the norm. Children who do not attend school are disadvantaged. Nations commit themselves, and international funding organizations allocate funds to Education for All. Education is viewed as a precondition for economic growth. As such, education has assumed a greater role than before as national investment and as a critical component of development strategy. At the same time, the "necessary but not sufficient" role of education provision in social and economic development is recognized.

Advances in information technology have eliminated many of the strictly geographical barriers to information and to participation in the global economy, opportunities for some and marginalization for others. Though often observed in the breach, self-determination is now recognized as a right of all human beings. More people than ever before have a voice in choosing the government under which they live.

Awareness of the Strength of Tradition

In the context of change, some things persist. Educational improvement has a long history. There have been many cries over the past several centuries to launch bold new initiatives and to discard the bad practices of the past. Among the most dramatic, the Russian Revolution replaced the tsar with a new Soviet government. Soon thereafter the Soviets launched a new Unified School, which rejected the hierarchy and religious beliefs of Tsarist Russia while drawing extensively from the pedagogical principles of the Tsarist period. Similarly the French Revolution proposed a new system of schools yet staffed these new schools with teachers from the old system.

The early modern period resulted, we feel, in six distinctive education models—German, French, English, American, Japanese, and Russian—that have had a profound influence around the world. Institutionalized into the "culture" of education systems, these models continue to play a formative role in shaping the direction of change in many contexts. Four of the six historical models were relatively centralized, and thus the centralized approach became widespread as new education systems were established. The American, Russian, and Japanese models have placed the greatest emphasis on basic education and the inclusion of all young people in schools. However, the more elitist French and English models were most highly diffused throughout the British and French colonial empires. Thus in most parts of the world, the education tradition is not particularly favorable to improving basic education for all. Only in the areas where the American, Japanese, and Russian models are prevalent have predispositions toward basic education been stronger.

The implications for education reform? National systems of education differ in important, somewhat understandable, ways. Education systems are not blank slates, but institutions. Reform involves institutional change as well as changes in policy. History and context are critically germane to the policy process.

Shift from the State as Sole Actor in Formal Education to Multiple Stakeholders

Formal education has always been a signature project of the nation-state, one of its primary instruments and responsibilities. Traditionally the state has assumed a primacy of authority over education within its borders. And while it is arguably true that many states may never have had the management and resources capacity commensurate with their authority, the assumption in planning and policy has been the primary, perhaps exclusive, authority of the state.

But with globalization and many states' failures to provide sufficient education, other organizations, both large and small, are increasingly claiming a stake in education and policy. As a result, more education systems share responsibility for the provision and policies of education—explicitly or implicitly and more or less willingly—with parents and communities, with nongovernmental organizations (NGOs) in local communities and larger national communities, as well as with international and intergovernmental organizations. Many education decisions are made or influenced by actors outside government, such as international funding organizations and NGOs.

Globalization has also limited the role of government in decisions external to the education system but which affect education, such as the economy. For better or worse, government is no longer (and maybe never was) the sole decision maker. Therefore the role of government in planning has shifted to a less directive, more negotiated and facilitative nature. This requires partnership on the part of government, often with organizations previously not involved in education, such as NGOs, international business, intergovernmental organizations, parents, community organizations, etc.

Effective partnership, we argue, involves appropriate and periodic rebalancing of responsibilities among partners—what governments do, what they allow others to do, and what they guide through regulation or negotiation. The particulars will vary from context to context. In some contexts, rebalancing of responsibilities may mean allowing other organizations to assist in the provision of education, while providing appropriate regulation and guidance. In other contexts, rebalancing may mean, for example, developing in-country technical expertise while assuming a more proactive and directive role in negotiating with multilateral lending agencies so that sectoral reform packages correspond more closely to national objectives.

Still, to the extent that government has legitimacy and a greater accountability to the larger national public good than either international or community organizations, we argue the state has a unique role in upholding the national interest. The nation-state retains responsibility for education, a responsibility that has increased according to the rise of rights-based claims to basic education. Among institutions, government alone has the authority and the resources to support systems of education. Therefore, the responsibilities of government, while shifting and often explicitly shared, remain critical.

Shift from a Preoccupation with Supply to a Greater Responsiveness to Demand

During the time when governments quickly moved to build formal schools and provide "education for all," the emphasis was naturally on access. Understandably, planning focused heavily on the supply of inputs, a task relatively well suited to central government. But over time, a gradual, but profound, change began to occur, and governments' preoccupation with supply shifted subtly to a greater responsiveness to demand. Governments began to realize the limitations of central provision. Budgetary constraints forced greater reliance on local resources to supplement what the government was unable to provide. Effective implementation of government policies often required more than compliance on the part of local education officials. Achieving government objectives required cooperation, even active engagement on the part of parents, all of which entailed increased responsiveness on the part of government to the demand side of education. This shift has manifested itself in a variety of ways, discussed as follows.

Increasing Concern with the Quality of Education

In many countries, rapid expansion of access resulted in large school systems of low quality. In many cases, school facilities were seen as poor quality, teachers were ill-prepared, and learning materials became outdated or insufficient in number. High proportions of children enrolled in school, but completion rates were low. It became clear that provision of schools was insufficient to ensure adequacy of education. In response, planners and policy makers began to call for a greater emphasis on quality.

Higher quality suggests that more attention be paid to the value or the worth of education provided. However, Adams (1993) and others have pointed out that quality can be defined in different ways, such as in terms of selectivity, reputation, inputs and resources, processes, or outcomes. In all cases the calls for higher quality reveal a perception that schools are not measuring up.

Attention to quality often focuses attention on schools' utilization of inputs, instructional processes, practices, and personnel. A focus on quality tends to focus attention on the outcomes of education, and, by implication, the measurement of outcomes. When measurements of learning outcomes reveal that children are not learning at expected levels, concern for quality leads to questions of accountability. Until recently, few nations, neither advanced nor poor, systematically ascertained if their children were actually learning the desired curriculum.[1] Often the first look is shocking, with many fewer children acquiring the intended curriculum than expected. Thus, a growing concern with the outcomes of education has led nations to reassess their approach to education planning and provision. The implications for education planning and policy are that reformers must think beyond the provision of inputs to the processes and outcomes of education: difficult aspects to quantify or to manage from the center.

Shift from a Top-Down, Command and Control Model of Management toward More Collaborative Models of School-Focused Instructional Support

Corresponding to the move from government as sole force and provider of education to government as one (leading) stakeholder of many, there is a shift to more collaborative roles—of government guiding rather than ordering, coordinating rather than providing, and influencing rather than controlling.

Similarly, management of an education system that is working to improve quality, responding to demand, or reaching marginal children requires a different approach than a system aimed primarily at the supply of inputs. Improving quality is likely to require attention to teachers and their behavior, both of which are far from the center and difficult to manage by central fiat. There must be both adequate levels of inputs available, and the teachers must make effective use of these inputs. This involves teacher engagement and professional judgment, neither of which can easily be compelled.

Similarly, marginal children typically require special programs to be enrolled, retained, and educated successfully. Often, these programs are best provided by organizations outside, but closely linked to, the school. The implications for planning and policy are that education ministries need to learn more collaborative modes of operation, more sensitivity, and a greater ability to respond to demand. However, ministries of education and education planners are often unpracticed in responding to demand.

The need is to shift from a dictating mode to a learning mode. At the same time, ministries, bearing the national responsibility for education of all, need to maintain an appropriate balance between coordination/oversight and initiative-stifling control. The focus shifts from school officials' compliance with central directives to a focus on the professional judgments of school leaders, informed and supported by higher-level offices and officials. In a less centrally driven, demand-focused system, top-down approaches to control are shifting to multidirectional change initiatives. Ideally, the entire system works to support the school-level delivery of service. Needs are communicated from the "bottom up," while the "top" and others stakeholders respond by providing resources and technical support.

All of which is easy to say, but difficult to carry out. This book is an initial attempt to locate top-down and bottom-up approaches to policy-making along a continuum of planning and policy options.

Increased Role of Market Mechanisms

Increased demand for education, fixed or declining treasuries, and adoption of neoliberal finance policies have led to increased reliance on market mechanisms in education. These market mechanisms may range from user fees to various forms of community finance, vouchers, private schooling, other "demand-side financing" measures (see Patrinos & Ariasingam, 1997). Market mechanisms serve to reduce the control of the state, which is seen as a positive move by those who consider the state's role problematic, and a danger by those who see the state as primarily protective. There is little systematic knowledge of the effects of different market mechanisms on formal education systems, which have been primarily state-run. In general terms, market mechanisms run the risk of increasing inequalities while increasing the options and vitality of segments of the system able to capitalize on new opportunities. However, these effects appear to vary greatly, depending on the particulars, the context, and implementation.

Blurring of Stages in the Change Process

Repeated failures to implement large ambitious plans have led to a shift from front-loaded, "blueprint" approaches to more iterative, non-linear strategies for change. Traditionally, policy-making and planning have been understood and practiced as a series of distinct stages, each with its own set of discrete actors—planners plan, then turn implementation over to implementers, after which evaluators assess the extent to which objectives were achieved. Research into the failures of implementation suggests that involvement of implementers in planning greatly enhances the chances of implementation and sustainability. And so, planners and policy-makers have begun to think in terms of more integrated approaches—implementation is considered in planning, plans are revised during implementation, and initial evaluation informs later implementation. Rather than designing the perfect blueprint at the outset, planners now work to design a planning process that can be altered as conditions change. The implications are that planning and policy-making are ongoing processes. Planners and policy makers need to remain involved in the entire process of reform. As noted, this shifts the focus of planning from provision of inputs to their utilization, outcomes, and the adoption of new practices on the part of the education system. Policy makers must concern themselves not only with formulation, inputs, intentions, and plans, but also with implementation, processes, and results, as well as the institutions and contexts in which change is to happen.

Shift from Project to Sector

Over the past decade, another major shift has taken place, in which the sector has substantially replaced the project as the focal point for reform. This shift is a result of awareness of three problems. Despite implementation of numerous education projects, many successful, national systems of education have often remained the same after decades of reform. Thus, curriculum reform, improvements in teacher training, and other initiatives, while important in themselves, have failed to improve the *system* of education. Secondly, funding organizations in many countries have supported a variety of projects, each in line with its organizational mandate but which were poorly coordinated as a whole. Thus, while individually important, the portfolios have failed as coherent programs of reform. Thirdly, education ministries have often lacked a comprehensive and self-directed strategy for sector finance and reform. Initiatives were planned and funded, but often without a strategy for improving the whole.

Sector-wide reform strategies were developed to address these issues, by promoting development of national sectoral frameworks, to coordinate and prioritize reform initiatives in the sector. As would be expected, sector-wide approaches are quite demanding in terms of their planning requirements, and they are subject to the implementation problems associated with overly front-loaded plans. Still, they provide a more coherent framework for planning than a project-driven approach. At the same time, sectoral strategies tend to concentrate reform, placing most of its "eggs in a single basket," thus centralizing decision making and increasing the stakes of failure if program theory fails to play out as expected.

Shift from Universal Technical Solutions to Context-Sensitive Strategies for Informing Social/Political Solutions with Technical Input

The trends of increasing sensitivity to demand (and markets); greater integration of planning, implementation, and evaluation; and increased participation in education decision making suggest that universal technical solutions developed out of social and political context are less likely to be successful than strategies in which a legitimate decision-making process makes use of technical information to inform political choices. Like politics, all implementation (and institutionalization) is local.

Planners and policy makers are aware of the distinction between questions that are technical in nature and those that are not. Some questions can be answered with technical information, while answers to other questions depend on values and preferences, although the trade-offs associated with different choices can often be informed by technical data. Planners and policy makers work in both technical and non-technical arenas. There are two basic strategies for dealing with such decisions. One approach is to separate the two domains, conducting the least politically influenced technical analysis possible, and then working to implement that solution with as little political interference as possible. But this approach is possible only if there is agreement on the basic goals of the initiative. Agreement can be achieved through a legitimate political process, or, less democratically, by marginalizing those with incompatible goals. Alternately a second strategy for decision making is to design a process that is recognized as legitimate, incorporates mechanisms for different groups to express their interests and preferences, and informs stakeholders of the likely implications of different courses of action using technical analysis. Decisions made using the second strategy, while more difficult to reach, are, we would argue, more likely to be implemented and sustained.

Increasing Awareness and Concern for Marginal Children

Pressures to enroll all children, coupled perhaps with a greater emphasis of demand on the part of governments and international

agencies, have led to increased awareness of the numbers and the difficulties of educating children who are, in one way or another, marginal.
The heightened concern for children on the margin can be seen in the
attention given to them in the 2000 Education for All initiatives.
Depending on local conditions, such children might include girls, linguistic or ethnic "minorities," the poor, rural children, children from
indigenous communities, the disabled, displaced and refugee children,
children affected by and participating in conflict, working children,
dropouts, sex workers, children who have been abused or trafficked,
AIDS orphans, children with AIDS, the malnourished, and so forth.
Marginal children are more difficult to enroll and retain, and often need
additional psychosocial, academic, and economic support. They may
lack the family and community supports available to mainstream children. Standard education provision strategies tend to be much less
effective with marginal children. The implication for education planning and policy is that a single model of education provision is unlikely
to be effective in reaching all children. Alternative models need to be
developed, including the provision of services and support unfamiliar
to many educators. Education systems tend to be rather brittle, and not
adept at outreach.

Increasing Emphasis on Access to Secondary School and Youth

A final trend to highlight is the increased emphasis on secondary
education and on youth. As greater proportions of children complete
primary school, questions of access shift toward secondary school, for
example, how can more children be educated through secondary school
affordably? While failure to educate young children is socially and
economically wasteful, the consequences of uneducated youth are
potentially more serious. Uneducated youth are more likely to have offspring for which they are unable to care, to be unemployed and economically unproductive, and to contribute to political and social unrest and
conflict. Addressing the full range of youth needs, however, remains
complex, requires policies and programs to extend beyond the purview
of education ministries and involve coordination across government

bodies, service organizations, employers, and schools. Meeting those needs represents one of the important challenges of the next decades.

A CHANGED CONTEXT FOR PLANNING FOR REFORM

In earlier periods, when virtually all education decisions were made at the national "center," a variety of techniques were developed to assist elite decision makers in formulating their national strategic policies and plans. But the general disrepute befalling central planning has challenged the utility of such techniques, and has increased local and international entities' involvement in decision making about national school systems.

Planning, though widely heralded in the first decades of international development, has come, in recent years, onto hard times. The apparent failure of central economic planning and the rise of market-oriented development strategies have raised questions about the value of central planning. Moreover, central governments, in large part to compensate for the shortage of public resources, have partnered with local community groups in the provision of education. As local groups have become involved in education, they have sought a voice in education decisions. Whereas education was once thought to be uniformly conceived, planned, and provided by a central government office, today's schools are increasingly anchored in their local settings, with each local community playing a role in deciding some aspects of the school's program. Moreover, as noted, globalization; the increasing profile of education in Education for All, the Millennium Development Goals; the interest of international organizations in education policy and provision; and the involvement of large international NGOs in education have resulted in increasing international involvement in decisions about national education systems.

It is clear that few, if any, central governments can assume the entire burden of education. Increased local and international participation in the finance and management of education is a fact in most systems. Increased local involvement in schools has led critics from "bottom-up" perspectives to urge abandonment of dated central planning techniques in favor of a myriad of unique local initiatives. The trend toward local and school-based management is an important one, we would argue, with significant potential for improving schools. However, the expanded participation of local and international groups, increases, rather than decreases, the importance of policy-making and planning. Local groups must articulate policies and plans to defend their proposals before their communities, to secure additional support from new benefactors such as religious groups and NGOs, and to coordinate their activities with government. Government needs to play, at minimum, a coordinating and legalizing role, ensuring equity and the use of education to meet the public good.

We suggest the best outcomes in education will result from a context-appropriate utilization of both bottom-up and top-down approaches—with each stakeholder in the overall system making a distinctive contribution. In the absence of clear methods for achieving such a balance, we offer a series of approaches and options, to initiate the learning process.

What Do We Mean by Policy, Planning, and Reform?

Policy Definition

A number of definitions of policy have been proposed. Haddad and Demsky (1994) provide a functional definition:

> an explicit or implicit single decision or group of decisions that may set out directives for guiding future decisions, initiate or retard action, or guide implementation of previous decisions. (p. 4)

A simpler and more straightforward definition would be as follows:

> a formal declaration of the way a system should operate, often accompanied by a timetable for implementation and a statement on financial backing.

In a formal sense, organizations seek to clarify their overall objectives and operational procedures with broad statements that usually are referred to as policy statements. Formal policy statements may have been developed over an extended period of time, based on careful

review by top leaders from both the operational and political or fidu-
ciary components of the organizations. In the case of governments, policy statements are typically promulgated by the executive office having
overall responsibility for the government and/or by the ministerial
offices responsible for the respective sectors. Government policies may
or may not be approved by the legislative body (Parliament, Diet, Congress) depending on the nature of the governmental structure and the
importance of the model. Similarly, in the formulation of policy, governments vary in the extent to which they seek inputs from the stakeholders likely to be affected by policy.

In effect though, policy operates less formally. We use *policy* to refer
both to formal statements and to the implicit or explicit decisions on
how a system should operate. Policy representing the common and
unquestioned assumptions of a group of people may never be formally
articulated into a policy statement. Policy may appear in a variety of
formats, such as formal policy statements, budgets, memoranda, and
speeches. Moreover, policy need not originate only from the leadership. Those implementing a policy, for example, may play an informal
but important policy-making role in they way they interpret and implement policies, as suggested by the term *street-level bureaucrat* (see
Lipsky, 1980).

Finally, policy-making can be understood in two ways. In the first,
and more common approach, policy-making seeks to bring about
change within the context of existing organizations and power relations. This need not be the case. Policy may make current political
arrangements the focus of change. (See discussion of organizational
versus political model, below.) In all cases, however, policy represents
the normative expression of a group of people, while reform refers to a
systemic change in policy.

Policy Scope

Policies vary along a number of dimensions. One useful dimension
is the *breadth* of policy scope. Some policies are limited to very specific issues, such as the working hours of a bureau or the number of
days of leave allowed. Others have much broader implications, for
example, a curriculum revision or reform of secondary education. Pol-

icy may cover an entire sector, as with a national education and training policy. Finally, a policy may work across sectors, including, but not limited to education, for example, a workforce or economic development policy. The breadth of policy scope might thus be described at one of four levels:

1. specific aspect or issue in system—for example, daily hours of instruction, posting of teachers
2. subsystem—for example, curriculum revision, primary education
3. system or sector—for example, education and training policy
4. multiple sectors—for example, workforce development

Policy scope may also vary in terms of *depth*, or in the kinds of change it seeks to promote. Larry Cuban (1988) distinguishes between first-order changes, or improvements in the effectiveness or efficiency in achieving existing objectives and goals, and second-order changes, which alter the fundamentals, the "goals, structures, and roles" of schools, or education systems (p. 342). First-order changes target more superficial aspects of the school system tending not to address the organization or the core goals of the system. Achieving many of the goals of education, however, requires deeper changes to the structure and culture of the education system. Thus, for example, when reformers talk of the need to improve not only the policies and practices of the education system, but to develop the capacity of the education system to make and implement good policy, they are talking of second-order change. In similar ways, Fullan (1999) writes of "deep change," or changes in the way organizations and systems operate. Deep change usually entails cognitive, affective, and behavioral dimensions of the people in an organization—attitudes, perceptions, behaviors, relationships, and the way people collaborate—in order to change the "culture" of the organization.

It may be helpful to visualize these ideas in the context of a model of education systems developed by Lockheed and Verspoor (1991) (see Figure I.1).

In general, the more specific, narrower, and shallower a policy is, the easier it will be to implement, but the less the chance it will have of bringing about deep and permanent reform. The broader and more gen-

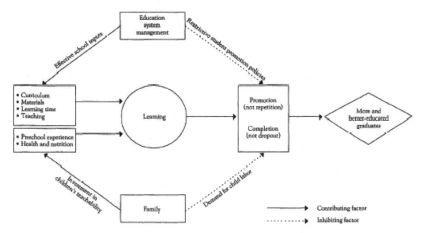

Figure I.1   *Lockheed and Verspoor's Model of Education Systems*

eral a policy is in scope, the greater the chances of deep reform, but the more difficult to implement.

Dimensions of Policy-Making

Haddad and Demsky (1994) differentiate major approaches to policy-making along two dimensions: decision makers and process. These dimensions apply to policy decision making at all levels of a society, from the policies decided by local school boards to those promoted by central governments.

Decision Makers: Organizational versus Political Models

The first dimension focuses on the locus of decision making. In an organizational approach, the decision emanates from a process of orderly review in which various units of a large organization and invited stakeholders participate. Thus the final decision reflects the consensus emerging from consultation with the various units. Such a model is almost invariably top-down, though it would be theoretically possible for an education system to develop an orderly bottom-up review process.

In contrast, a more political model exhibits how key political figures representing societal-based constituencies are also the key decision makers, and have their own political interests in mind as they negotiate policy decisions. In the extreme case of the political model, a particular politician may have sufficient clout to insist that the decision narrowly reflect his/her preferences. Political models could also incorporate bottom-up initiatives, assuming those on the bottom had political clout. Somewhat similarly, political models could also include those who seek to change the existing power relationships among decision makers and stakeholders in education.

Process: Synoptic versus Incremental Models

Another critical process distinction is between grand, inclusive, or *synoptic* approaches to policy, and *incremental* strategies developed step by step. The synoptic approach characterizes centralized societies with strong planning agencies that work to develop and implement long-term plans. Incremental policy-making is more characteristic of highly participatory societies with dynamic political and economic environments. The synoptic approach assumes a relatively high capacity to collect knowledge and predict the future, a broad agreement on the criteria for policy decisions, and a commitment by policy makers to maintain support for particular policy decisions over an extended period of time. In contrast though, the incremental model permits imperfect knowledge, uncertain criteria, and a disposition to adjusting decisions according to the circumstances. The incremental approach would seem more favorable to bottom-up initiative, but a synoptic approach could resolve local resistance to bottom-up participation, such as in the 1960s with the federal government's role in desegregating schools in Southern states.

A Consolidated Model

Assuming these two dimensions capture important differences in approaches to policy-making, a *consolidated* model depicts the combination of both approaches in Figure I.2. Particular patterns can be located at different points in the figure. More despotic authoritarian

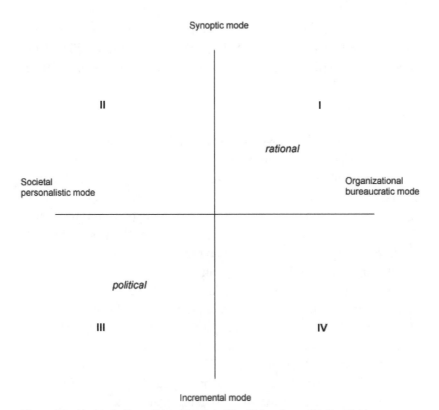

Figure I.2   *Haddad's Consolidated Model of the Dimensions of Policy-Making*

patterns would be located in quadrant II, whereas more democratic approaches shaped by the guidance of strong bureaucracies (such as possibly Japan or Chile) would be located in quadrant IV. Highly centralized and disciplined patterns (such as in Singapore) would be located in quadrant I, and yet others (certain local governments in the United States) would be located in quadrant III.

The ways in which different education societies make policy decisions tend to endure over long periods of time, because the politics of education decision making are deeply rooted in local political culture and traditions. This topic is elaborated in more detail in chapter 2. A clear understanding of the nature of a system's approach to policy-making provides important insights into the types of policies that will be possible (comprehensive in scope or incremental), the particular criteria that will be important in policy-making, and the likelihood that policy makers will support decisions over an extended period of time.

Planning

Education planning provides a set of rational tools and strategies for organizing the deployment of resources toward the achievement of objectives within the education system. Policy statements tend to project actions over an extended period. Some policy statements include target dates for realization of the respective components of the policy. For example, governments proposing to achieve "Education for All" are likely to specify a specific year for realizing the target of 50% enrollment, 75% enrollment, and so on.

Policies may serve simply as a kind of political support for some desirable goal, or they may include a practical plan for the realization of this goal. Multilevel government systems face complex issues in devising plans, as the various levels have their respective responsibilities for funding and administration. In such cases, the top-most level may decide to announce a policy while bypassing the funding issue. Alternately, as often occurs in the United States, the central government may offer funding incentives to local governments that actually decide to adopt the federal policy (e.g., in the area of school lunches, special education, technical training) or disincentives to local governments that fail to adhere (e.g., concerning racial and gender discrimination). To the extent a policy statement is accompanied by a forward projection of a target and an indication of the resources required to realize the target, it includes planning. More casually, we use policy to refer to the intent of change, while planning refers to the means and, particularly, the schedule and resources. Planning is useful to the extent that it leads to implementation of systemic changes, which in turn improves outcomes for beneficiaries and yields a system more capable of producing those outcomes.

Once a plan is set, a government may choose to rigorously adhere to it for the projected period; review and revise the plan periodically, as with some of the more dynamic contemporary nations (e.g., Japan, Singapore); or review and revise the plan less systematically. The ability of a government to revise its policies and plans partly depends on the extent to which the government has a well-developed system of information for reviewing its performance, and a free press and active intellectual community providing critical feedback on the policy's effectiveness.

Reform

Reform is the goal of policies aimed at *improving a system* of education. Reform suggests a change not only in what is done but in the ways things are done. Reform, we would argue, is better understood as what is implemented and sustained on the ground and the effects, intended and unintended, on intended beneficiaries and on the system, rather than only what is intended.

In recent years, the word *reform* has been used widely, almost promiscuously, to refer to almost any policy initiative. The casual use of the word *reform* runs the risk of suggesting that a great deal of change is planned or under way, when little of real substance, is changing in a system. This phenomenon can usefully be understood in terms of first- and second-order change (and perhaps a confusion of wishes and reality). Discussion in this book refers to both first- and second-order change, but we suggest the policy maker remain aware of the level type of change being enacted. Of course, organizations and their policy makers tend to espouse deeper levels of change than they are willing, or able, to enact.

Policy Makers, Planners, and Change Agents

We also use *policy maker* somewhat interchangeably with *planner* and *change agent*. All three work to improve education. Policy makers and planners are usually government officials, with policy makers working to organize and articulate intents for change, while planners flesh out concrete plans by which change will be brought about. Use of *change agent* highlights the fact that change may be promoted by individuals outside as well as inside government, with or without an official role.

DEVELOPING AN APPROACH TO REFORM

Nonformal or Nonrational Approaches

The first, and still quite common, approach to policy-making might be called a nonformal, or nonrational approach. Nonrational approaches do not use empirical evidence and analysis as the basis for policy formation, but instead rely on something else—habit, custom, or tradition (e.g., add 4% to last year's budget); politics (free primary education as a political move); informed judgment (seems like one supervisor per 20 schools is about right); external pressure (funding agency priorities); or strong belief (I believe it's the right thing to do). Nonrational approaches have characterized education policy-making from the outset. They can also be seen, more beguilingly, when data are used to justify a conclusion reached before data collection and analysis. Nonrational approaches often smooth the way for policy adoption, for they tend to address the political constraints of a particular context, either directly, by crafting policy to address the needs or interests of those with political power, or indirectly by not challenging the status quo. Such approaches may be used when problems are too complex to grasp, or when empirical evidence is lacking or inconclusive. Nonformal approaches, however, are likely to result in ineffective use of resources and failure to reach system goals. They are inefficient, lead to inequities, and are poor guides to action under conditions of rapid change. Nonrational theories-in-use might be expressed as follows:

Reform = Habit, Tradition (politics, informed
judgment, external pressure, belief)

Rational Approaches

Rational approaches to policy-making base policy decisions on empirical data and analysis (albeit not necessarily quantitative data). Rational approaches are a major advance over less formal methods in that they attempt to view and ground policy recommendations in "reality"; to systematically plan to articulate, evaluate, and achieve system goals most efficiently; and to avoid bias. Rational theories implicitly or explicitly assume:

Reform = (good technical) Policy & Planning

Much of the policy analysis literature, and many academics, takes the approach that the task of the policy maker is to develop the best technical analysis of the problem and propose solutions that best meet system goals within the constraints of finance and feasibility.

Rational approaches often organize the process of policy-making into a policy cycle, composed of a series of stages.[2] The first stage, *assessment*, analyzes the situation facing the education system and defines and ranks the problems in order of priority according to specified criteria. A comprehensive assessment is helpful in gaining a holistic grasp of the problems and context. Often, assessment is treated as a straightforward, often quantitative, description of the state of an education system: numbers enrolled and out of school, measures of internal efficiency and achievement, costs, and so forth. This approach works well when the process is not problematic, that is, when there is consensus about goals; when data are understood to be sufficient, legitimate, and accurate; and when stakeholders feel their interests are adequately represented.

When those conditions do not hold, the process becomes problematic and assessment is subject to questions: Who carries out the assessment? What are the problems facing the system? Which issues are more problematic? Who makes these decisions? What are the criteria? Whose knowledge is valued and reported? What is the process for resolving these issues?

Goal setting, the second stage, determines the direction of intended change. A full understanding of the articulated as well as unspoken goals and objectives of different members of the system is important to establish direction and priority in reform.

At the abstract level with unlimited resources, goals are easy to agree to. Who could disagree with the goal of greater access to basic education? More specifically however, when trade-offs are necessary, disagreement over goals are inevitable. Should the system continue to expand if expansion means a lowering of quality? Does equity require redress of historical inequities, even if some people are currently disadvantaged? These issues are often resolved by the couching of policy in terms of lofty goals about which there can be little controversy. In such cases, the real goals are likely revealed in the details of the plan, particularly in terms of what is and is not funded, or in the reality of what is implemented. Sometimes potential conflict is resolved by quiet adoption of the goals of the minister, policy maker, or funding agency, without broader consultation.

Education policy makers usually work toward a combination of four overarching goals—access, equity, quality, efficiency—and these are the primary goals discussed in this book. Less commonly articulated, but often quite significant, are other goals of education: economic growth; preparation of the workforce; global competitiveness and integration into the global economy; building of a national, ethnic, or in the case of socialist regimes, international identity; reproduction of the (current) social order; maintenance of the current political order.

The third general stage, *generation of policy options*, seeks to broaden the awareness of policy and decision makers to include unexamined options. In this stage, policy makers are cautioned not to make decisions, especially in favor of the first strategies that come to mind. But policy makers should brainstorm and develop a comprehensive listing of ideas and possibilities. It may be useful to explore the experience of other countries or organizations facing similar problems or to consult with the policy literature.[3] Again, questions of participation arise: Who is permitted to raise options? What process is used to generate options, and make the policy decision?

The fourth stage is the *policy decision*, whereby an option or strategy is selected from among possible options, granted resources and political approval, and the decision promulgated. Haddad and Demsky (1994) suggest that policy choices be evaluated on the basis of desirability, affordability, and feasibility. At this point, trade-offs must also be faced, which means selection of one policy option entails foregoing other options. Decisions about trade-offs are difficult, for some priorities will not be achieved and the interests of some stakeholders will not be addressed. After the decision is made, the policy decision must be operationalized, a budget, schedule, rules, and regulations of sufficient detail prepared, along with an implementation plan and a mechanism to monitor implementation.

The fifth stage is *implementation*, where the policy decision is carried out. Implementation is the stage where most policy failures take place. How often have you heard the policy makers' lament, "The plan was sound, but it wasn't implemented properly"? While policy makers are hardly responsible for the success or failure of all policy, policy makers must do their best to anticipate implementation difficulties. It is insufficient to develop a "good" plan that cannot be implemented. A good plan that was not implemented well may not have been a good plan after all.

Evaluation, the sixth and final stage, assesses the extent to which initial objectives were achieved, in effect looping back to the first stage. Evaluation may look beyond expressed objectives to assess unintended as well as intended effects. Based on results of evaluation, new options may be generated, new policy decisions taken, to address remaining or newly arising problems.

These stages, while not as sequential and discrete as suggested by the model, are a useful checklist and heuristic device for thinking about what to do next as part of a well-considered policy-making process. Skipping a stage may lead to less than full consideration, for example, of all potential options for achieving a given objective.

The problems with rational approaches are not with what they do so much as with what they fail to do. Rational approaches tend to avoid politics as biased, separating technical analysis and political process. Yet policy and reform involve both technical and political dimensions. Policy decisions reflect both informational needs and value judgments and preferences. Though value judgments and preferences cannot be ranked on technical grounds, the technical implications of different courses of action can be mapped. Policy debates often refer to larger unresolved conflicts in a society. The recommendations resulting from technical analysis must be implemented in an institutional, that is, political context. To be sustained, policy must be institutionalized in an organization.

At their most basic, rational approaches assume a single consensual goal; the task is to identify the best means to reaching that goal. In many cases, however, there is no consensus as to goal or values. The best technical means to reaching an educational goal depends on which goal one is maximizing. Technical policy makers tend to focus on the means, and not to problematize the question of multiple goal structures. However, when questions are not raised, the goals of the policy maker, her minister, or the funding agency tend to assume primacy, often in a process opaque, or cloaked in a technical rationale. And so, we would argue, rational approaches are necessary but not sufficient.

Evaluation Perspective

In a complex world of poorly understood cause and effect, and where policy makers have limited control, formation of good policy and implementation of good plans do not ensure the achievement of expected results. It is always wise to check to see if an education intervention has achieved the desired results. Often, it is wise to look more broadly, to see both expected and unanticipated consequences of intervention. In the broader context of reform, it is useful both to know if a particular intervention worked, and, more broadly, to learn more about which interventions work well, which do not, how and under which condition they are most effective. In these ways, evaluation can contribute to the body of knowledge about education reform and, if the organization can bear it, to an organization's learning. From this perspective:

$$\text{Reform} = \text{Policy \& Planning} + \textit{Evaluation}$$

As with other aspects of reform, evaluation entails both positive and normative dimensions. Evaluation, by definition, involves values, and effectiveness depends on the criteria used. Values often differ by stakeholder group. Teachers, system managers, and parents are likely to have very different perspectives, for example, on the effectiveness of a policy of linking teacher salary to performance. And so, evaluation often raises the question of *effectiveness for whom*, a question that is not easily resolved by rational approaches.

Implementation Perspective

Implementation is the graveyard of good policy. Even when there is agreement on goals, when policies are well formulated and plans well developed, policies often work out differently than anticipated. Sometimes, the deviations are innovative; often they are not. To reflect this reality, the implementation perspective suggests that good ideas and good policies are not sufficient for successful reform. Policies are rarely implemented as planned. The appropriate metaphor for education reform is less a blueprint, or a machine that operates according to the laws of physics, but something more social in nature. Warwick (1982) suggested a "transactional" framework, according to which policy represents a direction, political commitment, resources, and some basic parameters; all of which are enacted through a series of transactions among policy makers, various levels of organizational officials, field implementers, and influential local stakeholders. At each stage, the policy changes, albeit slightly. Hopefully, the policy was designed with "initial intelligence," technically sound and politically astute. The final, implemented form of a policy, however initially intelligent, depends on the results of these transactions. Policy makers cannot control the final form of policy, though they may influence it through strategic awareness of the factors likely to affect implementation, and what Warwick calls "ongoing intelligence," or appropriate responses to the changing conditions that arise during implementation.

We suggest that policy makers adopt an implementation perspective in their planning so as to anticipate and plan, to the extent possible, for likely barriers to implementation. According to the following perspective:

$$\text{Reform} = \text{Policy \& Planning} + (successful)$$
$$Implementation + \text{Evaluation}$$

At this point, we reiterate the position that systems seeking to improve learning outcomes are in particular need of an implementation perspective. Access, and equity to a lesser extent, can be improved largely with a centralized, top-down strategy of provision of resources. Local actors must receive the inputs and comply with central regulations, but relatively little professional judgment is needed. Improving learning outcomes, however, requires professionalism on the part of teachers. Even with the best curriculum and classrooms, a rare case in poor contexts, teachers must use the materials appropriately, in ways that can be learned but not prescribed, to produce learning. Of the factors Heneveld and Craig (1995) found to influence student learning (see Figure I.3), most are under the control of the teacher and cannot be mandated from the center. Thus the improvement of quality requires a

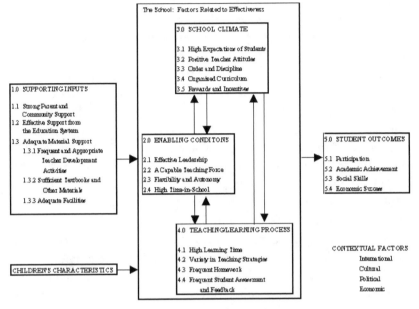

Figure I.3   *Heneveld's Model of the Classroom Learning Process*

more collaborative relationship between central ministry and schools than does a program working to increase access.

Process Orientation

As discussed earlier, many governments have chosen, or been forced by financial and logistical constraints, to seek partnerships in the management, and particularly the funding of education. Thus, in addition to a new relationship between central ministry and teachers, ministries are developing new relationships with a variety of stakeholders. These "partnerships," in addition to the organizational changes called for by efforts to improve quality, raise questions of process: How are the voices of various stakeholders to be heard? How are and can their interests be addressed, within a coherent national policy framework? How can stakeholder buy-in be assured? At the same time, how can participation be structured so that technically sound policies and plans are developed? How can policy-making and planning avoid becoming simply another forum for politics to win?

These questions suggest an explicit focus on the structuring of the policy process. They suggest the possibility of broader involvement of stakeholders than is traditional in education planning, a greater reliance on empirical analysis than is common in political debates, as well as a transparent process for managing the dialogue.[4] From this perspective, the process by which policy decisions are researched, analyzed, and made is of very high value, alongside, in importance, the content of policy analysis. Moreover, we would argue, more participatory approaches to policy are not only a good thing to do, they represent a sound empirical research strategy: Who knows the conditions there better than people closest to the desired outcomes? Participation offers the potential for better information as well as better implementation and sustainability.

There are implications at each stage of the policy cycle. A process perspective would ask who is involved in assessing the state of the system, setting goals, generating policy options, making the decision, planning and carrying out implementation, and evaluating results. A process approach would also ask how information is brought into the dialogue and how the dialogue and policy formation processes are organized to maximize participation and information, and even who interprets data.

In recent years, the widespread use of sector-wide assistance programs (SWAPs) has led to comprehensive planning exercises among government and funding agencies. These exercises have variably involved stakeholders outside of government and donor agencies. At the same time, the emphasis has typically been placed on the admittedly formidable task of developing comprehensive sector-wide policies and plans, sometimes less on broad participation in formation and implementation.

As a result, the process perspective sees reform as:

Reform = *(good) Process* + Policy & Planning +
Implementation + Evaluation

There are four dimensions to this conception of process:

- *Participation*: What stakeholders are involved and how?
- *Information*: What information is needed to make good decisions, and how can it be brought into the dialogue process?

- *Structure of dialogue*: How is dialogue structured to maximize participation and information?
- *Implementation*: How is the policy process organized to foster "ongoing intelligence?"

Context + Institutionalization + Organizational Learning

From the outset, we have argued for a contextualized understanding of policy-making and reform. Reform, we have maintained, is not only a matter of developing and enacting the right policies, but developing the system's capacity to develop and implement good policies on a continuing basis. Sustaining sound policy-making, we argue, involves attention to the macro and micro contexts of reform as well as to the institutionalization of good practice. Failure to do so is likely to lead on the one hand to one-size-fits-all solutions fitting no one well at all, and, on the other hand, to a constant need for reinvention of the wheel, as solutions fail to fit context.

Organizations are naturally resistant to profound change, and school systems, due to their loosely coupled nature, are among the most difficult to change. Thus, in addition to the influential traditions discussed in chapter 1, the micro-contexts of education as well as the macroeconomic context play an important role in what is implemented and the possibilities for change.

Institutionalization is important for the sustaining of good practice and the development of capacity. Institutionalization of good practice involves a stance of learning on the part of the education system, a willingness to allow and then correct mistakes. School systems, we argue, are experienced at teaching, but are much less adept at learning, especially ministries of education. Institutionalization requires attention to what might be called social and institutional sustainability, a complement to the emphasis on financial sustainability.

Finally, reform should (admittedly) ideally include an increased willingness and capacity on the part of an education system to learn. Reform is not simply about institutionalizing the right policy for all time, but in learning how to continue to make good policy. These issues are discussed in more detail in subsequent chapters. At this point, it is sufficient to complete the model:

Reform = *Context (macro & micro)* + Process + Policies &
Planning + Implementation + Evaluation + *Institutionalization*
+ *Organizational Learning*

CONCLUSION: CAN ONE PLAN FOR REFORM?

Externally, education planning has been used both to respond to developments in the larger society and, more ambitiously, to lead those developments. Planning was introduced after World War II as a way of speeding up the development process. Not surprisingly, the more modest the objectives, the more successful planning and policy are in achieving them. Thus, for example, it has always been easier to plan for the successful implementation of a new curriculum than for the successful provision of technical skills among the citizenry at large (in response to technological change). Even more difficult is successfully planning of education to grow the economy. While there is a general consensus that education is a facilitating, even necessary condition for economic development, it is difficult, at this time, to believe that provision of education is *sufficient* to lead directly to economic growth.

Yet despite the difficulties of planning, many of the development problems that led to the expansive and overly optimistic uses of education planning remain unsolved. The development agenda remains unfinished. In some cases, problems have even worsened over the past twenty years. Education plays an important role in their resolution, but the relationship between provision of education and development is not as simple as once hoped. Increasingly, education is understood as one of a number of essential factors in development.

Since the heyday of education planning with the emergence of independent nations in the 1960s, a great deal has been learned about how—and how not—to plan the improvement of education systems. Over time, education policy and planning—as internal strategy, as means of responding to developments in the larger society, and as strategies for directing those developments—have become more realistic in their expectations, and savvier and more strategic in their operations. So, yes, one can and should plan. Education planning and policymaking provide a set of rational tools and strategies for organizing deployment of resources toward achievement of objectives within the education system. This sort of planning seems prudent, even essential, for effective management of education systems. But one should plan and make policy humbly, with a greater regard for those interested in, affected by, and actually implementing education, all the while cultivating a greater respect for the unexpected.

The following four chapters discuss these ideas in more detail, after which we bring them to policy process, discussed in chapters 5–9.

NOTES

1. Indeed, while examinations have long been used as gateways to higher levels of education, these examinations have generally been used as selection mechanisms rather than to assess learning.

2. A number of policy specialists have devised similar schema for describing the policy cycle. Haddad and Demsky (1994) provide a particularly clear description.

3. To this end, William Cummings has developed the SHARE database, an online compendium of one thousand abstracts of educational research and policy or project interventions in developing countries. The SHARE can be accessed by contacting Prof. Cummings, at wkcum@usa.net.

4. See Reimers and McGinn (1997), as well as Crouch and Healey (1997), for discussion and examples.

Part 1

THE CONTEXTS OF REFORM

CHAPTER 1

How Education Systems Form and Reform[1]

In promoting educational change, we have argued, it is useful to understand the contexts of reform. Shaping contemporary reform efforts as they do, historical traditions and models are an important contextual component of reform. This chapter summarizes six traditions with special reference to their administrative and organizational structures, and the ways diverse ethnic, class, and gender groups of their respective settings are accommodated.

The first steps to launch modern education occurred on the European continent (which is best broken into the Prussian and French variants, with the Lowlands as a third possibility), then by the English, the American, the Japanese, and the Russian socialist patterns. The distinctive characteristics of each of these patterns can be summarized with an ideal-typical schema (see Table 1.1).

Each modern pattern was unified by a core set of ideals (much like the genotype of biology) that can be at least partially captured in a slogan, such as the educated gentleman, which is an aristocratic England's ideal of the 19th century, or the continuous development of the individual, in the American case. Over subsequent decades these national ideals were continually refined, but the six cases under consideration were never fundamentally altered. Thus these ideals had an enduring influence on various structural features of their respective systems, including the type of school that is most esteemed, the range of subjects covered, the prevailing theory of learning, and preferred teaching methods. In other words, there is a *gentle degree of determinism* implied (Müller et al., 1987) with the ideal, placing some constraints on curriculum, learning theory, and so on. For example, to realize the comprehensive education goals implied in the Anglo concept of the educated gentleman, a boarding school is essential along with close monitoring

Table 1.1 Core Education Patterns

	Prussia	France	England	U.S.	Japan	Russia
Period of genesis	1742–1820	1791–1870	1820–1904	1840–1910	1868–1890	1917–1935
Ideal	Loyal mandarin	Technical elite	Educated gentleman	Continuous development of individual	Competent contribution to the group	Socialist achievement
Representative school	Primary schools	Lycée/grande école	Public school	Comprehensive high, liberal arts college	Primary school	General schools
Scope	Whole person, many subjects, humanistic bias	Cognitive growth in academic subjects arts/ science	Academic subjects, civic & religious values, culture & curriculum	Cognitive development, civic values, social skills	Whole person, wide range of subjects, moral values, physical & aesthetic skills	Whole person, broad curriculum, technical bias
School and classroom technology	Lectures & self-study	Lectures & exams	Tutors, co-curriculum boarding school	Individualized courses & instruction	Teacher-centered, groups, school as units	Collective learning
Learning theory	Natural unfolding	Mental discipline	Hereditary brilliance	Aptitude & growth	Effort	Interactive
Administration	Quasi-decentralized	Centralized	Private	Decentralized	Quasi-decentralized	Centralized
Admin. Style	Autocratic	Authoritarian	Leadership	Management	Cooperation	Collective control
Unit costs	Moderate	Moderate	High	Variable	Moderate	Moderate to high
Source of finance	Local state	State (church)	Fees	Local taxes	State	State

by tutors; and because a gentleman is expected to dabble in everything, the cocurriculum is highly valued. In contrast, French formal education was intended to train experts. While students were outstanding in a particular intellectual area, there were no expectations that they play cricket or polo.

The core patterns emerged at different periods in the global process of modernization. In each instance there were unique confluences of internal and external forces, necessarily inviting distinctive responses. Several generalizations about the nature of education reform can be derived from these accounts:

- Education reform is closely associated with political shifts; economic forces are an important contextual factor;
- The magnitude and abruptness of the political shift influences the extent of the education reform;
- Political shifts are closely associated with major class realignments, and these in turn influence the focus of the education reform;
- Education reform, while bold on rhetoric, tends to focus on a limited set of changes concerning a particular level of schooling at least in the short run;
- Education reform, while often mentioning foreign examples in its rhetoric, draws extensively on indigenous resources, indigenous ideals, and indigenous education practices (both past and present);
- Thus even after a seemingly dramatic education reform, the memory of past ideals and practices will persist to exert influence on the new, possibly even returning at a later date to replace the new;
- Thus education reform, in its particulars, tends to turn inward, reproducing and creating indigenous patterns, rather than turning outwards, converging on internationally approved patterns.

These patterns were developed in the core nations of the world system and later diffused by their respective colonial and/or ideological systems. Thus the French variant became influential in Africa, Indochina, and Latin America, while the English pattern was widely diffused through Asia and Africa. Likewise the American pattern had early influence in Asia, and later, following World War II, a global influence. The Japanese pattern had a profound impact on Korea and Taiwan and more limited influence elsewhere, while the Russian Socialist pattern influenced China, Eastern Europe, Cuba, and many other developing societies.

THE FIRST STEPS TO SYSTEMATIZING EDUCATION

Modern education is one among several projects launched by the modernizing state. It is essentially a new venture, and at least for the first states embarking on the project, there was no clear design or master plan. How many different types of schools would be required? What should be the mix of academic and technical training? Who should be allowed to attend these schools? Who should pay for them—the state, the students, or private benefactors? These questions were some of the design issues for which no ready answers were available. And so in the early years, especially for the first modernizing societies, there was much trial and error.

The first steps focused on the design of a particular "representative" school that best reflected the most pressing needs of the modernizers. Building on this first venture, these same modernizers and their successors added other schools to respond to other needs—for different skills, regions, and interested groups. As new schools were established, the elites had to decide on the relations between the respective schools. These decisions gradually led to an overall design for the emerging modern education system. Germany was the pioneer in these endeavors, and France followed. Victor Cousin, for example, prepared a detailed report on German education, which played a critical role in the reforms of the 1830s promoted by Guizot. Numerous Americans traveled to Germany and France in the 1830s and 1840s to gather the insights that were later expressed in the U.S. Common Schools Movement. And, following the Meiji Restoration of 1868, Japan sent several missions to observe education practices on the European continent, in Great Britain, and in the United States. Those states beginning later drew extensively from the lessons learned by the pioneers, thus helping the latecomers to complete their task of systematization in a briefer time span. As a result, Japan completed its major systemic decisions within the first two decades of the Meiji Revolution, and the Bolsheviks took less than fifteen years to draw up the decisive education law of 1931.

The shape of the emerging systems can be compared in terms of two dimensions: (1) the differentiation/integration of various education opportunities both through vertical and horizontal divisions, and (2) the segregation/inclusion of different social groups in the various education opportunities primarily through horizontal segmentation/tracking. We suggest distinctive differences exist in both the structure of the respective systems and the means by which the respective states establish direction. Among the means available, states can influence the direction by establishing standards, accreditation, finance, admissions, and examinations.

Once the state is satisfied with the direction of modern education, it may delegate most education decisions to boards or other decision-making bodies, composed primarily of educators. But now and again the state intervenes with a new wave of reform in an apparent effort to get education back on track. These waves of reform symbolize the reality that the processes of systematization and expansion are never complete. Yet while these later reforms generate much interest and concern, some observers suggest they amount at most to fine-tuning. Ravitch (1983) finds that later reform often involves merely recycling old practices, thus creating only an illusion of reform.

THE POLITICAL AND ADMINISTRATIVE SETTING

Of the modern states, some were more centralized than others, and some were more inclusive or "democratic." In centralized systems, according to Margaret Archer (1977), the flow of education decisions likely reflects the pattern for other sectors, such as the judiciary, the police, and public health. In decentralized societies, education decision making may vary between locales. Thus in the United Kingdom, local education authorities were established that seldom overlapped with other government offices. In the United States, some states decided to assume a primary role in education decision making, while others left this task to local communities.

To the extent a polity is more inclusive, a greater array of stakeholders will more likely be offered a role in the systematizing decisions. In the United States and the United Kingdom, it is common, when considering major education reforms, to create consultative bodies that include representatives from the various political parties, the different levels of education, and the different working groups involved in education practice, such as the principals' association and the teachers' union. To the extent the polity is more narrowly constituted, the state will more likely consult with a small group of interests, such as corporate leaders, the military, and religious elites.

The priority that the polities of the core societies assigned to their education project also varies. Especially from the early 19th century, Prussia/Germany became concerned with its national identity and increased its emphasis on the education project. The education project also received exceptionally high priority in the late developing cases of Meiji Japan and Bolshevik Russia as both centralized states were determined to radically depart from their immediate past, looking to education as a prime asset for the new, nation-building agenda. In the United States, the federal government was constituted in such a manner that it could not assume responsibility for education. However, in several of the U.S. states, local governments came to stress the importance of education as a means for cultivating an informed citizenry. In the other core nations, education was assigned a lower priority.

VERTICAL DIFFERENTIATION

The first modern schools were established for a specific need high on the agenda of the modernizing elite. Tracing a couple of examples may suggest the approach in which the architects established the first schools, and how those first steps then shaped second steps and so on.

In the long-established nations of Germany, France, and the United Kingdom, aristocratic and middle-class families were familiar with an established precedent of schools. Early education was often provided in the homes by tutors and parents. When children reached a certain level of competence, they entered appropriate preparatory schools. Thereafter children in France gained entrance to the *lycée*, in Germany to the *gymnasium*, and in the United Kingdom either to public schools or grammar schools. Thus in these societies a system was already partially established. Still remaining was the development of a formal approach to the primary level for the children from ordinary homes, who lacked the cultural or financial resources to tutoring and home schooling. Also, in both France and Germany, the modernizing education leaders took steps to transform the structure and curriculum of higher education institutions. In France the *grandes écoles* were diversified and strengthened. In Germany, universities were provided new support and new rigor was introduced to the process of selecting students.

While a system was already in place in these long-established societies, there was ample room for clarification. Of many notable administrative accomplishments, Napoleon drafted the law of the university. While the term *university* normally refers to a tertiary level institution, Napoleon used the concept in its literal sense as the organization for the promotion of all learning. For him, this meant learning from infancy to adulthood. Napoleon's university specified that there be several vertically differentiated levels of education, the *école primaire*, the lower secondary boarding schools, the colleges and *lycées*, and the *grandes écoles*. These respective levels of schools would be provided by the administrative units corresponding to the commune, department, academy, and university. Each administrative level was to provide the physical plants for the schools at the respective education levels, while the university rector was to provide the academic program. The rector was to be appointed by the emperor, as were the members of the oversight board. Those responsible for administering, operating, and supervising lower levels of the system were to be appointed by the rector or his delegates. Exceptional for its administrative clarity, Napoleon's law of the university has greatly influenced subsequent thinking in the field of education administration.

In Japan the Meiji elite had no prior experience with an elaborate multilevel education system. Samurai simply came to fief schools that consisted of several grades with a provision for further individual tutelage. Keenly aware of their technological backwardness, the Meiji leaders declared their intent "to seek knowledge throughout the world." To gain access to this knowledge, they recognized that their emissaries would require a command of foreign languages. As a result one of their earliest acts was to establish a translation bureau that was essentially a small college. Given their technical focus, they also established several engineering schools. Several of these early colleges later were consolidated into Tokyo University, which was recognized as the first Imperial University in 1886. At the same time, the Meiji elites declared their intention of developing a new postfeudal social structure that would enable the entire population to contribute to national development. In addition, elites established a national army that would be staffed by conscripts from all social groups, including offspring not only of the former samurai class but also of the peasant and commercial classes. To prepare youth for their roles both in national development and national defense, planners looked to the primary school as an important agent of initial socialization. Thus in early Meiji Japan, both the primary school and the university were given high priority in the first decade of the design period.

The first recruits for the early Japanese "universities" were the legions of bright samurai who had received a Confucian education in the old feudal system balanced with self-education in foreign languages and books. But once this cohort entered the new higher education institutions, the Meiji leaders had to decide what would be required to prepare the new wave of primary school students for tertiary education. Their first step was to establish several middle schools to provide further training for the primary school graduates. In the late 1870s, there was only one place in the middle schools for every twenty graduates of the primary schools. Yet the middle school curriculum insufficiently prepared students for the new higher education institutions. To fill this gap, numerous private specialized schools (*senmon gakko*) were rapidly established, specializing in foreign languages and the study of selected foreign books. The government response was slower, depending on the discussion in various official committees. Finally in 1886, with the establishment of the Imperial University, the central government established a number of higher schools, modeled on the German *gymnasium* and the French *lycée*, to complete the transition from the middle school to the university. Reflecting the orderly thinking of that era, these higher schools were given the names "No. 1 Higher School," "No. 2 Higher School," and so on. Meanwhile, the government distinguished between higher education institutions focused on higher learning from those focused on specialized learning. With this distinction, various new regulations were issued outlining the types of the post-primary (or secondary) level experiences appropriate for the respective higher education courses.[2] As will be noted below, in effect these regulations initially reduced the value of the now extensive private sector of post-primary specialized schools.

In decentralized systems, the process of filling the gaps between different levels of the system was less uniform. The U.K. system was highly segmented, reflecting class distinctions, with prominent educators reluctant to introduce refinements out of concern of lowering the barriers between the established classes. In the United States, first there were many colleges, with a patchwork of preparatory institutions underneath these colleges. Most notable were the grammar schools to start youth in their schooling, but often lacking was an intermediary institution to bridge the gap between the grammar schools and the colleges. Partly to address this issue, grammar schools would have many grades, sometimes as many as ten. Then students might go to an independent preparatory school or even a preparatory school attached to one of the colleges. Over time, various intermediary arrangements were introduced, the most common being the four-year high school. From the mid-twentieth century it became more popular to have a five- or six-year primary school, a three- or four-year middle school, and a three-year high school.

Comparing these approaches to vertical differentiation, they can be said to reflect several different approaches to the "serious" business of education. In the continental systems and to some degree in the United Kingdom, this serious business was carried out at the secondary level in schools that were originally intended for aristocratic and middle class families—the *gymnasium* in Germany, the *lycée* in France, the public school in the United Kingdom. In contrast, in the United States, serious education began in the college. And in Japan and Russia, where modern education was established in part to break down old aristocratic traditions, serious education for all began in the primary schools. These differences in tradition are reflected in such diverse aspects as the quality of education materials, the workload expected of educational personnel, their compensation, and finally the pace of student learning. Simply put, *things get better in each system at the level where that system gets serious.*

HORIZONTAL DIFFERENTIATION OF SEGMENTS AND TRACKS

Studies of education structure make a distinction between two principles for accommodating group differences:

- *Tracking* (or streaming) occurs when different curricula are offered to young people based on some form of testing of their motivation and/or ability. Occurring as early as the primary grades, students are placed into parallel tracks or streams that are more or less difficult. For example, in Malaysia there exists the A stream for the top third-graders, the B stream for the runners-up, the C stream for the average student, and so on. In later grades, the curricula for the different tracks may differ qualitatively, as for example between an academic track that prepares students for tertiary education, and a vocational/technical track that prepares students for a manual labor role in the workforce.
- *Segmentation* occurs when members of the two groups are clearly identified and explicitly routed into separate schools. These separate schools may have ostensibly similar features, as claimed by American states as separate but equal schools for white and black children. Or, schools may vary in certain respects as in the British colony schools that, on the one hand, provided members of the colonial government with a rigorous academic curriculum in the English language, while only providing for natives a more practical curriculum in the vernacular.

Tracking is explained as a strategy for optimizing human resource development. With limited resources, the state asserts a responsibility to prepare sufficient numbers of students in the different spheres of the modern workplace. While evident even in the primary grades in the early modern period, most systems subsequently abandoned tracking, concluding that it was both too difficult at that early age to truly evaluate aptitude and placed too much pressure on young people to make these judgments. Hence most systems introduced tracking following the primary grades, with the track assignment based primarily on academic performance during the primary years and/or a primary school leaving examination. Typically the academically proficient students were tracked to the academic schools, and the less proficient were tracked to the vocational schools. This form of tracking at the secondary level was accepted in most of the early modernizing societies, though the extent seems to have been determined by the prominence of the business class in operations of the state. In Germany and France, where business classes were most prominent, the diversity of vocational/technical tracks seems to have been most extensive, whereas in the United States and Russia there were fewer tracks.[3] Indeed, in many U.S. school systems, there were essentially no opportunities for vocational and technical training.

The degree of centralization of a system also appears to have influenced tracking. In centralized systems, authorities were responsible for the entirety of the national labor force, and were thus inclined to carry out systematic studies of labor force needs. These studies naturally led to conclusions about vocational/technical areas that were both over and undersupplied. From these inferences, the central government authorities then might propose new policies for alterations in the composition of vocational/technical education to address future needs. Decentralized governments, lacking such an overarching perspective, were less likely to make such recommendations.

In the actual practice of tracking, certain social groups, for example, minorities or children from the lower classes, are more likely to end up in less esteemed tracks. This is justified as a function of meritocratic selection. In some cases and at different times, societies, or at least elites, have strong feelings about the need to preserve ascriptive differences: Girls should receive a different education from boys, aristocrats should not mix with commoners, whites and blacks should not mix, etc. Where these sentiments have prevailed, the respective groups may be segregated in horizontally segmented education systems that may begin from the first day of schooling. We will have more to say about segmentation below.

Horizontal Segmentation to Serve Different Groups

All of the modernizing societies were composed of young people with diverse backgrounds and gender differences. Marxist reinterpretations tend to suggest the major issue confronting the modern reformers was equality. While equality was an important issue, far more pronounced at the early stages of the modern transformation was the concern to build a new national identity that superseded separate religions, ethnicities, and racial identities. Though initially a lesser theme, equality of social classes increased in salience over time. Gender equity was rarely considered—a woman's place was to help her husband and family. While national integration was a major concern, there was always the question of how far to go in bringing people together. The other side of this question was to ask whether the members of these diverse groups wished to mix with each other.

Religion

The German states launched the modern transformation with the Reformation. While many states broke with the Roman Catholic church, others did not. For many decades, wars took place to force a common policy. Ultimately a truce was negotiated that allowed each state to go the way of its prince. And these differences were preserved as the German states were consolidated (Lamberti, 1989). Religious differences were allowed to persist according to locality, reflected in the school's religious curriculum, while integration was achieved in other subjects. It should be noted that the German solution recognized two major religious groupings—Catholicism and Protestantism, while other religions, notably Judaism, were not acknowledged.

France rejected the German solution by separating church and state, a solution adopted in the United States as well as in Japan and Russia. Of course, in each setting there were subtleties. While church and state formally separated in the United States many schools featured religion until well into the 20th century. As Bellah (1975) notes, American schools featured a religion of American civic virtue. In Japan, public schools were religiously secular except they allowed, even promoted, worship of the emperor. And in Soviet Russia, the schools were also religiously secular but celebrated Soviet heroes.

However, in all of these "secular" cases, powerful religious groups were discontented, and continuously lobbied for independent education systems. In the United States and elsewhere, this was ultimately allowed, often under the conditions that religious schools could receive no support from state funds, and that they would conform to basic establishment standards for the secular subjects. Therefore parallel systems emerged in America, with the main public system supported by the state, the second independent.

Major schools in the United Kingdom had always been religiously based, and British leaders rejected the continental theory that the church and state could or should be separated. Influential at this time was Edmund Burke's commentary on the disastrous French Revolution. In earlier times, the English aristocracy and their schools conformed to the dictates of the Catholic Church. Henry VIII replaced Catholic orthodoxy with the Anglican Church; after an awkward period, both the nation and its schools accommodated. Thus Britain preserved the role of religion in the schools. Most schools included a chapel along with classrooms. By the mid-19th century the United Kingdom became more relaxed about these matters, allowing different Protestant sects to practice. Similarly, it allowed different schools to feature different religions.

Class

An emerging theme of the modern revolution was the promotion of equality. Class differences clearly troubled the German leaders, but they chose to use the education system to preserve class distinctions (Mueller, 1984). In the United Kingdom some mobility was permitted by allowing able commoners to buy a position in the upper class. But especially in France there was much tension as the bourgeoisie were largely excluded from the royal court. The imperial government levied exceptionally heavy taxes on the commercial and peasant classes in order to carry out its policies of national defense and conquest. And so the concern with equality was increasingly articulated and became a clarion call of the French Revolution. But, as soon became evident, the revolutionaries were interested in limited equality—for the bourgeoisie but not for the workers or peasants. And the education reforms that followed mainly focused on opening up new opportunities for those resident in cities and towns.

The entry-level schools in the urban areas were generally of superior quality in Germany and France, giving the upper class an advantage.[4] In Britain the upper classes were unwilling to leave their destiny to chance and retained a system of independent public schools that preserved the right to select students based on such criteria as lineage and upbringing.

The United States was essentially a rural nation so these issues were less salient. But ultimately America followed the continental pattern by instituting the norm of neighborhood schools. Residential class segregation led to class segregation in access to education.

Japan was unique in recognizing the threat of class segregation. The new leaders, who were themselves from relatively peripheral fiefs, were determined to give commoners, especially those from peripheral rural areas, a chance at mobility. They set up schools throughout the nation, including rural areas, and put in place financial regulations requiring the government to actually spend more on rural than on urban schools. Moreover, within a given geographic area, a hierarchy of middle schools and high schools were established, with strict meritocratic criteria enforced for entrance to the best schools. As it turned out, the former samurai did better on average, but many commoners also succeeded.

Russia also was concerned about class equality. Indeed in the earlier stages, the revolutionary general schools actually favored children from worker families over those from upper- and middle-class families.

Ethnicity and Race

All of the modernizing states were formed through bringing together people of diverse cultural backgrounds. Most notable is the United States, which is often depicted as a nation of immigrants. But in the European states there was also much diversity as the new nation-states were composed of numerous principalities with their distinct traditions. Similarly, Soviet Russia was composed of many nations, languages, and religions. Even in supposedly homogeneous Japan, the Tokugawa system spanned a far-flung archipelago. There had been such diverse developments of the supposedly common Japanese language that natives of Kyushu Island in the south were unable to understand natives of central Kyoto, not to mention those from the northeastern areas of Tohoku and Hokkaido. For most of the modernizing states, modern education was seen as a mechanism for blending ethnic differences. As long as children could do well in the official language of the state, they were included in the common school.

The United States was somewhat unique in its unwillingness to include one subgroup, African Americans, in its conception of equality. This reluctance varied by region, but in most Southern states, African Americans were held as slaves and provided no social rights, including the right to education. After the Civil War, African Americans obtained citizenship and became eligible for equal education. But the response in many states was to provide "separate but equal" schools. Race was not an official consideration in the other core societies, except possibly for Japan where a separate system was set up to provide education for certain "immigrant" groups, most notably Koreans.[5]

Gender

Finally, in virtually all of the core societies, gender was treated in a special way. German laws discuss girls in the same breath as boys, yet a distinct curriculum was prepared for the two sexes. Japan was explicit about separation. Girls were to become good wives and wise mothers, while boys were to become productive members of the economy. Especially after the primary school, distinct tracks were established for Japanese boys and girls. Through World War II, girls were not admitted to the Imperial Universities. Only in Bolshevik Russia was there no separate formal provision for boys and girls.

As outlined in Table 1.2, different patterns of tracking/segmentation preserved religious, class, racial, and gender differences.

Vertical Integration of Levels

Rules are created to build links between the different types of schools. The most significant are those relating to student admissions and passage from one grade or level to the next.

Table 1.2   Segmentation Principles for Different Groups

Groups/ Nations	Religion	Class	Race & Ethnicity	Gender
Germany	Protestantism and Catholicism allowed	Tracking by locality	Equal as long as able in national language	Equality but implicit tracking from upper elementary
France	No religion in schools	Tracking with urban bias in school location	Equal as long as able in national language	Equality but implicit tracking from upper elementary
U.K.	Anglican religion featured in all schools	Elite schools use ascriptive criteria for admissions	Equal as long as able in national language	Equality but implicit tracking from upper elementary
U.S.	No religion in public schools, but independent Catholic segment allowed	None, except neighborhood admission principle	"Separate but equal" segmented school systems for whites and blacks	Equality but implicit tracking from upper elementary
Japan	No religion in public schools, but independent private schools allowed to include religious instruction	Resources favor periphery schools	Equal as long as able in national language	Explicit girls' track after the primary grades
Russia	No religion in schools	Admissions may discriminate against descendents of old ruling class	Equal, and local languages allowed in primary schools	Gender equality

Perhaps the most dramatic initiative of modern education was to declare that all children had the right to education. The various German states asserted the right to education from the middle to the end of the 18th century. The Revolutionary Council of France made its declaration in 1794. Britain debated this question for several decades, but did not actually issue a formal declaration until 1902. Both Japan and Russia asserted every child's right to education within a few years of their respective revolutions. The declaration of the right to education placed responsibility both on the state to provide education opportunities for all, and on the parents to send their children to school (or otherwise provide for the education needs of their children).

Whereas schools in the past selected new students from a larger group, now they were expected to accept all who applied. In some systems, this new obligation led schools to attempt to design a school atmosphere that adjusted to the needs of all of children, regardless of their sociocultural background. In others, notably France, all students were accepted, but stiff barriers were placed in front of those who did not adjust to the school routine. In the early modern French primary schools, children were given academic tests at the middle and end of each academic year in each subject, and those children who failed even one test were expected to repeat the school year. Thus the early French system was characterized by high repetition rates, leading to frequent dropouts. In contrast, the Japanese and Russian systems from early on adopted a philosophy of automatic promotion that placed considerable pressure on the schools to find ways to reach out to their slow learners.

While the approaches for the early years varied, most systems developed procedures for measuring the academic potential of their primary school graduates. The continental schools relied exclusively on summative examinations. In contrast, in the United States, Japan, and Russia, schools tended to combine course grades with summative examinations in determining academic achievement. Elsewhere we go into greater detail on the examination procedures of the different systems (Cummings, 2003).

As these decisions were being made, another highly contentious issue was the assignment of formal responsibility for decisions on admissions and promotion to those school levels beyond compulsory education. In that the state was footing at least some of the bill for public education, the argument was advanced that it should have this responsibility. On the other hand, educators were inclined to assert that academic matters were their responsibility. In the more centralized systems, the state won these debates. Thus in France, the examinations were prepared by the center. In contrast, in the United States, teachers in the respective schools assumed responsibility for examinations. In the other systems, the responsibility varied depending on the level. To the extent that evaluation was the responsibility of frontline educators, there was a tendency for multiple criteria to be used (and in the U.S.

case written summative examinations might be excluded from these criteria). However, when the responsibility rested with the state, the hard criteria of performance relied on a national examination.

In the cases of Germany and Japan (Amano, 1990; Ringer, 1974) schools and universities were initially invested with the responsibility for examinations. But in time, the respective states sought to insert their authority in the process. Among the various reasons put forth was the argument that the education institutions were training future civil servants and thus the state needed to be involved. The university counterargued that in certain fields such as medicine the state lacked the competence to manage sensible examinations. The actual responsibility for different examinations seesawed back and forth. Eventually both ran their respective examinations.

In the United Kingdom, a variant of the examination system known as "payment by results" was introduced in the 1870s (Reisner, 1923, p. 282) to allow individual schools considerable autonomy in the conduct of their programs but to subject their students to an annual performance test. Schools that did well in these examinations were provided with increased resources, whereas those who did poorly had their allocations cut. Once schools came to understand the impact of this system, they began to dismiss low-performing students and recruit superior students from nearby schools. The result was so disruptive of the lives of young people that it was discarded within a few years. The reader may appreciate the similarity of the British "payment by results" approach and recent reforms proposed for the United States.

As the objective of these measures was the assurance of quality control, some systems also considered alternative approaches, such as supervision or accreditation. In most of the centralized systems, inspectors were appointed to visit schools and evaluate their education programs. Where these inspection systems were well staffed and considered reliable, the process of inspection of the whole school could substitute for an evaluation based on examining the performance of each student in the school.

Recognizing the possibility of external imposition of quality control measures, educators in the United States from the late 1800s devised an alternative approach of voluntary evaluation where several education institutions joined in an education association, set their own standards, and carried out their own evaluation exercises (Selden, 1960). The evaluation involved a statement of institutional mission and a report on the resources available to realize that mission. If peer institutions felt the resources were appropriate for the mission, the institution was accredited. In this way, the schools and universities of the decentralized American system sought to forestall opportunities for the state to intervene in their autonomous education activities. Accreditation came to be widely practiced in the United States.

VERTICAL INTEGRATION OF SCHOOL AND ECONOMY

An important factor thought to influence equality of opportunity is the way the different systems link to the labor market. A major goal of modern education is to provide human resources for the various positions in the economy. The salience of this goal varies across the societies. In late-developing societies such as Japan and Russia, one of the strongest arguments advanced for the establishment of particular institutions was their vital importance in preparing elites or cadre for particular jobs of national importance. Indeed in Japan, vocational schools were set up first, and factories followed as the first cohort of graduates finished their commencement ceremonies. While the rhetoric was more muted, the United Kingdom looked to its top universities for recruits to join both the civil and colonial services.

The economies of the core societies varied considerably in terms of their "work systems," with some economies having a greater prevalence of daily wage and entrepreneurial opportunities, emphasizing organizational jobs, and yet others emphasizing professional jobs. To the extent that the former types of job are prevalent, employers are more likely to stress the importance of vocational-technical education, and to the extent that the latter jobs are prevalent, the stress will be on academic training preparing young people for first and second degrees in the higher education system. Distinct from the demands of the labor market is the overall philosophy concerning the role of the state in preparing young people for work. In all of the core societies, lip service is given to job preparation. But in socialist societies, the state tends to guarantee every school graduate a specific job. And in corporatist societies there tends to be a relatively close alliance between employers and the education system both at a policy level and through personnel connections. Thus every Japanese secondary school and higher education institution has a network of employers with which it works for placement of graduates, and these education institutions consider it their responsibility to place every one of their graduates who seek employment.

In the socialist and corporatist systems, the education system is expected to prepare youth for work. Thus these systems have a well-developed vocational/technical education system for blue-collar workers. And even in their academic system, the various programs are specialized in nature (e.g., three-year professional first degrees) as contrasted with the liberal arts degree prized in the United States or England. Thus in the socialist, as well as the Japanese systems, young people move directly from schools into jobs and receive all of their training on site and fully funded by their employers. In Germany, training is also offered on site and largely funded by employers. Ironically, the more democratic systems build the sharpest division between schools and employers. Since these links are weaker, the public sector spends relatively more on postschool training programs. In the United Kingdom, training may be on the premises of (prospective) employers, but the state provides large subsidies for this training. In the United States, training is provided in job training centers managed and paid for by the state with minimal support from employers. And participation in these centers provides limited connections with employers and no guarantee of actual employment. The several patterns are depicted in Table 1.3.

PRIVATE SECTOR OR NOT

In the premodern education systems, most schools were private and usually associated with religious organizations. Germany's folk schools were supported by local churches and communities, France's schools were provided by the Catholic Church, and most schools in England were affiliated with the Anglican Church until the 1870 Education Act.

Table 1.3   Links of Schooling with Human Resource Training Programs

	Philosophy	School Education	Secondary Education	Human Resource Training Programs	Job Search
U.S.	Market	General	Mainly general	Pre-hire, mainly at training schools, public funding	Individual responsibility
England	Market	General, but with tracking	Mainly general but with voc-tech tracks	Pre-hire, mainly at work sites, public funding	Individual responsibility
France	Market and corporatist	General, but with tracking	Half general and half voc-tech	Pre-hire, mainly at work sites, public funding	Individual responsibility
Germany	Corporatist	General, but with tracking	Half general and half voc-tech	Pre-hire, all at work sites, corporate funding	Individual responsibility
Japan	Corporatist	General	half general and half voc-tech	Post-hire, all at work sites, corporate funding	Schools help
Russia	Socialist	General	More voc-tech than general	Post-hire, all at work sites, public funding	State guarantees

The modern education project is normally thought of as an initiative of the new nation-state, and in this initiative the state may absorb prior private initiatives in order to realize its self-proclaimed mission. Indeed in France, the Revolutionary Council sought to nationalize the Catholic education system. Also, whereas the private system played a major role in Japanese and Russian education both prior to the respective revolutions as well as in the early years afterward, the new states were determined to launch major education initiatives aimed at eliminating the private sector. In the Soviet case, all private schools were closed, and in the Japanese case the state at one point indicated that no young person who had received training in a non-state school need apply for position in the national civil service, a regulation with potential for severely undermining demand for private schools.

But even in these instances, private educators played an important role. Fukuzawa Yukichi's Keio Juku is regarded as the first modern school in Japan, having been established in 1855, thirteen years before the Meiji Revolution. Even in the first days of the Russian Revolution, there were important groundbreaking private initiatives. And while the French revolutionaries threw out the Catholic schools, they rehired the former teachers who abandoned their monastic robes to assume positions in the new revolutionary schools.

In the United Kingdom, while Parliament procrastinated, only the private sector responded to popular needs for education. Similarly in the early decades of the American experience, all education opportunities were provided by private institutions.

While making important contributions, the private sector was nevertheless viewed as a threat by most states. These states questioned the advisability of allowing private education. A prominent theory argues that these states were persuaded to permit private schools as they became convinced that private schools had the capability of responding to special needs that important sectors of the public wanted but that the state, with its limited resources, did not consider essential. Indeed, Estelle James (1987) has identified two distinctive ways in which private schools can serve special needs. On the one hand, private schools meet the differentiated demands, or needs, of particular class, religious, or gender interests that are not prioritized by the state. On the other hand, private schooling may respond to the excess demand for education opportunities above those which the state is prepared to meet. According to this theory, private education will accordingly have two patterns—a set of differentiated schools from grade 1 through higher education for key interest groups, such as the Catholics in the United States, and a set of excess schools to meet the popular demand for secondary and higher education in societies where education expansion is still in its early stages as in 19th-century Japan or a contemporary developing society.

While interesting, this theory has numerous exceptional cases: for example, in a number of contemporary societies where the entire education system is provided by the private sector (Cummings & Riddell, 1992). There are several societies in Africa and Latin America where the private sector is prominent at the elementary school level but less at the secondary level. These exceptions suggest a simpler explanation for the prevalence of private schools than that proposed by the above theory. From the institutional perspective, the several core nations develop unique political solutions for the recognition of private education institutions. Later, these solutions are imitated by the newly emerging societies as they draw on the models of the core nations to develop their respective systems.

The solutions of the core nations were as follows:

- In Germany, the states were in control, but depended on local/private support for folk schools.
- In France, private schools were initially disallowed. But France had insufficient resources to develop a public system, and allowed the church to play a major role in primary education in the early years. Later, when the state was able to collect more resources, state policy toward Catholic schools vacillated.
- In Britain, the private sector prevailed—the so-called public and independent schools that start from the lowest grades and go through college. These schools were firmly entrenched and the state never considered the option of disbanding these institutions or interfering in their operations.
- The United States was influenced by French thought, which placed a strong emphasis on the separation of church and state. Embodied in the U.S. Constitution, this thinking profoundly impacted private education in America. During the early decades of the 19th century, young children were not allowed to attend religiously founded schools. But from the second half of the 19th century, religious schools were allowed so long as they provided the curriculum of public schools and independently secured adequate financial resources. These changes led to the opening of a prominent Catholic school sector at all grade levels. Of course, private institutions also thrived at the tertiary level.
- In Japan, private schools were initially allowed without restraint, and thus many were created at all levels, especially at the secondary and tertiary levels. But the state became nervous perceiving some private schools as politically too liberal, and was shocked that the Christian schools taught that there was a god other than

the emperor. These concerns peaked in the 1880s with the procla-
mation of the new constitution and various education laws that
included much stiffer rules for the founding and operation of private schools. Though these regulations were later relaxed, the private sector had been dealt a blow. Although private schools were
able to regain an important foothold at the secondary and tertiary
levels, they were unable to reestablish prominence at the primary
level.

• In Russia, private schools were closed soon after commencement
of the Revolution, and were not tolerated through the period of
Soviet rule.

And so in every system, the private sector is restrained, but the pattern
varies. These systemic solutions were first practiced in the core societies and then later exported around the world. Thus when Cummings
and Riddell (1992) reviewed the prevalence of private education in 129
countries, they found that most of the countries had developed a public–private education mix that resembled one or the other of the above
patterns practiced by the core nations.

Systems with a modest private sector are able to accommodate the
demands of certain interest groups without significantly jeopardizing
core policy objectives. In contrast, in systems with large private sectors
such as Japan where over half the places in secondary and higher education are in private schools,[6] it is difficult to preserve certain policy
objectives, in particular, the principles of uniform quality and equal
access.

SUMMARY: THE INSTITUTIONAL NATURE OF REFORM

This chapter has focused on three areas where the state has sought to
shape education: establishment and finance, examinations, and
employment. In these three areas, each state has established distinctive
systems. These systems vary in their complexity as indicated by their
different degrees of vertical and horizontal differentiation, as well as
by the extent and locus of their integration. Some systems took all levels of their education systems seriously, whereas others put particular

emphasis on one level or other. Similarly, some systems put more effort into monitoring and smoothing the transition from one level or segment to another, whereas others allowed these differentiated parts to stand as obstacles for the young people going through the systems. While several states devoted most of their effort to influencing these three levers of control, they evidenced less interest in other matters, such as the recruitment of teachers or framing the pedagogy—all to be taken up in the second major volume of this study.

This review of the reform experience of the core societies has the following implications for the analysis of reform elsewhere:

- Education systems throughout the world have been profoundly influenced by the institutional patterns developed in the core societies. Any attempt at reform needs to take that influence into account.
- Education reform in the core societies was never easy. Major reforms were usually stimulated by associated ideological, political, and economic change. Thus, in analyzing the prospects for reform in a particular environment, it is essential to look beyond education to the broader societal context.
- Factors such as leadership, resources, theoretical fit, and persistence are conducive to successful reform.
- Even after a reform is launched, its trajectory is likely to be shaped by residual interests such as the demands of class, ethnic, and religious groups. Thus, the reform plan is but the first step in an uncertain journey of implementation. What finally emerges from this journey may only faintly resemble what was envisioned.
- The persistence of institutional forms and memory shapes the possibilities of reform. As a result, efforts at reform often lead to first-order rather than second-order change.

NOTES

1. This paper draws on arguments presented in William K. Cummings, 2003, *The Institutions of Education*, Oxford: Symposium Books.

2. The Ministry of Education's (1980) *Japan's Modern Educational System* provides an excellent summary of the various regulations.

3. While there were relatively fewer tracks differentiated in the Soviet Russian system, at least during the early decades, the proportions of general school graduates channeled to these tracks were perhaps as large as was the case in continental Europe. In these systems, a smaller proportion went on to the academic track. In the United States, the proportion sent to the vocational-technical track was always comparatively modest.

4. Mueller (1984) argues that the Prussian king, William III, following Napoleon's defeat in 1806 of the German states, intentionally favored the urban schools so as to improve the prospects for the recruitment of the urban middle classes into the Prussian civil and military services (pp. 143 ff). The king felt aristocratic nepotism had weakened the quality of these services, and, moreover, he doubted the loyalty of many of the aristocrats.

5. Nations that favored segmented education at home such as the United Kingdom and the United States replicated this pattern in their empires. The British set up separate schools in English for the colonial officers and in the vernacular for the "natives." While the French and the Japanese "welcomed" everyone in the colonies to a single school system, these schools set such high academic and linguistic standards (classes were only in the language of the colonial administration) that most locals failed.

6. See William K. Cummings, "Private Education in Asia" in Cummings and Altbach (1997) for an explanation for the very large private sectors in the educational systems of Eastern Asia.

CHAPTER 2

Recent Phases of Education Reform

The previous chapter discusses the process by which education systems became institutionalized and developed their distinctive characteristics. The shape of the first modern education systems was developed in six core modern nations to serve the nation-building interests of the respective ruling classes. While these first systems differed significantly in many features, they represented an acceptable fit (or at least a winning accommodation of the various interests) in their respective contexts and the issues that were salient at the time of their creation.

Over the subsequent course of development, modern education[1] has been diffused to new settings. At the risk of oversimplification, we argue in this chapter that there have been six approaches or phases to this diffusion, focusing on distinctive models of education development/change.[2] Five of these models are sequential: (1) the original modern models and the colonial and neocolonial models exported by the core nations, (2) the postcolonial centralized (or state-led development) model(s), (3) decentralized regionalization models promoted by multilateral agencies; (4) neoliberal decentralized–sectoral reform models also promoted by multilateral agencies, and (5) emerging community- (and school-) based models. Finally, a sixth approach has persisted throughout the period in a transformative model, an approach that questions the dominant models of change and seeks, instead of reform, to transform the education system and the society. We seek in the pages below to review these models in terms of:

- Where they are most prevalent;
- How they are organized, administered, and financed;
- What the main characteristics of their education delivery are, such as buildings, curriculum, instructional materials, teacher preparation, stress on student mastery;

- What their implications are for bringing about change in developing country education systems.[3]

We see the evolution of models of reform as an ongoing process of trial and error. Each new model developed in reaction to perceived problems with the previous models. As a result, a great deal more is known about what *is less likely to work* than what could be successful. Typically, failed approaches are examined, failures diagnosed, and new strategies adopted to overcome the limitations identified in past approaches, but without systematic evidence—evidence which would be counterfactual at best—that the new approach will work better. Each dominant approach is based on the prevalent ideas at the time.[4] Needless to say, none of the efforts has been perfect, as illustrated in chapter 4, but like all ideas, most efforts have fit best in the settings where they were first developed and less well in other settings.

A BRIEF HISTORY OF SIX APPROACHES TO EDUCATION REFORM

Prior to the modern era, education was primarily provided by parents and religious/social groups. The Jesuit and Franciscan orders of the Catholic Church were noted for their education activities in the geographic regions where the Catholic Church was prominent. The Anglican Church was active in the United Kingdom. In areas where Islam was prevalent, local rulers and communities supported *madrasah* and *pesantren* to provide religious instruction to young men. And in Eastern Asia, widely prevalent Buddhist temple schools introduced young people to religious principles and practical skills, while Confucian schools focused on the principles of governance and leadership.

Core Nations and Their "Metropolitan" Models

With the emergence of the modern nation-state in Western Europe, these various forms of religious education were significantly transformed and even suppressed out of a conviction that they taught traditional and irrational beliefs. The modern school sought to focus the attention of young people on the new agendas advanced by their national leaders, including the promotion of national identity, industrialism, and world empire. The modern schools were first developed in the core nations as described in chapter 1, and subsequently exported, often in reduced form, to the colonial territories of the core nations. Colonial schools in French territories closely resembled the schools of the French motherland, the colonial schools in British territories closely resembled those in the United Kingdom, and so on. The main aim of colonial education was to serve the colonial government and the metropolitan motherland. Rarely was colonial education well organized to serve the leadership or development needs of colonial subjects. Still, just as there were important differences in the schools of the core nations, so also were there important differences in the schools in their colonies.

After World War II, the vast majority of the colonial territories gained independence and hence autonomy in the management of education. Initially, the new countries perpetuated the education systems they had inherited from the colonial era. The current governments of former colonial regimes supported this inclination, arguing that the new states deserved the same quality of metropolitan education as the old states. Bilateral assistance also tended to sustain the old models. France directed the majority of its bilateral assistance to its former colonies, much of which was used to pay the salaries of French nationals as teachers in the former colonial schools. Similarly, the United Kingdom, the United States, and Japan directed much of their bilateral assistance to areas where they had once been dominant. With the Cold War, the Soviet Union and the United States directed assistance to areas where they were seeking an increase in influence. Newly independent countries often found it worthwhile to continue in the familiar traditions, while former colonial rulers supported practices with which they were accustomed. These practices, having been institutionalized in the former colonies, likely seemed to colonial leaders to represent "good education practice." In these ways, the practices and beliefs of the old system were effectively sustained by leaders in the new system, and bilateral assistance served to perpetuate colonial patterns of education rather than to sponsor radical new initiatives.[5]

A particular interesting case, in showing the persistence of colonial features, is the Cameroons, which was formed through the consolidation of geographic areas formerly under the British and the French. Even to this day the education system of the Cameroons is comprised of two systems, one taught in French and the other in English, one with a structural nomenclature similar to that in contemporary France (cycles, *lycées*, etc.), and the other with English nomenclature (forms, ordinary level and advanced level exams, etc.).

In these ways, colonial schooling, though formally ending with independence, has continued to persistently influence the subsequent development of education. On the positive side, metropolitan models have provided relatively coherent models of education, linked via curriculum, language, and other ways to the global system. On the negative side, the metropolitan models, like all colonial institutions, were transplants, seldom top of the line and often culturally invasive. Colonial models neither fit the varied context of the colonies, nor served their developmental needs. Continuing dependence has constrained natural adoption and adaptation of international models of education. Instead, metropolitan models remain intact, often ill-fitting, yet vested in the national economy and social order.

Multilateral Assistance: Centralized (State-Led Development) Models

Following World War II, a large number of colonial territories gained independence from the former colonial powers of France, the United Kingdom, the United States, Holland, and Japan. With more than one hundred new states being recognized within two decades, the sudden emergence of new states led to a scramble to build new systems for governance, law, and the delivery of social services. The United Nations, established in 1945, took the lead in this new challenge of nation building. Among the main priorities of the UN, as expressed in its charter, was the promotion of education as a human right.

To help the new nations in the development of their education systems, the United Nations established the United Nations Educational, Social, and Cultural Organization (UNESCO) in 1946 and asked the French government to host this institution. For a variety of reasons, UNESCO, from its very early days, promoted a centralized, state-led approach to development of education, an approach that closely paralleled the centralized Francophone model. Likely reasons include UNESCO's Paris location and the special responsibility of the French government for launching UNESCO, the widespread belief at the time in the efficacy of central planning, the prevailing optimism of education planning that development could be substantially led by investments in education, and the "natural" focus on newly independent central governments as the locus of policy and planning for national development. One feature, for example, of the Francophone model was a uniform curriculum for schools through the nation with a common set of textbooks for every grade of every school. An early UNESCO initiative recruited a large cadre of subject specialists to work with educators in the new states to develop such a curriculum. Another feature of the French system was the systematic planning of school construction and support based on annual school surveys and reports. UNESCO developed guidelines for school construction of a six-room primary school that it presumed would be appropriate throughout the developing world. UNESCO established the special International Institute for Educational Planning (IIEP) to assist the new states in developing their planning and monitoring capacities. Over time, IIEP trained a large proportion of the staff in national ministries of education. As outlined in the introduction, rational planning—characterized by centralized, state-led, inputs-driven strategies—became the dominant approach to education reform.

Generally speaking, the centralized model assumed developing countries' education systems lacked technical expertise, funding, and the variety of materials, things, and systems requisite for a functioning education system—high-quality textbooks, modern ideas of pedagogy, appropriate pay scales, and so forth. This deficiency model led to a clear role for international funding and assistance agencies, to help developing countries acquire the know-how, funding, material inputs, and systems they needed. Given this emphasis and the importance devoted to planning, centralized approaches paid considerable attention to institution building and, of course, to the provision of inputs.

Despite limitations, the centralized model represented several advances over metropolitan models of reform. However influenced by metropolitan institutions, the new systems were run by national officials. Central governments assumed a rightfully (in our view) central role in providing and organizing education to their citizens. No one else had the charter, or the capacity, to do so. In poor countries, it made sense to focus scarce management resources where they could do the greatest good for all. Rational planning, despite its shortcomings, represents a substantial improvement over nonrational approaches to policy—tradition, favoritism, and so forth. As a result of various efforts largely carried out under the centralized approach, school enrollments increased dramatically throughout the world during the period of the 1950s through the 1970s. More children than ever before in history were attending school.

Still, several decades of state-led education planning suggested shortcomings. Centralized models were premised on the dubious assumption that the new modern states had their foundation in compliant societal or national groupings that sought a common national identity. An implicit assumption, among others, was that all people within the geographic boundaries of Indonesia wanted to be Indonesians or all within the boundaries of Nigeria Nigerian, but the majority of new states contained long-standing ethnic and religious divisions. Initial centralized education plans largely ignored these divisions, proposing instead a common education in a particular language, agreeable to some while foreign to others. Additionally, the initial centralized models assumed new school entrants had a level of intellectual preparation similar to young people in Western Europe, or perhaps elites in newly independent nations. Consequentially these misguided pedagogical assumptions led to high repetition and dropout rates in the newly established schools, especially in rural areas and among ethnic minorities.

Over this same period, the reputation of international agencies formed to promote national development waxed and waned. UNESCO began as a modest institution with an eminent director and high-quality staff. By the 1960s, it had grown to be the UN's largest special agency, employing over 20,000 staff around the world. While UNESCO claimed to use high standards for recruitment, it also was committed to regulations ensuring proportional representation of its member states. Over time, critics saw a decline in staff performance, with over half the staff working out of Paris as contrasted with the field. For these and other reasons, many came to perceive UNESCO as ineffective and inefficient. In 1981 the conservative Reagan and Thatcher governments of the United States and the United Kingdom, both key funders, withdrew, thus undermining the preeminence of UNESCO.[6] During the same period, centralized planning assumed a certain disrepute as influential governments around the world adopted neoliberal market policies. Moreover, the successes of central planning were often overwhelmed by other forces in the development experience, including weak and corrupt indigenous governments, domestic conflict fanned by neglected minority groups, declining revenues for agriculture exports, rapid population growth increasing the demand for social services, increased borrowing from donors to cover the provision of social services, mounting national debt, continued domination by external economies, and dependence in the global economy The case of Indonesia, as summarized in the following box, provides an illustration.

Finally, centralized models often assumed an unrealistic role for central government in the planning and provision of education. In its purest form, overly centralized systems made virtually all decisions at the center, or top, of the system. The knowledge and potential agency of local school officials, community members, and others outside the center was not utilized. In a number of countries, overly centralized systems collapsed under their own complexity and expense. When systems couldn't keep up, they tended to fail, starting with peripheral peoples and areas and moving inward to the core. Higher education and elite secondary education were often preserved, but the basic education system suffered along with poor and other marginalized people. Overly centralized systems are inclined to front-load, putting most of their energy into the development of the best blueprint possible. Implementation and formative evaluation are less valued. Centralized systems tend to lecture rather than to learn.

Thus, in many new nations, an initial decade or two of optimism in the possibilities of education was followed by a period of despair. In all fairness, the multilateral centralized model may have never had a chance. Given the poverty of most developing country treasuries, and the multiple development needs of government, education arguably has never been funded at sufficient levels for effective work. Was the failure of centralized models a failure of funding, or a failure of the model? An academic question at this point perhaps, given the costs and subsequent macroeconomic developments.

NATIONAL DEVELOPMENT IN INDONESIA

Indonesia is an island nation of great geographic and cultural diversity. Java, the central island, has been formed from a series of volcanic eruptions (several of which are still active), with a rugged topography and exceptionally rich soil. While the majority of the population lives on this island, the nation is composed of several other large islands and over 1,000 smaller islands. To the west is Sumatra, which among other assets has rich oil reserves. And to the east are numerous islands sometimes known as the spice islands because of their extensive export of various spices. Across hundreds of islands there is considerable cultural diversity with hundreds of ethnic groups, at least 14 major languages and many dialects. While the majority of the people adhere to Islam, most of the inhabitants of Bali are Hindu and many in the eastern islands are Christian.

Following long periods of Portuguese and British presence, the Dutch colonized Indonesia in the mid-19th century. Their primary concern was resource extraction through plantation farming and mining. Thus they invested modest resources in infrastructure development (few roads or railways) or in social services. Distinct from the colonial education system, the Muslims established *madrasah*, and Christian missionary work led to the establishment of many schools in the eastern islands. With the conclusion of World War II, an independence movement that engaged in a fierce struggle with the Dutch emerged. The movement finally succeeded, and the new Republic of Indonesia, first proclaimed in 1946, was widely recognized by the international community in 1951.

The new government proposed a constitution celebrating unity within diversity, and declared the trade language of Bahasa Indonesia as the national language. With this language as the common medium of instruction, efforts were launched to establish a national education system. During the first decade, Indonesia attempted a democratic form of government, but experienced much strife. With rapid population growth and limited economic success, education and other social initiatives faltered. The national debt soared. Separatist movements emerged to challenge the government, and in response President Suharto encouraged a shift toward communism.

This was reciprocated by a military coup leading to a strong military government and the firm implementation of new policies in all spheres. Population growth was slowed and the economy began to show an upturn. Education and other social services also improved. But there was much underlying tension. While the "New Order" persisted for 30 years and Indonesia overall prospered, many inequities emerged and became foci for controversy. Moreover, as time passed, the New Order government began to bias its policies to the majority group, exacerbating ethnic and religious tension. To respond, the New Order government encouraged a limited decentralization of government services. For example, basic education was delivered in local languages, and the various provinces were encouraged to add local content to the national curriculum. But these and other measures were insufficient to appease critics.

Ultimately the New Order government was toppled in the mid-1990s and a new cycle of nation building has ensued. A key focus of the current political dialogue is increased autonomy for the various regions. Indonesia most reluctantly allowed East Timor its independence in the late 1990s and now is facing similar demands from Aceh, the westernmost province. In the education sphere, community-based models are being encouraged, though still under considerable central control.

Multilateral Assistance: Decentralized Models

Concurrent with the decline of UNESCO, other multilateral actors became more interested in education. Most notable was the World Bank, which from the mid-1960s began to argue that education was a sound investment with a return equal to or greater than investment in physical capital. (This argument was later refined to say that, among the different education investment alternatives, primary education yielded the highest social rate of return, and was therefore the best investment.) From the 1960s the World Bank began to make loans in education. Over time the bank's loans to the education sector occupied increasingly large shares of its portfolio and of total donor expenditures on education. Similar trends can be noted in other international banks, notably the Asian Development Bank.

At first the World Bank followed the UNESCO model in programming its loans, and on many occasions relied on UNESCO as a subcontractor. However, from the early 1980s the World Bank began to express increasing concern with the weaknesses of the centralized approach—associating centralization with "bloated" national bureaucracies, for example, or with programs that were unresponsive to local needs. Gradually, the World Bank moved to a more decentralized model, sometimes with a market-orientation. Representing a broad range of strategies, decentralization is unified by the movement of government functions away from central government toward multiple local units, and often, to markets. Decentralization models have taken several forms.

The Decentralized Regionalization Model

On the one hand, in some large diverse countries, decentralization was promoted in the form of what might be called regionalization, whereby geographic regions often concurrent with cultural groupings were allowed considerable autonomy in some aspects of education decisions. Such moves accorded well with governments facing regional challenges to national authority. In addition, one problem with the international funding agencies taking a decentralized approach is that the World Bank, for example, is required to have a formal government partner that can take responsibility for a loan. Bilateral agencies such as USAID (United States Agency for International Development), JICA (Japan International Cooperation Agency), and GTZ (Deutsche Gesellschaft für Technische Zusammenarbeit) have more flexibility, but agreements are nonetheless made between (central) governments, thus posing a problem for decentralizing reforms. In many cases, this shift essentially meant that the locus of attention shifted to regional as contrasted to national governments. Once the World Bank began such practices, other important multilateral actors and a number of bilateral agencies followed suit. Thus, in large countries such as Indonesia and Pakistan, a familiar recent pattern of donor support emerged in which the World Bank supported education development in certain states/provinces, while other donors, notably the Asian Development Bank, or USAID, focused attention on other states/provinces.

This so-called decentralized approach has the advantage of promoting capacity building at the regional or state level. Also, the major inputs such as curriculum development, textbook production, and teacher training can be prepared in the official languages of the respective states.

At the same time, while the content of education is potentially more sensitive to regional variations, regionalization may not change the underlying hierarchical nature of relationships within the education system. The actual approach to the delivery of education may continue to be top-down, with regional governments identifying the sites for school construction, building schools with the standard grades 1–6 (or in some countries grades 1–8) designed with a single classroom for each grade irrespective of the likelihood of attrition, and posting teachers trained in the urban centers to schools throughout the region. In sum, without other changes, the "decentralization" achieved by this new multilateral approach is no more likely than "centralized strategies" to reach deep enough to address the felt needs at the grass-roots level. Table 2.1 outlines implications of these approaches in terms of decisions about the delivery of education.

The Decentralized Sectoral Reform Model

Decentralization also took the form of sectoral reform, for which a brief background is useful. Around this time, many (though hardly all) economists concluded that export-oriented economic and structural reform strategies offered the best hope for economic development among poor countries. Governments were encouraged to implement structural adjustment packages, as preconditions for economic assistance from the global financial institutions. Typical among recommendations was a reduction in the size of public sector spending, with dramatic implications for sectors such as health and education. Central government, generally, was understood as less efficient and effective than decentralized government units and markets. Market mechanisms were promoted in the social and other sectors (without a great deal of evidence, we would argue, of their effectiveness).

These larger conditions, combined with the weaknesses of central planning discussed earlier, led to development of decentralized-sectoral approaches to education reform. Sectoral approaches emphasized

Table 2.1 Decisions about Delivery of Education

	Centralized	Decentralized-regionalization	Decentralized-sectoral reform	Community-based	Transformative
What are the assumptions behind educational policy	Education is to promote national development and a national consciousness	As nation is composed of distinctive ethnic groups, education should be responsive to the majority of the respective regions	Education should be responsive to parents, students, community members, civil society, other social groups	Given the constraints governments have faced in reaching out, communities are looked to for educational initiatives	Education should lead to a more just order & the empowerment of the oppressed
Who decides on education goals	The centralized state in consultation with donors	The state in consultation with local governments and donors	Stakeholders, clients, "consumers"	Local communities in consultation with government, civil society	Participants, especially the poor and disenfranchised
Who funds	Central governments with donor support	Central and local governments with donor support	Central government, donor support, users, others groups	Local communities provide a substantial sum, with some outside help	Unspecified
Who decides curriculum	Central government	Central government may define structure, with allowance for local content and local language for instruction	Negotiated among stakeholders, particularly consumers	The central government may define goals, but local schools decide content and may rely on local language for instruction (often with assistance from sponsor)	Participants and teacher-facilitators
Who decides on educational personnel	Central government	Regional governments following central regulations	Negotiated with levels of government, external stakeholders	Local community possibly in collaboration with sponsor	Participants & teacher-facilitators
Who decides on admissions	Local officials, based on central regulations	Regional officials	Negotiated with levels of government, external stakeholders	School head and community, perhaps in consultation with sponsor	Participants & teacher-facilitators; Ideologically, open to all

the institutional restructuring of relationships between groups within government and with institutions, that is, civil society and the market outside government. On the one hand, the role of central government was to be reduced through decentralization and restructuring. In a typical decentralization initiative, a number of functions were moved away from central government to lower levels of the system, in an effort to promote responsiveness and efficiency.

At the same time, sector-wide approaches have promoted comprehensive development and funding strategies for the entire education sector, thus giving central government an even more central coordinating (though not necessarily provisionary) role.

Sectoral approaches developed, in part, from awareness of the limitations of centralized approaches. The natural emphasis of centralized approaches on provision of inputs and specification of processes led to unwieldy central bureaucracies attempting, at their worst, to micromanage local processes, albeit with insufficient local capacity to do so effectively. Specification of project inputs and processes sometimes took place at the expense of consideration of outcomes or of education agents and units working outside the center. A project was judged successful according to whether inputs were provided and processes followed as planned, rather than according to improvements in outcomes. Moreover, the natural impulse of external aid agencies to help countries meet deficiencies led to a multiplicity of development projects in many countries that failed, it appeared, to improve the overall systems of education. Education programs in some countries had become so donor-driven that education ministries spent most of their time managing external projects instead of developing their own strategic priorities.

The operating assumption in the decentralized sectoral reform approach is that developing education systems need to change the way they carry out their operations, a "deep" conception of education improvement. It is in this sense that the word *reform* appears so frequently in recent education development discourse. While decentralization and restructuring, sectoral reform initiatives, and market mechanisms all aim, in slightly different though resonant ways, at basic changes in how education systems operate, these changes are wrought indirectly, by structural changes to the institutions, incentive structures, locations of power, and to the "rules of the game." Decentralized sectoral reform approaches spend relatively little time building planning and policy-making institutions, detailing how goals are to be reached, or assisting implementers in reaching program goals. Instead, efforts focus on the desired objectives and incentives, leaving the means to implementers. Although working well when micromanagement by government is the primary problem, decentralized sectoral reforms are much less effective when implementers and implementing organizations lack the capacity to achieve specified targets.

The decentralized sectoral reform model was born in the financial crises of the 1980s, when the multilateral finance agencies, in particular the International Monetary Fund (IMF), the World Bank, and the regional banks, made structural reform—including openness to markets, reductions in public expenditures, balancing of budgets, relaxation of currency and price controls, and so forth—a condition of continued financial assistance. Given the economic dependence of developing countries, this assistance, and hence structural adjustment, was essential to continued economic and political viability. Debt was rescheduled, loans and aid packages were negotiated between governments and the World Bank/IMF, with funding disbursed in several increments subject to fulfillment of certain conditions of "reform," conditionality.

Adapted and applied to education and other sectors, the rationale for decentralized sectoral reform was the following:

1. Education reform needed to be approached in a systemic, not piecemeal fashion. Therefore, a sectoral rather than project-centered approach was preferred. Ideally, the sectoral approach would involve a country developing an overall analysis of its entire education sector, along with a statement of deficiencies, prioritized objectives to overcome those deficiencies, and a coordination of external funding and technical assistance efforts within the government plan.
2. National systems needed to develop the capacity and ownership to manage their own affairs. Therefore, the management and leadership of reform were to be located in the host country government, as opposed to being managed or overly advised by external agencies and experts. Technical assistance would be pro-

vided as necessary, but the purpose was to enable governments to take over as soon as possible.

3. Measurable reform objectives, both outcomes and intermediate outcomes, would be negotiated by government and donor. Funding would be provided to the host country government, to help it reach its objectives, and subject to achievement of the negotiated intermediate process objectives and longer-term outcomes.

While showing some successes, sectoral reform strategies are vulnerable to the problems associated with front-loaded plans, the difficulty of specifying meaningful intermediate and outcome indicators of reform, and the vagaries of international funding (see Moulton et al., 2002). Sectoral strategies have been developed largely on theoretical grounds, grounded in neoliberal readings of neoclassical economics. Sectoral strategies make explicit attempts to revise the "rules of the game," the institutional roles and authorities of different actors, and to bring new actors such as nongovernmental organizations (NGOs), national and international, into a more active role in the education system. The attempt is either to weaken the central state, or reduce its relative power in relation to other stakeholders. The introduction and use of a variety of market mechanisms in education in contexts that have previously been a near government monopoly have had important effects. NGOs, for their part, have come, in many countries, to assume a significant role in education.

"Decentralization," in its various meanings, has attracted a great deal of interest, appealing to what has been called the "democratic wish"—to break up concentrations of power in the distant unresponsive center; redistribute it to disbursed agents closer to beneficiaries, consumers, and "the people"; and to create "civic space." As we have suggested, whether or not the people gain a greater voice is not automatic but likely to depend on the particular form and manner of decentralization. Decentralization is particularly appealing, we would argue, to U.S. and U.K. sensibilities. It resonates with the culture of their inherited models of education, its efficacy perhaps more a matter of belief than of evidence. Nonetheless, the apparent weaknesses of central approaches, coupled with the rhetoric of decentralization, have given fresh impetus to community-based models of education, discussed more fully in the following section. At the same time, the top-down, unduly hierarchical nature of many education systems has meant that neither local education agents nor the communities and parents of schoolchildren have had authority under centralized or regionalized systems to participate actively in schooling. Decentralization has been used, among other things to rebalance these relationships, or at least to talk about it.

Community- (and School-) Based Models

While the rhetoric of the 1980s emphasized neglected areas and peripheral groups, the strategies mobilized by the major bilateral and multilateral actors proved inadequate. As noted, less-central government offices were often as unresponsive as national governments to the needs of peripheral groups, local schools, and communities. Top-down organizational cultures typically value authority over "customer service." The lack of focus on schools, communities, and peripheral groups is a natural consequence of centralized approaches, which emphasize central bureaucracy, planning, provision, and standard inputs over "field" sites, variable needs, implementation, utilization, and outcomes. Decentralized and sectoral approaches, while speaking of the redistribution of power and systemic solutions, often did not reach "down to" communities, schools, and peripheral groups. Sectoral approaches emphasized outcomes, but stayed out of the "business" and location of the production of outcomes, thus never quite getting into the school or community. As a consequence, perhaps, and as a result of declining public expenditures on education due to weak economic growth and structural adjustment, the record of education improvement over the 1980s was disappointing.

Recognizing the stagnating situation and seeking to reignite the global commitment to education reform, the United Nations Children's Fund (UNICEF) and the World Bank teamed up with a variety of other education actors to convene the World Conference on Education for All at Jomtien, Thailand, in late 1991. Drawing on UNICEF's experience with mass mobilization for childhood immunizations, the conference produced a clear confession of past inadequacies. Detailed estimates of the numbers of children and young people that had been deprived of schooling were developed, noting that young girls, minorities, and those in peripheral areas were most neglected. New partnerships with private and nongovernmental organizations were called for as part of a grand strategy to provide basic "education for all" by the year 2000.

Justifying the focus on education, the fundamental developmental role of education was discussed in terms of its contributions to fertility decline, improvements in health, economic competitiveness in a global economic terms as well as traditional economic growth, and national development (see, for example, McMahon, 1999). Lawrence Summers captured the tenor of the times in his statement that education of girls was the most "influential investment" a developing country could make.

Among the many important themes of the Jomtien conference was the recognition that alternate, often indigenous, models for the delivery of education had great potency for reaching neglected groups, which sometimes included millions of people. Jomtien featured presentations by Escuela Nueva and the Bangladesh Rural Advancement Committee (BRAC), both innovative alternative forms of community-based education. Following Jomtien, donors began to channel some of their development funds to local and international NGOs to further develop alternate indigenous and community models. Over time, there has been a blossoming of new endeavors in virtually all continents of the developing world.

These community school models have many characteristics in common. Schools tend to be small and thus can be located close to the children's homes. They rely extensively on local community planning and support, often in the construction and maintenance of schools, sometimes in management and finance. "Community schools" favor a flexible schedule tailored to the various obligations of young people; they encourage a relevant, sometimes indigenous, curriculum; the classes tend to meet in existing buildings or those of low-cost construction. Often recruited locally, teachers may lack extensive preservice training, but are supported by highly skilled consultants, who ease them into the instructional routine. Teachers adhere to careful procedures for monitoring the progress of each student. Sometimes the instructional schedule in these schools is more demanding than the schedule in nearby public schools, though the range of subject matter varies. Disadvantaged students, previously poorly served by public schools, often make rapid progress in their studies, for example, completing as much in three years as a public school completes in four. Especially notable are the high completion rates at these community schools and their ability to "reach" many of those children that standard public schools do not attract. In some contexts, notably BRAC in Bangladesh, community schools have achieved what the regular system has long been unable to obtain.

The theory underlying community- (and school-) based approaches is simple: interventions should begin at the level of the system where the essential mission is enacted, that is, the school or community, and work backwards from there in providing support.

Community schools, though not necessarily low-cost when all expenses are included (Tietjen, 1999), provide modest levels of education to peripheral children previously unreached by schools at moderate cost, by shifting expenses from one domain, for example, extensive preservice teacher training, to another—extensive supervision and instructional support. Community schools have highlighted rigidities in the overstandardization of schooling, and demonstrated alternatives, in terms of teachers, infrastructure, curriculum, instruction, access, achievement, community participation, and so forth.

At the same time, several questions have been raised about community schools. They typically offer only lower primary grades. Higher level instruction requires more highly trained, and better paid, teachers. Transition to the formal, public school sector can be problematic, and community school students may lack the language skills to perform well in traditional schools. Investments in community schooling do little to enhance the capacity of the formal system and may undermine or drain resources from the regular system in favor of a parallel system of arguably lower quality. Some community-based schools are truly indigenous to their communities, while others are imported by international NGOs, who largely take on the role of donors. Then too, development of a multitude of community schools may enroll great numbers of children in basic schooling, but does a mass of schools comprise a coherent system? What about the higher-order skills and knowledge necessary for global competitiveness? When government is weak,

NGOs can substitute for government rather than increasing the availability of services.

Supporters answer that the current formal system, despite its noble intent, has failed to provide even basic education to vast numbers of the world's children. At current rates, many nations are not on target to reach even the revised Education for All targets for 2015 (see discussion in chapter 4).

Alongside and resonant with community-based school approaches are what might be termed school-based models of reform—strategies that work at the school level to bring about reform. The most extensive site of school-based reforms is in the industrialized nations of decentralized persuasion, that is, the United States and the United Kingdom. Adherents include a number of well-known educationists including Michael Fullan (1991), Thomas Sergiovanni (2003), and Richard Elmore (1982) in the U.S. context and Ward Heneveld and Helen Craig and others (1995) internationally. Though not as strong a tradition internationally at this point as other reform models, school-based initiatives are influential and sometimes introduced in conjunction with other approaches. Their common characteristic is their persistent reminder of the need, in any education endeavor, to focus explicitly on what happens in the school. Like community-based models, school-based approaches do not explicitly address the larger system. Unlike decentralization models, school- (and community-) based reforms devote substantial time to building the capacity of schoolteachers, officials, and community members and truly local organizations.

Though growing from different roots, community- and school-based models are resonant with complexity theories, which emphasize the "self-organizing" nature of "complex adaptive systems" (see, for example, Byrne, 1998; Lewin, Little, & Colclough, 1982). Complexity theories emphasize the difficulty of controlling the direction and nature of change in a complex system. Complex systems are systematic but not organized or directed by a central authority. They can be influenced, with an understanding of "leverage points" but the final consequences cannot be planned in any definitive way. Table 2.2 below contrasts some of the education characteristics of the community-based models with those of centralized and decentralized-regionalization models.

Table 2.2   Approaches to the Delivery of Education

	Centralized	Decentralized-regionalization	Community-based
School organization	Sequence of graded classes that cover full cycle of basic education	Sequence of graded classes with some schools focusing only on lower grades	Can be a multigrade class, or a single common grade class, sometimes several grades
School size	Minimum of 180–200	Based on number of students	Circa 30 students in the locale per class
Location	Tend to be near central government offices	Each region decides on school sites	Where there are 30 eligible students, teacher
Permanency of school building	Solid structure, often brick or ferro-concrete according to donor plan	Solid structure, designed locally and built with local materials	Simple structure, may be of local wood or bamboo
Curriculum theory	Public schooling targets the normal pattern of development	Target normal pattern while recognizing diversity of local cultures	Every child can learn at their own pace
Language of instruction	National language	Regional language	Often vernacular
Instructional materials	Primarily textbooks in national language	Primarily textbooks in local languages	Likely to be modular, with extensive reliance on local examples; Highly structured; Basic subjects
Teacher recruitment and posting	Teachers recruited, posted nationally, generally not to home areas	Teachers recruited, posted regionally	Teachers recruited locally
Teacher preparation	Attendance at normal school; Full certification	Attendance at normal school, or on the job	Possibly only a short course, for outstanding primary cycle graduates generally not certified, though may work toward
Monitoring student progress/promotion to next grade	System end-of-year tests with high repetition rates	State test or classroom teacher tests	Continuous assessment, master learning so all move forward at same pace

Transformative Models

Alongside these dominant models of reform have been persistent calls for much deeper and broader change, leading to transformation of the education system and the broader society. What we are calling *transformative models* represents a variety of more radical critiques of education and their roles in reproducing or transforming social inequalities and the domination of some groups and countries by others. Traditional education plays a pivotal role both in legitimizing oppressive economic, social, and political systems and in spreading ideologies that mask oppression. Dominant reform strategies work either to focus attention on less salient dimensions of the system or to further the oppressive cause. Neoliberal policy is particularly dangerous in this regard, for it seeks to reduce the public good nature of education, weaken the potentially protective role of the central state, and open the education and other systems up to markets and global forces. From such a perspective, even apparently bottom-up initiatives such as community schools serve the larger, but hidden, interests of making the world safe for the accumulation of capital. Traditional education, from this critical perspective, serves the function of domestication, whereas liberatory education works to heighten the critical consciousness of the oppressed, helping to realize their role as subjects in the building of the social order (Freire, 1993). Transformative models have played a relatively minor policy role in recent years. However, they informed a number of national experiments in education in socialist countries: Cuba, Tanzania, Guinea-Bissau, and Nicaragua (see Carnoy et al., 1990), as well as helping to inform the ideology of resistance to apartheid in South Africa and Namibia. Though not widely implemented, the transformative model provides a vision of true change and, perhaps more importantly, a critical counterbalance to totalizing views of education and development.

Table 2.3 contrasts the six models in terms of their approach to the process of reform.

SUMMARY: EVOLVING UNDERSTANDING OF REFORM

Over the decades following World War II, several distinctive education visions have emerged. The initial vision was simply a perpetuation of

Table 2.3 Approaches to the Reform Process

	Metropolitan	Centralized	Decentralized-regionalization	Decentralized-sectoral reform	Community/School-based	Transformative
Role of education in development	Education is consumption item; Education is for preparation of elites	Education is to lead national development and national consciousness	Education is to lead development, foster regional, maybe national, consciousness	Education as individual and social investment	Education should help local people live better lives. Education is focused in schools and in communities	Education should transform society, reduce inequality and oppression
Basic assumption of reform	Developing countries (DCs) need to build a strong system, like "core" systems	Deficiency—DCs lack technical knowledge, funding, systems, educational stuff	Local deficiency—DC regions lack technical knowledge, funding, educational stuff	Dysfunction—DCs need to restructure, to use stuff they have better and focus on outcomes	Education reform must start at point of service	Education can domesticate, but its real purpose is to liberate.
Prescription	Emulate metropolitan models	Technical assistance and funding through projects	Move decision making closer to people—the region	Changes to "operating system" (maybe more stuff); Sector-wide strategy	Begin reform with school, community	Remain critical; Develop alternative sites of power.
Who initiates reform?	Metropolitan leadership, or designees	National leadership or designees. Donors	Regional leadership, or designees. Donors	Any stakeholders who can gather influence. Donors	Schools or communities	Oppressed
Role of central government	To implement metropolitan decisions	Provider, implementer	To set parameters, leave much as possible to regions	To set rules, monitor implementation, evaluate outcomes	Support schools and communities	To promote transformative change
Role of local education agents	To comply with metropolitan	To comply with national	To comply with regional	To help shape policy, practice	To lead reform	To raise own and others' critical consciousness
Attention to local needs	Very little	Standard provision (to extent possible)	Standard provision of regional models	Participation of local, external agents encouraged	Very high	High
The "truth" of each model	There are different ways to organize an education system. Ed systems are institutions.	Coordination is necessary; Important to see big picture; Technical assistance, funding, capacity building are necessary.	One size does not fit all; Regional variations should be attended to, especially in instructional decisions.	Importance of systemic reform. Need to change way things work, not just more of same. Outcomes are important.	Reform must get inside the school. Alternatives exist to standard models of education provision.	Education often fails to free the poor. Dominant approaches to reform tend to benefit the powerful disproportionately.

the education practices of the former colonial powers. Subsequently, multilateral donors first devised a model following many of the assumptions of highly centralized systems, especially the French. This was followed by a more decentralized model that reflected greater sensitivity to the heterogeneity of cultures and interests within national boundaries, but which did little to change the top-down relationships of system managers with communities and school-level personnel. Over the last decade, a more ambitious decentralization variant has developed, one which seeks to restructure relationships and broaden participation within and outside the education sector. Around the same time, indigenous and international nongovernmental organizations have demonstrated considerable success in devising a variety of new models that draw on the aspirations and resources of local communities. At the same time, the focus on local conditions of education has fostered a greater appreciation of school-based dimensions of reform. Finally, transformative models question the real purposes of education: to fill students with knowledge or to help them become active subjects of social transformation, to accept and fit into the social order or to challenge it.

In a given country, two or more of these visions may coexist, serving different constituencies. For example, in the Cameroons two neocolonial models, British and French, coexist, serving different regions of the country. In Bangladesh, the centralized model generally prevails in the more urban areas, whereas in the rural areas NGOs are fostering their distinctive community-based models; perhaps the most notable is that sponsored by BRAC, which currently reaches out to several million children, primarily young girls, in peripheral areas throughout Bangladesh. A given reform initiative may seek to combine the insights of different models of reform.

Though the promoters of the respective models might not agree, each of these models has strengths and weaknesses. The neocolonial as well as the centralized models may have the greatest potential for providing a high quality of education geared to enabling young people to succeed in the upper grades of modern schooling. Unfortunately, these models are relatively insensitive to the needs of young learners and hence foster high repetition and dropout rates. Moreover, it is difficult to deliver education along the lines of these models to children in the more isolated peripheral areas, or to children who are, in one way or another, out of the mainstream. The decentralized-regionalization and especially the community-based models are most effective in reaching out and providing an education experience that harmonizes with local cultural needs. When carefully monitored, the community-based models can also deliver high-quality education at least through the early grades, but there are few effective examples for the later grades of schooling. Sectoral models provide the hope of systems transformed, but it is difficult to see, in fact, how such proposals will play out. The community-based models may involve less expense in some areas, but they place a greater burden on beneficiaries and thus in that sense are less equitable. School-based approaches highlight the essential nature of within-school processes but lack a systemic vision. Transformative models keep the focus on equity but are difficult at this point to see being implemented on a national scale.

As suggested, we believe we are between paradigms, as it were, well aware of the limitations of past models and of the requirements for a new approach to reform but not yet possessed of a coherent vision of what such a model might look like. Chapter 3 continues the discussion of context and process by focusing on internal contexts and theories of change. Before moving on, however, we take some time to discuss broad trends and indicators of success in education reform.

ANNEX: THE CONCEPTUAL HERITAGE OF EDUCATION REFORM INDICATORS

Educators have proceeded through several phases in the systematic planning and analysis of education systems, generating a complex and sometimes contradictory (or at least counterintuitive) language for discussing accomplishments.

Early Developments

Systematic efforts to provide education on a national scale were first begun in the 18th century, most notably in Sweden and Prussia. At that time local governments were the primary units in national plans, and national governments were concerned with providing at least one school for each administrative unit. Additional schools were allowed and subsidized if enough children enrolled to justify such a move, but these early efforts failed to take into account those areas outside the de facto jurisdiction of local governments—nor did they concern themselves with those children who did not seek schooling. Central authorities prescribed a curriculum outline but provided only minimal supervision and instructional support.

Progressivism

From about the turn of the 20th century, particularly in the United States and under the leadership of the "progressive" political reformers who sought to de-politicize and rationalize public services, education planning acquired a more systematic character. Principles of scientific administration (inspired at least in part by the engineering models of Taylorism) were applied to examine the efficiency of schools, primarily relating the actions of school personnel to efficiency in graduating students. This approach highlighted such problems as dropouts and repetition, with less attention to such goals as quality and values education. Various forms of psychological and achievement tests were devised to help education administrators in their work, but these tests had little direct impact on planning.

At the same time, reformers such as John Dewey in the United States and a number of educators in Europe and Japan sought to humanize and democratize education. A variety of alternative approaches were developed to educate children, especially those of preschool and primary school age. Efforts were made to attend to the holistic needs of the child.

Socialist Planning

Concurrent with and a derivation of Taylorism was the development of systematic planning in the newly formed Union of Soviet Socialist Republics (USSR). Committed to mass education and faced with a vast territory and population, the socialist educators also developed a vocabulary stressing efficiency. On the one hand, they focused on issues of internal efficiency, that is, the strategies that would enable children to complete school in a minimum amount of time, thus providing room for new cohorts of children; such strategies included automatic promotion, the use of tutors, and instruction in local languages. On the other hand, the socialist planners were concerned with placing every graduate in a productive job—external efficiency. This led to extensive studies of the relationship between education and the needs of the labor market. One practical outcome was the development of various forms of vocational and technical training for many of those youth who had completed a basic education course. Ultimately techniques of manpower planning emerged, and external efficiency measures of the degree of fit between education experiences and labor market needs were proposed.

Access and Mobility

Refinements of these engineering models of schooling were still dominant in education planning through World War II, and left a strong imprint on early UNESCO work in developing national planning capabilities throughout the world. The main concern of many of these agencies was to develop measures of internal and external efficiency.

An additional refinement, in view of the United Nations declaration and the increasing acceptance of children's right to education, was the development of measures of access, initially crude, through dividing the number of children in school by some measure of total or school-aged population (typically developed by another agency). During the 1950s sociologists became increasingly interested in questions of access and began to investigate the relative openness of education systems cross-nationally. They then related this education openness to the relative openness of occupational systems, attempting to understand the extent to which education contributed to social mobility. These studies concluded that education promoted social mobility when nations expanded their industrial sectors. However, when economies remained stagnant and primarily agricultural, education expansion led primarily to educated unemployment. Refinements of early mobility studies included the development of education attainment models.

Returns on Investment in Education

As nations expanded their education systems to provide mass and universal access, education budgets grew, and planners began to investigate the cost-effectiveness of these expenditures. Their efforts were accelerated by the increasing interest of economists in the relationship between education and overall processes of development. Whereas the earlier language of efficiency had generally been phrased in terms of physical ratios, by the late 1960s new financially based measures had gained prominence.

A focus of these studies were calculations of the private and social rates of return to a nation's investment in education. Studies suggested that such rates were surprisingly high, compared with investment in the industrial infrastructure, for example. Primary education generally yielded a higher social rate of return than secondary or higher education. A second focus involved an examination of the relative returns on different types of education investments such as expenditures on teachers, textbooks, and school buildings.

Education Quality

During this period, some analysts began to argue that the task of providing access to schools and even of developing relatively efficient education processes had essentially been achieved. The question arose of whether children were learning anything, especially in systems with automatic promotion. Were children receiving a "quality" education? Increasing attention came to be devoted to determining what children learned in school and what features of the overall process were related to their accomplishments. One severe limitation in this new area of effort was the scarcity of reliable measures of learning. While reasonable measures for such subjects as language, mathematics, and science could be devised, though infrequently used, researchers experienced difficulty in developing measures of other desirable skills or values. As a result, determinations of quality came to be based on traditional academic subjects. In many countries, national assessments have only recently been undertaken to determine the extent to which children are acquiring the intended curriculum. Instead, most countries have relied on national examinations almost exclusively as a means of selecting students for higher levels of education.

In the 1960s James Coleman and others (1966) conducted an influential study in the United States that concluded that minorities and poor children received a lower-quality education than did members of the majority group, and did not fare as well on tests of achievement. Coleman and colleagues also observed that differences in the quality of education inputs were not the most important factor in explaining the lower achievement of minorities and poor children. Instead, he pointed instead to various "out of school" factors such as the home environment and family socioeconomic status (Coleman et al., 1966). Coleman-type studies have been widely replicated both by individual researchers and in the International Education Achievement (IEA) survey; various analysts, comparing the pattern of findings from these numerous studies, reported that school factors have had a much greater impact in developing countries than in industrialized nations. Recent research suggests, however, that the Coleman effect may be spreading and that differences in school inputs are more weakly associated with differences in learning outcomes than found in the 1960s (Baker, Goesling, & Letendre, 2002).

Effective Schools

While Coleman's and other such studies focused primarily on the relationship between academic achievement and what went into schools (parental background, teachers, textbooks, buildings, etc.), educators in recent years have urged that greater attention be given to what happens inside the schools. They point out that certain schools, while objectively no different from other schools in terms of these inputs, nevertheless have a much greater impact on children's academic achievement. These educators have sought to detail the features of these effective schools, and suggest that such factors as leadership, clear goals, a positive school climate, and discipline make a difference. A recent theme has been to suggest that schools that have considerable discretion in managing themselves tend to achieve greater effectiveness than those whose actions are circumscribed by large bureaucracies.

Community Participation

While the mainstream of education planning focuses on formal units within the governmental structure and education bureaucracy, a countercurrent has always urged greater attention to the concerns of the recipients of education. Leading spokespersons for the increased involvement of parents, communities, and NGOs stress the rigidities and limitations of bureaucracies and the vital importance of capitalizing on the wisdom and energy available in traditional organizations (Korten, 1980; Shaeffer, 1992). This participatory tradition relies primarily on qualitative evidence to illustrate its proposals and recommendations.

These traditions, the problems they address, and the data they use to answer their questions can be summed up in Table 2.4.

Over time, education planners have multiplied the criteria employed to evaluate education systems. Early criteria were relatively easy to measure, while those proposed in more recent years are more complex, requiring greater care and expense to realize. At the same time,

Table 2.4   The Heritage of Indicators

	Problem	Indicator
Bureaucracy	How many schools are there?	Basic statistics
Progressivism	How well are they run?	Internal efficiency
Socialism	Are graduates working?	External efficiency
Access	Who gets in?	Enrollment ratios
Social mobility	Does education increase an individual's chances?	Mobility rates
Economic returns	Should the public support education?	Rates of return by level
Costs–benefits	Which inputs are most beneficial?	Costs, quantified benefits, measures of effectiveness
Education production	Do schools make a difference?	Student achievement
Effective schools	Why do some schools do better than others?	Aspects of school climate
Participation	Who controls schools? Who pays?	Measures of parental attitudes and satisfaction

increased calls for accountability have led to an increased reliance on indicators of individual and system performance and process. We would argue that our capacity to measure, limited as it is, still outstrips our capacity to manage accountability.

NOTES

1. We use the term *modern school* to refer to formal schooling based on the "Western" model, consisting of formal, graded schools, offering credentials and serving as a prerequisite for entry into higher levels of schooling (Williams, 1997).

2. While this volume emphasizes the development of education systems according to a limited number of patterns, other scholars emphasize the convergence of education institutions (see, for example, Chabbott, 2003; Meyer & Hannan, 1979; Fuller & Rubinson, 1992).

3. Throughout, the discussion refers most directly to basic education in the formal system, though there are implications for higher education as well.

4. We use the expression *publicized* to highlight the politics of good ideas. Interested organizations and stakeholder groups are rarely neutral with regard to how change should be approached. Those with more access to publicity are more able to promote their ideas as the best available.

5. Despite the general tendency to retain much of the colonial system, a number of governments made conscious efforts to break with the past: Tanzania, China, Guinea, Ghana, Cuba, Nicaragua, for example. These efforts were more or less successful, though all encountered resistance, and all, with the possible exception of Cuba, have retreated from their most revolutionary claims (see Carnoy et al., 1990).

6. Still, UNESCO has continued to play an influential advocacy and technical assistance role, though overshadowed somewhat by the bilateral agencies and multilateral banks.

CHAPTER 3

Thinking about Contexts and Processes of Change

Previous chapters have considered what might be termed the macro-contexts of education change: chapter 1 discussed dominant traditions of education that, institutionalized during formative periods, continue to influence the thinking and activities of education actors and their institutions long after their introduction. From this analysis, we draw several insights. First, despite underlying commonalities among forms of the "modern school," there are important differences across systems, differences that have important impacts on the lives of education actors and that frame the possibilities for reform of education institutions. Despite convergence at some levels, there are, at other levels of analysis, influential, and persistent, institutional differences in the organization and operation of education systems. These differences suggest the possibility of policy space for change. In addition, the discussion of traditions of education reminds us that education reform is nowhere undertaken on a blank slate. Any effort at change takes place in context, among people with history, traditions, institutions, and memory. In this way, reform would appear to involve a substantially deeper level of institutional change than is considered in many policy and planning exercises. At the same time, national education systems are not unique unto themselves. They tend to share features with other systems, based in part on common background and the resilience of institutions.

In the context of these influential models, chapter 2 then elaborated a roughly historical typology of approaches to the education development process. Chapter 2 ends with the assertion that, given the problems of current approaches, the profession lacks a coherent paradigm for managing systematic change in education. At the same time, the expectations for reform have grown: reform is charged not only with putting in place a new curriculum, for example, but also with developing the capacity of the system to develop, implement, and evaluate curriculum on its own on a continuing basis. Not only is reform called upon to complete the job of the reform in a technically effective manner, but it is also tasked with collaborating in that process with new and various groups of stakeholders and managing different actors in the system. Reform is charged not only with making needed improvements in the delivery of education services but also with transformation of its own system and ultimately of society.

Working to achieve such objectives—indeed any changes to the deep structure of education systems—requires critical attention to "local" as well as macro contexts. This is not to deny the salience of macro conditions, especially in the face of powerful external forces and organizations. But the effects of the external on reform take place locally. Regardless of technical rationality, local political, organizational, and social factors and local implementers can decide the fate of an initiative. And so, this chapter discusses some of the issues of context and process that affect the change process. In particular, the chapter discusses:

- multiple contexts of education change—the policy and the organizational contexts in which change is decided and enacted; the larger social contexts within the country; and the external political economy.
- processes of education change—surfacing and testing implicit change theories-in-use; development hypotheses, program theories, and their empirical bases; factors affecting organizational learning; and (more and less useful) models of the change process.

Looking ahead, chapter 4 turns to the outputs and outcomes of education in different national systems, particularly in light of international efforts to mobilize education systems to meet targets associated with Education for All (EFA) and the Millennium Development Goals. The remainder of the book elaborates strategic options for change agents seeking to bring about reform.

MULTIPLE CONTEXTS

Contexts of Change

The first insight we would offer is a simple one, though relatively infrequently observed: the effectiveness of reform must be understood (and plans made) not primarily in terms of intent, but in terms of what is implemented and then what is sustained or institutionalized. Accordingly, the change agent's job is not simply to develop a technically sound and financially viable plan but to plan for implementation and (help) develop a process that will sustain and institutionalize the desired change. At a minimum, then, at least three contexts are directly relevant to this view of change:

- the context of policy formulation and planning;
- the context of implementation; and
- the context of institutionalization.

However well designed a policy is from the perspective of actors in one context, it is likely to look quite different to actors in another. A decentralization initiative, for example, may be intended by those in the formulation/planning context primarily as a means of enhancing the authority of actors closer to the "action." However, to those implementing the reform, the same initiative might appear, for example, to be an unfunded mandate, a "decentralization" of problems the center is incapable of handling, even an unwanted increase in workload. Thus, to enhance chances of effective formulation, implementation, and institutionalization, a policy should "make sense," initially and on an ongoing basis, in all three contexts. We use the term *naïve planning* to refer to change initiatives that are uninformed by the multiple contexts of policy, for example, policy developed with only the policy-making context in mind.

How important is awareness of context? That depends. The greater the need for economies of scale or national mobilization of resources, the greater the reliance on central expertise or coordination, the greater the importance of systemic linkages or of national political leadership or law, the greater the importance of attention to the contexts of formulation and planning. In terms of attention to the "bottom," or "enacting contexts" of reform, the more the reform relies on buy-in on the part of implementers and sustainers—immediately, or over time—the more the reform requires professional judgment on the part of implementers and/or sustainers, the more change agents need to consider the differential contexts of implementation and institutionalization in their plans. Similarly, the more local contexts vary in important or unknown ways, or the more unpredictable the course of reform in local contexts, the greater the need for awareness, and consideration, of local context in planning.

We would argue that three questions are particularly salient:

- *Are enactors able to?* Are implementers and sustainers able—at individual and organizational levels—to implement/sustain the policy or change? Ability includes resources, know-how, and organizational wherewithal.
- *Do they have to?* How free are implementers and sustainers *not* to implement/sustain the policy?
- *Do they want to?* Does it make sense for implementers/sustainers—on balance, given other choices, everything else going on, history, and the costs and benefits from the perspective of implementers and sustainers—to implement/sustain the policy or change? Put another way, given the values, goals, competing claims on attention and time, the relative ability of authority to coerce, and the past, is it rational for implementers or sustainers to implement/sustain this policy? This cost–benefit calculus is likely to include organizational, economic, political, social, cultural, historical, and perhaps ideological considerations.

Participation of implementers and sustainers in the formulation and planning of policy is one useful way to work toward responsiveness to these contexts. *Participation*, of course is a fuzzy term, referring to a variety of particular strategies and begging for problematization. Indeed, participation can refer to very casual to quite meaningful involvement in decisions that affect one (see Shaeffer, 1992). Participation, whichever meaning is used, is not a panacea, but we would argue that participatory approaches likely offer a better possibility of contextually informed planning than nonparticipatory approaches.[1]

In addition, the organizational contexts in which policy maker, implementer, and sustainer work are likely to play particularly influential roles in shaping response to a reform initiative—the extent to which an organization's survival and well-being is threatened or assured; internal systems of accountability, reward, and support; the extent of hierarchy and cohesion within the organization; an organization's openness to change and learning; and so forth.

In thinking about context, it is important to be clear about the point or points at which implementation decisions are made. Thus, for example, if a policy aims to increase girls' enrollment in primary school, an obvious context of implementation is the family. (Local officials may promulgate, even promote, the policy, but the family is the critical implementer.) Does it make sense—given the family's economic conditions; other children; the availability, safety, and attractiveness of the school; and the family's cultural values; and in light of the government's ability and willingness to coerce—to send a particular girl to school? Regardless of the rationality of girls' education from a national perspective, or even from the long-range perspective of the family, a family is unlikely to enroll a girl in school if the perceived costs (physical, economic, social, cultural, etc.) of enrollment outweigh the perceived benefits and if no one compels enrollment. Many well-intended but centrally focused diagnoses of girls' education, for example, construe the problems and solutions only from the perspective of policy makers and planners, not, critically, from the perspective of those who will decide whether or not girls attend school.

If part of the girls' education initiative involves a pregnancy policy, for another example, whereby adolescent mothers are permitted to return to school after childbirth, then the school leadership is likely to be a critical context for implementation. If a school director has substantial discretion in implementing the policy, for example, his or her internal calculus of costs and benefits is likely to determine implementation (see Wolf et al., 1999).

A policy that enjoys widespread support is also more likely to be sustained, whereas one lacking such support, whether through opposition or the noise of competing claims, is likely to suffer from benign neglect. In contexts of choice, we have argued, the social, cultural, political, and organizational viabilities of a policy or change are as important to its sustainability as its financial feasibility.

We would argue that implementers and sustainers almost always act in ways that are rational, and can be understood, but these ways are rational in their own contexts. What might appear to be irrational on the part of an implementer and sustainer is often a misplaced projection of the rationality of the planner/policy maker onto the context of implementer/sustainer.

Planners working under the assumptions of "rational planning" and hierarchical authority are particularly prone to missing the diverse rationalities of the multiple contexts and players in policy reform. In an effort to solve education problems expeditiously and under the consistently tight constraints of funding and attention, overly rational planners tend to downplay the history and context of a problem, the meaning it has to different players. They tend to apply the technical rationality of solving a problem to the different rationalities of implementation and institutionalization, whereas solving a technical problem is only part of the process of implementing and institutionalizing change. In this way, outsiders may be particularly challenged, as compared with knowledgeable insiders, in developing implementable, socially sustainable plans, as they tend to lack a sufficient understanding of the particular local contexts.

At the same time, administrative authorities are prone to confusing legitimate or positional power with enforcement power. They are likely to assume a policy or plan will be implemented in the specified way because authorities, who are in charge, have made the policy decision. In this way, administrative authorities may be more challenged than outsiders to develop implementable, socially sustainable policies and plans, for they may be too close and too convinced of the power in their authority. We remember a regional decentralization initiative in one country where the central ministry announced as fully implemented the afternoon it was promulgated by central authorities.

Larger Social Contexts of Reform

Given the pressures of time, attention, and resources, and the desire to improve the system, a conscientious change agent is likely to focus on the problem and solution, to the exclusion of context. If a rational planner, she or he will tend to focus quite intently on the best technical solution to the problem. This makes sense given the logistical and organization challenges of getting policy on the agenda, marshalling support, and gaining approval, and the technical challenges of defining problems, gathering data, devising affordable and hopefully effective strategies to deal with the problem, all fast. Moreover, it is difficult for technical staff, sitting in a planning office, for example, to do much about the context, whereas the change agent *can* work on the proposals for change. From the longer-range perspective of implementation and institutionalization, however, and of working to bring about deep change in education systems, it makes sense to think about context.

Nowhere, as we have asserted, does reform start with a blank slate. Change agents who miss the larger context run the risk of proposing naïve, underinformed strategies for change. Failure to see the larger context may result in a misunderstanding of the full origin and dynamic of the problem, leading, for example, to treatment of the symptom, to use a medical metaphor, rather than the underlying cause. Still, understanding context is an enormously complex undertaking, and it may be useful to highlight some of the dimensions of context of likely relevance.

Social Context: How does an initiative look not only in terms of the problem and solution, but also in terms of the larger social context?

Historical Context: What is the history of reform in this context? What historical experiences are likely to affect development, implementation, and success of the reform? How does an initiative look, not only in terms of current problems and possible solutions, but also in light of the history of problems and solutions?

Political Economic Context: Which groups stand to gain and lose by the reform?

Economic Context: How will the reform be financed? Over the short and the long term? What are the relative costs and benefits? How will costs and benefits accrue to different groups?

Organizational Context: Does the ministry have the capacity to implement and institutionalize a reform such as this?

Sociological Context: How will the reform affect predominant divisions in society?

Technical Context: How is the solution going to solve the problem? Do the parties responsible for implementation have the general knowledge, the specific understanding of tasks and responsibilities, and the resources to carry out their responsibilities?

Cultural Context: Is the reform compatible with local culture(s)? What meaning will the reform acquire in the context of local culture?

Political Context: How will the reform affect the distribution of power in society? Are dominant coalitions in favor? Why is this issue coming to the fore now?

PROCESSES OF CHANGE

In addition to mindfulness of context, we highlight the importance of the change process, in five dimensions: (1) the nature of the problem to be addressed (different problems call for different processes); (2) the social mechanisms and potential for social resolution of policy issues (the greater the social capital and the more developed social institutions, the easier the process, all else being equal); (3) the empirical and theoretical foundations of development hypotheses and program theories (relatively few proposals are well-grounded in theory and research); (4) the surfacing and testing of implicit theories of change; and (5) more and less useful models of the change process.

Nature of the Problem

Reimers and McGinn (1997) list four questions that provide useful distinctions among policy problems. Participatory processes become important to the extent that a problem is divergent, involves multiple disciplines and levels of knowledge, involves negotiation or multiple actors, and operates in a democratic policy arena. From this perspective, most important problems in education require a more or less participatory process.

- *Convergent or divergent*? Convergent problems have single solutions as compared with divergent problems, which have many possible good answers. Convergent questions tend to focus on technical issues, such as: What is the cost of educating a student through secondary school? A related divergent question might be: Should the government invest more in secondary education? There is a tendency to answer divergent problems with convergent answers, rather than to use answers to divergent questions to inform a larger process of decision making.

- *Single or multidisciplinary/level knowledge*? Some problems can be addressed with knowledge from a particular profession or discipline or from one level of the system, whereas other problems require knowledge from multiple disciplines and different system levels. Testing specialists, for example, could well design a continuous assessment system on their own. However, the knowledge that teachers, administrators, parents, and others have of conditions in schools, classrooms, and communities would be needed to design a continuous assessment system that is likely to be implemented, and widely used as intended.

- *Single decision maker or multiple actors*? Obviously, the fewer the number of people and levels of an organization involved in a decision, the less negotiation is required. A simple policy decision about administrative matters, for example, might be made by a minister or her designee, whereas use of a new instructional approach in teaching mathematics would require a much more complex set of negotiations to be successfully implemented.

- *Soluble with technical knowledge*? Some problems can be addressed using technical knowledge, whereas other problems can only be resolved by reference to values and preferences, which often vary greatly. Compare two questions: Will the elimination of school fees result in more girls enrolling and completing school? Is the purpose of education to prepare students for the workforce or to transform society and redress past inequities?

Authoritarian or Democratic Decision Making?

Reimers and McGinn (1997) raise a fifth question about the context of decision making—top-down or participatory? On the one hand, policies are more easily developed and implemented in a more authoritative system. At the same time, we would argue, more participatory policy processes, which often become necessary in addressing complex policy problems such as those outlined above, are facilitated by a successful history of participatory decision making in a system; the existence of social and political structures outside education in which public participation plays an important role; and by social cohesion or "social capital" and an operational level of trust among important groups of stakeholders and social groups. At the same time, the need to make important decisions in education can provide an occasion for initiating new forms of participation, as there is near universal agreement as to the importance and value of education, if not the means. Regardless, a society's predominant approach to decision making plays an important role in determining appropriate process.

Empirical Basis for Development Hypotheses and Program Theories

While advocating appropriate structuring of participation in the process of policy-making, we feel such processes should also be as informed as possible by a solid empirical base. As Reimers and McGinn argue, virtually all important decisions in education involve both technical and normative dimensions. Unfortunately, education facts are rarely cut and dried. Answers tend not to be right or wrong so much as right *if* one wants to achieve a certain goal. Or wrong *when* certain conditions prevail. In cases of divergent problems, or where the answer depends on the differing values of stakeholders, information can serve to inform trade-offs and suggest likely consequences of different courses of action.

We have argued that the empirical basis for most reform efforts in education is extremely weak. Most of what is done, we would argue, even by the most rational of technical planners, is based on something akin to faith. Elmore (1996), for example, argues that U.S. educators do not know how to improve education on a system-wide basis. Lacking knowledge of what is *sufficient*, we develop intervention after intervention of *necessary* measures that may, or may not, achieve targeted goals. It is worth inquiring, at appropriate points in the policy process, how grounded the underlying theories of change are in research and/or practice. Will holding teachers accountable for their students' scores on standardized tests result in improved instruction for all students? It seems logical that it would, but what does the research say? Do students who are forced to repeat a grade learn more than similar students who are promoted? We don't really know. What are the effects of school choice, for example, on equity? In a particular community? Across a system? We don't know. Given such a murky theoretical foundation, it is useful to make as explicit as possible and to test the underlying hypotheses on which we expect change initiatives to work.

Surfacing and Testing Theories-in-Use

Deep learning becomes possible as change agents become aware of their own, and others' (implicit, and often inaccurate), theories of change and work to surface and test them. Such an approach places the change agent in a learning as opposed to a knowing stance, useful given how little is known.

At this point, it may be useful to digress a bit into some basic points in organizational theory. Argyris and other constructivist theorists argue that people use "mental maps" to guide their plans, actions, and assessments of situations (Argyris & Schön, 1978).[2] These mental maps can be considered theories; they have the characteristics of theory—generality, consistency, completeness, testability, centrality, and simplicity. They may explain a particular event: for example, why a class scored poorly on a test. Or they may explain how the class, or the world, works in a more general way: for example, why students in rural areas score lower than students in urban schools. Theories are simplifications. They are more or less accurate in explaining how things work and more or less useful in helping people make sense of the world around them. People take action on the basis of theories they hold. Argyris and Schön (1978) call theories that individuals, or organizations, use to guide their actions "theories-in-use."

Most theories-in-use are tacit, that is, they do not operate at a conscious level. Tacit theories enable people to deal efficiently with a host of daily events without questioning causality at each step of the way. Tacit theories determine (and limit) how we see the world (Howley et al., forthcoming). Though most people are generally unaware of their own theories-in-use, theories guide behavior. Tacitly held theories can create difficulties, for they often contain unexamined assumptions. They can color understanding of what's happening and restrict one's ability to respond flexibly, though they are difficult to identify, surface, and change. Theories-in-use can be deduced by observation of behavior and critical analysis. If a teacher only asks boys to answer questions in a classroom of mixed gender, one can infer that she does not think much of girls' ability to respond. There may be other reasons, of course, but she has a theory-in-use that causes her not to call on girls, whatever she says.

At a conscious level, people are aware of their "espoused theories," the theories they use to explain their behavior, and the explicit values they support. People's behavior is generally guided by theories-in-use, while explanations and self-understanding are usually governed by their espoused theories. The teacher, for example, may state, and firmly believe, that she sees girls and boys as equally capable of learning. There is usually a certain discrepancy between people's espoused theories and their theories-in-use, sometimes more than a little discrepancy. Argyris and Schön (1978) believe that the closer espoused theories are to theories-in-use, the more effective the organization or individual.

Like Argyris and Schön (1978), we believe that this "theory" of theories-in-use is usefully applied to organizations as well as individuals. We would further apply theories-in-use to practices of education reform in general; to the approaches to change of particular education organizations such as schools, ministries, and funding agencies; and to particular initiatives. In the case of general approaches to reform, we might use the term *development hypotheses* to describe the developmental effects expected to follow from a particular initiative. In the case of a particular intervention, we use the term *project theory* to describe the chain of causes and effects expected to result from project activities. (See chapter 8 for discussion of program theory in the context of monitoring implementation.)

Often, assumptions are not wrong so much as they are too general, in which case they need to be qualified to be useful or the conditions need to be specified under which the assumption will accurately describe a particular situation. Take for example the widespread assertion that decentralization will lead to improved school effectiveness. Evidence suggests that this may be the case, or it may not. Decentralization may lead to improved school effectiveness, for example, if decentralization provides schools with the resources and authority to make instructionally sound decisions (and if effectiveness is well measured by scores on cognitive achievement tests). However, this desirable outcome may depend on the capacity of schools to make good instructional decisions. Thus, while the theory that decentralization will lead to higher student performance is not exactly wrong, it is somewhat misleading as a guide to action. It can be examined, and refined into a more useful theory, which can then be used, tested, and further refined. In this process, of course, useful lessons are being learned about how to improve schools. Of course, it is also the case that some theories-in-use are simply, and verifiably, wrong. For example, the theory of the earth being flat limited national policy options in Europe and elsewhere for thousands of years. However, due to the high stakes of being wrong, very few people, for centuries, were willing to test it.

A second set of associated concepts relates to learning. Argyris and Schön (1978) see learning as taking place as a consequence of the detection and correction of error. When sensing an error, most people look for an operational strategy that will work within the "goal-structure," and "rule-boundaries" they commonly use. This is "single-loop learning," a simple feedback loop, where outcomes cause adjustment of behaviors, as with a thermostat. (A similar concept, *first-order change*, was discussed in the introduction.) A thermostat senses an "error," or gap between actual and desired temperature, and responds by following the rule that says "turn on the heat." People involved in single-loop learning accept the framing of the problem (not enough heat) and take steps to address the problem by following the conventional "rule" for such situations (turn up the heat). Single-loop learning takes existing goals, beliefs, values, conceptual frameworks, and strategies for granted without critical reflection. It may work to increase the effectiveness of the strategies used to deal with the problem, it may even adopt a slightly different strategy for reaching the same goal (within the same rule boundaries), but it leaves most of the existing ways of doing things, including dysfunctional strategies and assumptions, in place. It works finely when, as in our example, adequate heat is the goal, lack of heat is the problem, and turning on the heat is an effective solution. However, single-loop learning is not effective when the environment changes, or when heat, to continue the example, is not the problem.

In such cases, double-loop learning (discussed in the introduction as *second-order change*) is needed to modify the governing variable of the system—in this case, seek heat—to some other goal. Double-loop learning involves surfacing and critically reflecting on goals, beliefs, values, conceptual frameworks, and strategies. As such it leads to *deep learning* and the possibility of *deep system change*. Double-loop learning is critical in organizations and individuals who find themselves in rapidly changing and uncertain contexts, or when solving problems that are complex, ill structured, or that change over time. Double-loop learning, while arguably essential for organizational effectiveness in uncertain environments, is generally discouraged in organizational life. Double-loop learning, by definition, calls into question the status quo and the ways things are conventionally done.

Generally, of course, people lose awareness of most of the governing variables they rely on, and focus their efforts on implementing their existing theories-in-use—doing what they've always done, only harder, or again and again. In many such cases, a more effective approach would be to question the goal or the theory underlying their strategy for reaching that goal. Lacking awareness of their own theories of change, policy makers may continue to utilize change strategies long after they have lost relevance or effectiveness to the problem at hand.

Rondinelli (1993) suggests, perhaps playfully, that most development work ought to be undertaken as policy experiments. Indeed, a considerable body of research and practitioner literature suggests strategies such as these for organizational as well as individual development. Peter Senge, notably, has written numerous books about learning organizations (see, for example, Senge, 1994).

Some faulty theories-in-use might fall into a category we might call "Theories Where We Don't Know Any Better":

- Doing something necessary is (implicitly) sufficient to improve a system. Provision of quality inputs will (necessarily) lead to improved learning—a common assumption we have discussed. In the case of schools, good textbooks are generally necessary to high levels of student achievement. However, textbooks must be adequately utilized to be effective in promoting learning. Thus, provision of textbooks may not be sufficient to improve learning. Even so, how many development projects have focused on curriculum development and distribution, with the expectation that such steps will necessarily result in measurably higher levels of student achievement?

• Schools and teachers can improve student learning (if they want to)—holding schools and teachers accountable will lead to increased learning. A number of education systems have put accountability systems in place to track student achievement and to sanction schools or teachers when students do not score sufficiently well. Implicit in such policies is the assumption that teachers or schools are able to improve student learning—that teachers and schools have the know-how, the resources, and the organizational wherewithal to improve student acquisition of the desired material. It may be the case that many schools, especially the weaker ones, are not able. A policy that simply puts accountability systems in place, but does not provide support to schools in improving, may run afoul on this theory. Of course, failure to meet the specified standards will be understood as failure on the part of teachers and school rather than failure of theory.

In addition, a number of other theories-in-use fall into a category we might call, "Theories Where We Do Know Better." Though rarely stated as such, these implicit theories can be identified in the design of a surprising number of education interventions. (Of course, the problem with theories-in-use is not a matter of explicit knowledge or values, but of implicit beliefs and resulting behavior.)

• Policy will be implemented as intended. Though rarely stated as directly as this, change processes that include no feedback loops to check the implementation of policy are "in-use" of this theory of change.
• Implementation will (necessarily) follow the policy decision.
• There will be no unintended consequences.

- People will adopt an idea because it is a good idea.
- A project will be sustained because it is a good project.
- People will act according to the rationality of the planner's context.
- People will do something because they are supposed to (or because it is their job, or because an authority told them to).
- Authorities, by virtue of their authority, can bring about implementation of a policy.
- Policy is made (only) by "policy makers" and officials at the "top" of the system.
- Technical considerations can be separated from politics.

Ideas, even inaccurate ones, live long beyond their originators, as John Maynard Keynes famously observed:

> The ideas of economists and political philosophers, both when they are right and when they are wrong, are more powerful than is commonly understood. Indeed, the world is ruled by little else. Practical men, who believe themselves to be quite exempt from any intellectual influences, are usually the slaves of some defunct economist. Madmen in authority, who hear voices in the air, are distilling their frenzy from some academic scribbler of a few years back. . . . Sooner or later, it is ideas, not vested interests, which are dangerous for good or evil.

MORE AND LESS USEFUL MODELS OF THE CHANGE PROCESS

Many of these assumptions are legacies of rational and stages models of the policy process, discussed briefly in the introduction, and of command and control models of education governance. Stages models suggest that the policy process is usefully understood as a sequential series of steps, distinct in function and time. Haddad and Demsky (1994) present a typical cycle, composed of eight "policy stages":

- Analysis of the existing situation
- Generation of policy options
- Evaluation of policy options
- Making the policy decision

- Planning for policy implementation
- Policy implementation
- Policy impact assessment
- Subsequent policy cycles

Other models vary slightly in the naming and specification of stages. Some models, for example, include more explicit stages of agenda setting, whereby policy problems are placed on the national decision-making agenda. (See Grindle & Thomas, 1991, for a useful discussion of stages models of policy.)

This model of the policy cycle has a number of advantages. It is useful heuristically. Indeed, we use it here to organize the second half of this book. It parallels the individual process of cognitive decision making and permits analysis of a variety of policies across a diversity of institutional contexts and policy domains. It serves as a checklist of necessary steps and their most rational sequence. The wise planner, for example, will base his/her generation of policy options on a thorough analysis of the current situation, else a key element be overlooked. It is good practice to hold evaluation of policy options until after a complete list is generated; typically, there are more and better options than the first ones that come to mind. And so forth. In these ways, the model directs the policy maker to a next logical step in the change process.

Nonetheless, stages models have a number of limitations in describing and prescribing actual policy formation and implementation processes (Porter & Hicks, 1997): real policy-making is rarely as neat as described. Policies can be derailed at any point, by forces having nothing to do with the technical quality of analysis. Policy-making does not necessarily proceed through all stages, nor does it necessarily follow the steps in order. Steps may be skipped, or returned to at subsequent times. Rarely do policy makers generate and evaluate a full range of options. Policy agents may use rational policy processes to justify decisions already reached rather than to identify the best technical solution. Then too, a full discussion of the pros and cons of different strategies is counterproductive in a contentious political environment where agreement may be more important to the success of education than the technically best solution. Moreover, while the stages model may accurately describe an individual's decision-making process, it does not describe collective decision making well, which is much more diffuse and less linear. Finally, stages models tend to reinforce a false division of labor, between those who formulate the policy and those who implement it, for example. This is associated with one of the pathologies of education reform efforts, the development of "good" plans that are not implemented. Finally, stages models of policy tend to be front-loaded, with much greater attention devoted to the plan than to implementation and beyond.

Porter and Hicks (1997), building on the work of Kingdon (1984), suggest that it is more useful to think of the policy process in terms of multiple "streams." At any given time, policy elites can focus on only a limited number of issues, hence the useful concept of *policy agenda*. Given the many potential issues that could be targeted, a policy is much more likely to get onto the agenda and to be acted upon if it represents a viable solution to a politically important problem. (As such, the policy can be seen as lying at the intersection of three somewhat independent streams, the stream of problems, the stream of solutions, and the stream of politics.) Many social conditions, Porter and Hicks point out, exist, without being considered policy problems. Girls may drop out of school due to pregnancy, for example, and this can be experienced as private tragedy, or it can be defined as a policy issue by being linked to public awareness of the issue as one about which action can and should be taken, and by government.

Like problems, there are many solutions floating around in the solutions stream, most of which are not acted upon. Solutions, often generated by policy researchers, attract attention when they are linked with problems. Both problems and solutions, however, are unlikely to assume priority unless linked with salient politics. Like problems and solutions, politics typically moves independently in its own stream according to its own logic and imperatives. Indeed, each stream has a life of its own. However, when the three streams converge on a given policy issue, action is likely.

Like all models, the streams model is a more or less useful simplification. It accounts well, we feel, for the selective rationality of government systems in deciding on and implementing policy. At the same time, it allows for the multiple rationalities of politics, policy solutions, and potential policy problems. The streams need not flow in any particular sequence, a realistic portrayal, given the way policies are actually formulated and adopted in organizations. The streams model recognizes the fluid yet understandable nature of the policy process. Ideas are important but not determinative of the outcomes of policy processes. Bad ideas as well as good may be adopted. Individuals and groups, inside or outside of government, can play an important role in bringing about policy change, by focusing attention and linking problems with solutions to political issues. Indeed, the authors spend considerable time discussing strategies that policy entrepreneurs can adopt to influence the policy process.

Thus while we organize our discussion according to a series of rational analytic steps, the process of policy change itself may be more usefully understood as an advocacy process (even if one is advocating a policy one feels, through dispassionate scientific analysis, best meets the needs of the nation). Viewed in this way, bringing about policy change is a matter of identifying and acting on leverage points.

Finally, we see a parallel set of problems with common conceptions of agency in the change process. Command and control models of change underlie many strategies undertaken by government. At their most severe, such models assume complete passiveness, compliance, and capacity, on the part of field implementers. Managers have perfect knowledge of what needs to be done at all levels of the system. Their job is to specify tasks and monitor compliance. Field implementers, for their part, are required (and are both willing and able) to do what they are told. (See Table 3.1.)

In fact, these "ideal type" conditions rarely apply to any human organization, and especially not schools, where the primary task of instruction is one that cannot be specified well from afar. School systems, as Weick (1976) famously observed, are "loosely coupled systems," and orders from the top have only modest direct effects down the line. As a result, teachers have considerable discretion in how enthusiastically they implement central directives, especially those where judgment is required.

A further problem is that it is unclear whether central administrators have the information needed to make all education decisions. While central administrators may see the big picture, teachers have the best information about the conditions facing the children in their classroom.

Table 3.1   Two Approaches to Implementation of Change in Complex Systems

Aspect/Dimension	Command & Control	More Participatory
Aliases	Top-down; hierarchical	Bottom-up; top-down and bottom-up
Type of planning	Forward	Backward
View of reform	Stages	Nonlinear, at least recursive
Metaphor for plan	Blueprint to be followed	Structured negotiations
Metaphor for organization	Hierarchy, machine, bureaucracy	Forum; herding cats
Ideal for Implementers	Obedience, capacity to carry out tasks; compliance	Professional judgment, capacity to move toward goals in local context; discretion
What implementers need from central authorities	Clarity & training	Discretion & support
Role of center vis-à-vis plan & implementers	Enforcement	Support; direction
Causal effect of factors affecting implementation	Deterministic	Influential, but contingent on transactions
Approach to implementation	Develop a good plan and follow it	Transactional; develop good process
Approach to monitoring	Monitor for compliance and adherence to details of plan	Monitor expected inputs, activities, intermediate outcomes, unexpected outcomes; monitor critical transactions; monitor to see inputs have arrived, if activities are taking place as expected, if intermediate outcomes are resulting as expected, what unexpected outcomes have resulted, if theory holds; monitor progress toward goals of reform; monitor "ongoing intelligence"
Understanding of deviations	Mistakes; errors	Possibly adaptive, possibly not; possible innovations, potential source of knowledge about what works where & when; possibly a problem with people, possibly a problem with plan, process, or in context

Table 3.1   (Continued)

Aspect/Dimension	Command & Control	More Participatory
Dealing with deviations from plan	Tighten accountability, measures of central control; reporting, oversight	See what can be learned; check theory and actors; balance accountability with support, participation, discretion
Possible consequences of strategies of dealing with deviations	(Sometimes) defensiveness; denial, unwillingness to admit failure; diminished capacity to learn from mistakes	Possible continued deviations from plan (due to weaker accountability)
Management strategies	Funding formulas, formal organizational structures, authority, relationships, regulations, administrative controls—budget, planning, evaluation	Knowledge, problem solving on part of implementers, incentive structures, bargaining among key groups, strategic use of funds
Works well when	Goals are clear, consistent, enjoy broad support; program theory is accurate; implementers are committed to change, capable; organizational conditions are favorable; reform is supported by interest groups; contextual conditions remain favorable; when central government has power, and little consensus possible among powerful groups of stakeholders	There is some area of (potential) agreement, a goal to be achieved; different groups are willing to negotiate; skillful facilitator having credibility with different groups

Source: Elmore, 1982

The technologies of instruction are not well enough understood to specify with any precision. The improvement of instruction, from this point of view, is one of enabling teachers to make the best decisions, based on their professional experience and knowledge, according to the changing classroom conditions. Finally, given the frontline nature of teachers' work, the "bottom" of the school system would seem a potentially fertile source of policy ideas. So, given the professional nature of teaching and the loosely coupled nature of schools, central administrators need a more sophisticated system of acquiring teachers' cooperation, their compliance, and their ideas.

A number of observers see changes in the role of government, as governments decentralize and work with "partners" outside the ministry. Adams (2000) characterizes these shifts in several ways. The *role of government* is shifting from financier, designer, and evaluator of education development to catalyst and partner with local organizations. There is a corresponding shift from control and compliance to policy coordination, management, and monitoring of regulations. The purpose of policy planning shifts accordingly, from a primary focus on the allocation of public resources to public/private coordination, and the coordination and mobilization of interest groups. The focus of *strategic planning* shifts from control to setting a national vision, and providing leadership in equalizing services. *Management support and administration* shift from detailed monitoring of administrative processes to monitoring of national standards, and support of research and development. Government's role shifts from provider of (all) services to facilitator of good services.

All of this suggests that a more participatory, professional process of policy development and implementation may better help education systems reach many of their goals. The complex goals and technologies associated with education suggest that teachers are much more useful as active, intelligent agents working toward and helping define national goals than they are as passive implementers of policy decisions reached at the center. School-based reform models suggest that such a learning process is best fostered by neither the directiveness of centralized and regionalization models of reform, nor the lack of guidance implicit in decentralized-sectoral reform strategies, which provide the incentives but not the technical assistance. What is needed is a more engaged process of *instructional coaching*. Such a perspective suggests that central ministries shift their orientation from administration (enforcing rules and regulations) to management (maximizing resource use to achieve goals) to leadership (mobilization to define and achieve higher-order goals).

Finally, dynamic systems theories such as complexity theories or chaos theory caution against too optimistic an approach to change (Howley et al., forthcoming; Wheatley, 1994). Schools and school systems, as "complex adaptive organizations" are inherently unpredictable. Causality is difficult to trace, as direct linear relationships are rare. Adaptive systems cannot be controlled. However, would-be change agents can take advantage of "leverage points" to attempt to influence the direction of change. The Internet, as a common example, cannot be directed, but it can be influenced. In such a system, a blueprint approach to planning is much less useful than a more interactive strategy, with broad goals set but with flexible strategies that shift according to changing conditions. Everything we know about the reform process suggests that no plan can anticipate every development. Too much is unknown. There are too many variables outside the control of ministries of education. More useful than a specification of every detail is general agreement on broad goals, the political will to change, and, as we have argued elsewhere, a process that structures information and participation in negotiating, understanding, and moving toward goals.

SUMMARY: REFORM AS LEARNING

This chapter has discussed a series of micro-contextual factors likely to affect the reform process. We have discussed the importance of understanding "local context," specifically, the contexts of implementation and of institutionalization, as well as that of policy formulation and planning. Planners eager to institute system reform should pay attention to the sociopolitical context in which the reform will live, attending to the internal and external political, historical, cultural, and organizational factors likely to be relevant. Policy makers have also been urged to surface and test their theories of change and causality in education, to adopt a *learning*, as opposed to a *knowing*, or performing, stance. We have discussed ways the change process is commonly, and can more usefully be, understood, both in terms of how change takes place and how it is directed. Rather than a series of sequential, rational steps, policy adoption is better understood as the convergence of problems, solutions, and politics. Change agents can identify leverage points to bring about such convergence.

Rather than a top-down bureaucratic system of command and control, education systems ought to work better as more participatory organizations supporting the work of professional teachers, using an appropriate mix of carrot and stick, accountability and support, identification and mobilization around common goals. Education systems might operate more effectively as learning organizations rather than as knowing, declaring, or performing systems. Given the unpredictability of reform, front-loaded designs are likely less useful than agreement on the need to change and on the broad outlines of reform, and a legitimate process to organize discussion by stakeholders around values, the state of the system, the ways change can be promoted, and the desired direction and nature of reform.

NOTES

1. See *Current Issues in Comparative Education* (vol. 6, no. 2: Participatory Development: A Promise Revisited) for a critical discussion of this issue.

2. See also the relevant discussion of frame-shifting in Bolman and Deal, 1997.

CHAPTER 4

A Report Card on Education Reform

For over five decades, improvements in education have been promoted by national governments and international agencies, consistent with the 1948 UN Universal Declaration of Human Rights that stated that every child has a right to education. One of the main goals of the United Nations Educational, Social, and Cultural Organization (UNESCO) has been to foster universal basic education throughout the world. The argument for mass education was further bolstered in the 1960s when economists asserted that economic returns to basic education at 20% + annually were superior to investments in virtually all other developmental inputs. Government and donor allocations for basic education increased over the 1970s. However, due to high levels of debt and the demands of structural adjustment, many national governments cut back on their funding of education in the 1980s. However, following the Jomtien conference and the World Declaration on Education for All (EFA) of 1990, there was a resurgence of interest in improving education. Progress toward EFA was reviewed at the Dakar conference of 2000, and the global commitment to EFA became one of the nine core goals of the Millennium Development Goals (MDG) that now guide much of the current work in international development.

In this chapter, we seek to understand how much change has actually taken place over the past decade as well as where this change has occurred. Much of the evidence reviewed here was first considered in the Dakar conference of 2000 and in other forums.[1] A recent World Bank report updates the Dakar conference information with a "global scorecard" observing "that over the 1990s the average rate of primary school completion in the developing world (on a country weighted basis) improved only from 72 to 77%, far short of the progress needed to ensure achievement of the education MDG of universal primary completion" (Bruns, Mingat, & Raktomalala, 2003, p. 3).

What we add to these earlier accounts is a country-by-country report card of the current state of education reform. Our focus will be on the core concerns of access, equity, quality, efficiency, and relevance—to the extent that available data allows this.[2] Conversely, we also will highlight those settings where education is in decline, and seek to indicate what has gone wrong. The chapter ends by highlighting 22 countries *for which data is available* where reform is lagging. There are at least as many additional countries for which data is not available where EFA may be in trouble. Our aim here is to review a methodology for highlighting successes and failures in the international effort to promote EFA.[3] The intention is not to criticize particular countries, for most of the countries that are lagging in EFA have made major, albeit troubled, efforts to improve provision, and as we observe below they have encountered considerable obstacles, many of which lie outside of the education sector. At the same time, some countries have managed, for whatever reason, to advance.

WHY EFA?

Poverty, Malnutrition, Health

The fundamental rationale for EFA is the belief that the educated person lives a fuller and longer life and that educated countries are healthier, more equitable, and more prosperous (World Bank, 1993). Additionally, many advocates of EFA focus on the link with political stability and freedom. There are many studies that show direct correlations between the level of educational attainment of individuals and their overall well-being (Prescott-Allen, 2001). Similarly there are numerous studies that report a link between the educational development in nations and other indicators of national success (McMahon, 1999). Table 4.1 presents an example of these correlations for 1990, the baseline year of EFA. As can be seen, countries that have higher primary and secondary enrollment ratios and greater gender equity tend to have lower infant mortality, lower population growth, and higher per capita income; these relations are equally strong for the sample of developing countries (those with per capita annual income below $5,000, the second correlation in each cell of the table) as for the full sample of developed and developing nations (the first correlation).

Table 4.1 Pearson Correlation (r) of Indicators of Educational Access and Equity with Three Indicators of Well-Being, 1990 and 1990–2000

Indicators (1990)	Primary Gross Enrollment Rate (GER)	Secondary GER	Primary Gender Ratio	Secondary Gender Ratio
All countries (n= 145)				
Infant mortality	−.553	−.713	−.684	−.831
Population growth rate	−.380	−.494	−.367	−.538
GDP per capita (PPP)	.323	.670	.450	.733
Poor countries (n= 65)				
Infant mortality	−.649	−.702	−.650	−.759
Population growth rate	−.257	−.439	−.344	−.480
GDP per capita (PPP)	.394	.741	.518	.763

	Change in primary GER 1990–2000	Change in secondary GER 1990–2000	Change in primary gender ratio 1990–2000	Change in secondary gender ratio 1990–2000
All countries (n= 145)				
Change in infant mortality	−.103	−.220	.030	−.096
Change in population growth rate	.020	.200	.080	−.006
Change in per capita income in PPP	−.030	.359	.075	.178
Poor countries (n= 65)				
Change in infant mortality	−.134	−.234	−.037	−.204
Change in population growth rate	.078	.243	.163	−.004
Change in per capita income in PPP	.105	.484	.146	.178

Note: Poor countries are those with per capita income below $5000.

Distinct from these one-time illustrations of the value of education, is there a relation between change in education and change in societal well-being? Wheeler (1984) provided a sophisticated cross-national analysis of the link between educational improvement and both population and economic growth using data for the 1970s; here we update several of his findings.

The second half of the table suggests that many of the same relations continue through the 1990s. Countries that have improved their level of access to basic education during the 1990s have experienced a decline in infant mortality ($r = -.134$ for developing countries; $-.103$ for all countries) and an increase in per capita income ($r = .105$ for developing countries).[4] These are admittedly correlations of modest strength; one reason is that the majority of nations already reported relatively high levels of access to basic education in 1990, and for those nations the potential range for further improvement was modest. In contrast, there was greater range for improvement at the secondary level. The correlations of secondary-level expansion with the same indicators of well-being are considerably stronger. For example, concerning the link to per capita income, there is a stronger correlation with secondary educational expansion ($r = .484$ for developing countries) than with primary level educational expansion ($r = .105$). On the other hand, the correlations of educational improvement with change in the population growth rate are inconsistent; if anything educational expansion at the primary and secondary level and improvement in the gender ratio appear to be moderately positively associated with an increase in the population growth rate.

The Cultural and Institutional Heritage

Among the many factors influencing educational expansion and equity are the cultural and institutional heritage of each setting. In traditional Confucian and Islamic societies, woman's place was traditionally in the home so opportunities for education were not normally extended to young girls. However, during the modern era, most Confucian nations came to believe that basic education was equally important for boys and girls; currently these same societies are opening up the doors of secondary and higher education to young women. While Islamic societies have not gone as far as the Confucian group in opening up basic education, nevertheless, as illustrated in Table 4.2, the average levels of access and equity at both the primary and secondary level for Islamic societies is about the same as for all developing societies.

Somewhat distinct from the religious tradition of a nation is the type

Table 4.2   Cultural and Institutional Influence on Education Access and Equity in Developing Countries in 1990

Indicators	Primary GER (%)	Secondary GER (%)	Primary Gender Ratio	Secondary Gender Ratio
Confucian society	125.0	48.7	0.93	0.75
Islamic society	82.1	58.1	0.84	0.79
French colonial past	80.0	28.5	0.77	0.69
British colonial past	81.5	29.6	0.87	0.71
U.S., Japanese, or Russian influence	97.0	83.8	0.95	0.95
All developing countries	85.8	40.6	0.85	0.77

of education system provided during the colonial period, as discussed in chapter 1. At least five colonial patterns can be identified—French, British, American, Japanese, and Russian—and each placed a different emphasis on development of education. The French tradition was most restrictive, insisting that education opportunities be available only in the French language and at the same standard as observed in France. As a result, in French colonies, there were relatively few education opportunities at either the primary or secondary level, and all higher education took place in France. The British were somewhat more tolerant of local culture, generally favoring a dual system at the primary level with one stream in English and the second in the vernacular language. This opened up access to more young people, but at the secondary level most opportunities were restricted to those who completed the English stream. The American, Japanese, and Russian approaches were more liberal than these two examples, but these latter nations possessed fewer colonies and thus exerted less impact on the institutional heritage of education.

Interestingly, those with strong Confucian and Islamic traditions fare better than average in terms of both access and gender equity. While these cultural and institutional factors influence the starting level of developing countries, our analysis found little evidence that these factors influenced the rate of change to EFA over the past decade. Countries with a Francophone past, on average, improved at the same rate as those with an Anglophone past and so on.[5]

The Economic and Political Context for EFA

Education is a costly long-term endeavor. Nations that experience relative prosperity enjoy the revenues to support education improvement, while nations that are experiencing stress may be forced to cut back in order to finance more pressing issues such as national defense, food relief in the face of drought, or a health crisis. The 1990s were a difficult time in many parts of the world, especially sub-Saharan Africa. In this section, several of the competing claims on national resources are considered.

Economic Development

Economic development can be considered both a cause of improvements in education and a consequence. Indeed, while statistical models involving the introduction of time lags can be used in an attempt to determine the temporal ordering of these two variables, it is perhaps best to consider them as interrelated. Watkins (2000) reports a close relation between a country's rank in per capita national income and its rank in terms of education performance. Essentially this means that countries that are economically advanced have relatively more education opportunities (see also Table 4.1).

Concerning change over the 1990s, as already noted in Table 4.1, those countries that experienced more economic development were also likely to expand their education systems, especially at the secondary and tertiary levels. While it is encouraging to know that economic development is supportive of education improvement, it also should be noted that the 1990s was not a good decade for many national economies, especially those in Africa as well as several in Asia that toward the end of the decade experienced a severe financial crisis. So economic developments over the past decade have not been supportive of education improvement.

Political Stability/Domestic Conflict

Many observers point to political conflict as a major factor eroding economic growth over the 1990s, especially in Africa and parts of Eastern Europe. Several Eastern European nations went through the extraordinary transition from socialism to new political environments and from planned to quasi-market economies. In Africa, many societies experienced major disruptions. Civil wars raged in Nigeria, Sierra Leone, Uganda, Rwanda, Liberia, the Sudan, and Zimbabwe, to mention a few examples. Where there was conflict, public military budgets went up and private opposition armies also made heavy investments in weaponry—thus diverting the national economy from a focus on other activities. Where military budgets went up, education budgets suffered and education improvements stalled.

It is somewhat difficult to develop reliable indicators of the level of political stability/conflict for particular years—and hence to develop indicators for short-time periods of change in political stability. The World Bank has recently proposed several indicators of the political environment that rely on surveys of elites in the respective countries; the proposed indicators of government effectiveness and political stability are the most comprehensive, though they are only available for a limited number of years. On the other hand, there are indicators of changes in expenditures and changes in access to education. Concerning the synchronic correlations, government effectiveness and political stability are strongly correlated with relatively high allocations for education and health and somewhat lower allocations for the military. Table 4.3 below presents the correlations of the political variables and changes in economic and financial variables with three indicators of improvement in education.

In general, an effective government and a stable polity are associated with education expansion and, at least for developing countries, with an improvement in the primary-level gender ratio. While Table 4.3 does not illustrate this point, the analysis found that effective stable governments tended to allocate more money for social services and somewhat less money for the military. And countries that devoted more resources to the social sector showed greater progress in education expansion at both the primary and secondary level, as well as progress at the secondary level in improving the gender ratio. Countries that allocated more for the military had a poorer record on both education expansion and gender equity.

Table 4.3   Economic Growth, Political Stability, Sectoral Expenditures, and Education Improvement, 1990–2000

Indicators	Primary GER	Secondary GER	Primary Gender Ratio	Secondary Gender Ratio
Per capita income in PPP 2000/1990	.098	.259	.024	.178
Government effectiveness	−.128	.252	−.207	−.086
Political stability and lack of violence	−.095	.193	−.182	−.067
Percent of GDP for education 2000/1990	.109	.233	−.175	.155
Percent of GDP for health 2000/1990	.033	.040	−.223	.111
Percent of GDP for military 2000/1990	−.175	−.026	−.124	.012
Poor countries (n = 65)				
Per capita income in PPP 2000/90	.105	.485	.146	.178
Government effectiveness	.039	.303	.169	.113
Political stability and lack of violence	.121	.303	.034	.134
Percent of GDP for education 2000/1990	.125	.224	−.147	.189
Percent of GDP for health 2000/1990	.199	.176	−.143	.183
Percent of GDP for military 2000/1990	−.206	−.085	−.083	.131

Note: Poor countries are those with per capita income below $5000

Debt

Levels of national debt vary widely. Heavy debt is accompanied by heavy payments for debt servicing, which reduces the availability of funds for both public and private investment. Heavy debt is related to a variety of causes, including political instability and a poor record of economic development. International debt reached its peak in the late 1980s, after which some nations were able to decrease their debt burden and/or negotiate better rates for the servicing of these debts.

This analysis found that nations that had a heavy debt service burden in 1990 were spending less on the social services areas of health and education. Nations that had heavy debt also were less likely to receive assistance from international donors. On the other hand, those nations that received relatively more aid were able to make greater progress in reducing their debt. To the extent these nations were able to reduce their debt service burden, they were able to increase their expenditures on social services and hence to foster education improvements.

Discussion thus far has highlighted a variety of societal features that are associated with education change. The next sections turn to identify those nations that have made the greatest strides toward improvement in education—as well as identify another group of nations that regrettably have moved backward.

EXPANSION AND ACCESS

For 130 countries for which data is available, including both developing and industrialized countries, the average primary GER (gross enrollment rate) in 1980 was 92.3%, 93.0% in 1990, and 99.9% in 2000. Among the 65 nations with a low to modest per capita income, the average primary GER in 1980 was 76.2%, 87.4% in 1990, and 94.2% in 2000. So there has been a modest overall gain in access to primary education since Jomtien.

Underlying this modest gain is a complex pattern of ups and downs. In the first column of Table 4.4 are listed a large group of countries that showed considerable progress since Jomtien. Among them, Libya, Morocco, Bangladesh, Guatemala, El Salvador, the Dominican Republic, Rwanda, and Uganda would appear to have virtually achieved universal access.

Several countries had a low GER in 1990 and experienced little to no improvement by 2000, including Djibouti, Niger, Burkina Faso, and the Sudan. Many countries already had a high GER in 1990 and sustained this. China was one, with a GER of 125.2 in 1990 that shifted to 113.9 in 2000.[6]

Table 4.4   Countries with Significant Shifts in Primary Education Gross Enrollment Rates (GER) between 1990 and 2000

	Gainers				Decliners		
Country	GER 1990	GER 2000	Increase	Country	GER 1990	GER 2000	Decrease
Tajikistan	91.0	104.3	13.3	Congo, Rep.	132.5	84.2	−48.3
Lithuania	90.7	104.4	13.7	Azerbaijan	113.7	92.9	−20.8
Guinea-Bissau	55.7	69.7	14.1	Zambia	98.7	78.8	−19.9
Vanuatu	96.1	111.0	14.9	Iran, Islamic Rep.	112.2	93.0	−19.2
Gambia	63.9	78.9	15.0	Lesotho	120.3	102.5	−17.9
Senegal	58.9	74.1	15.1	Myanmar	106.5	89.5	−17.0
Switzerland	90.3	107.3	17.0	United Arab Emir.	104.3	90.6	−13.7
Belarus	94.8	111.9	17.1	Iraq	111.3	98.8	−12.5
Chad	54.4	73.4	19.0	Afghanistan	27.0	15.1	−12.0
Bolivia	94.7	114.8	20.1	Moldova	93.1	84.7	−8.4
Yemen, Rep.	58.3	79.2	20.9	Ukraine	88.8	80.6	−8.2
Guyana	97.7	120.2	22.5	Turkey	99.1	91.9	−7.3
Mozambique	66.9	91.1	24.1	Burundi	72.8	65.7	−7.1
Guatemala	77.6	102.0	24.4	Tanzania	69.7	64.0	−5.7
Jordan	70.9	97.0	26.1	Saudi Arabia	73.3	68.3	−5.0
Serbia & Montenegro	72.0	98.8	26.8				
Bangladesh	71.6	98.9	27.3				
Mali	26.5	54.0	27.6				
Dominican Republic	96.6	124.3	27.6				
Ethiopia	32.7	60.5	27.8				
Guinea	37.1	67.0	29.9				
El Salvador	81.1	111.2	30.1				
Kuwait	60.2	93.7	33.5				
Morocco	66.9	101.2	34.3				
Mauritania	48.7	85.4	36.7				
Benin	58.1	97.0	38.9				
Rwanda	69.6	116.9	47.3				
Uganda	71.3	133.9	62.6				
Libya	29.0	105.4	76.4				

Of the 130 countries for which data is available, 50 had a lower primary GER in 2000 than 1990; among these were several with relatively high levels of access that experienced minor shifts, shifts that may simply reflect the limitations of GER as a stable indicator. However, as indicated in Table 4.4, nine countries experienced significant declines (greater than 10%), most notable among them the Republic of Congo, Azerbaijan, Zambia, Iran, Lesotho, Myanmar, and Afghanistan.

At the secondary level, the list of countries reporting a drastic decline in GER is not as long—partly because the base-year GERs were lower. Among the countries experiencing modest declines are several in Eastern Europe and the Middle East as reported in Table 4.5; African countries are not prominent among the decliners.

Table 4.5 also lists the countries that experienced significant increases in GER between 1990 and 2000. The geographic focus of the countries experiencing an increase is quite dispersed, including Thailand and Vietnam in Southeast Asia; Bangladesh in South Asia; Turkey, Jordan, Kuwait, Oman, and Saudi Arabia in the Middle East; Mexico, Brazil, and Argentina in Latin America; and several African and Eastern European countries as well. Many of the countries making rapid strides in secondary level expansion resemble the profile of newly industrializing societies.

Table 4.5   Countries with Significant Shifts in Secondary Education Gross Enrollment Rates (GER) between 1990 and 2000

	Gainers				Decliners		
Country	GER 1990	GER 2000	Increase	Country	GER 1990	GER 2000	Decrease
Colombia	49.8	69.8	20.0	Tajikistan	102.1	78.5	−23.6
Mexico	53.3	73.5	20.2	Georgia	94.9	72.9	−22.0
Cyprus	72.1	93.4	21.4	Kyrgyz Republic	100.1	85.6	−14.4
Mauritius	52.9	76.5	23.6	Cambodia	32.1	18.1	−14.0
Fiji	56.2	79.9	23.7	Yemen, Rep.	58.0	46.3	−11.7
Saudi Arabia	44.0	68.7	24.7	Mongolia	82.4	70.9	−11.5
Serbia & Montenegro	63.4	88.7	25.3	Azerbaijan	89.9	79.7	−10.2
Argentina	71.1	96.7	25.5	Russian Fed.	93.3	83.3	−10.0
Turkey	47.3	73.3	25.9	Romania	92.0	82.3	−9.7
Bangladesh	19.0	46.1	27.2	Syrian Arab Rep.	51.9	42.8	−9.1
Iran, Islamic Rep.	55.2	82.4	27.2	Kazakhstan	98.0	88.9	−9.1
El Salvador	26.4	53.9	27.5	Iraq	47.0	38.3	−8.7
Macedonia, FYR	55.7	84.6	28.8	Moldova	80.0	71.5	−8.5
Paraguay	30.9	59.9	29.0	Belarus	93.0	84.6	−8.4
Belize	41.3	70.7	29.4	Armenia	93.3	86.0	−7.2
Botswana	42.7	73.2	30.5				
Oman	45.7	76.5	30.8				
Venezuela, RB	34.7	66.0	31.3				
Tunisia	44.9	77.6	32.8				
Vietnam	32.0	67.1	35.0				
Latvia	48.6	84.8	36.2				
Samoa	36.1	73.8	37.7				
Jordan	44.6	86.1	41.5				
Bolivia	36.6	80.0	43.4				
Kuwait	42.9	88.4	45.5				
Cape Verde	20.6	66.3	45.7				
Portugal	67.4	113.6	46.3				
Thailand	30.1	82.8	52.7				
Brazil	38.4	105.3	66.9				

Equity

Equity refers to the degree of fairness of providing opportunities between individuals and social groups. At the group level, education systems may be more favorable to particular ethnic, religious, class, or gender groups. While in principle it would be desirable to look at all of these dimensions of equity, the current practice of reporting international statistics only provides extensive information on gender equity. A common indicator of gender equity is the gender gap. However, the magnitude of the scores for this index is influenced by the total level of access; for example, the higher the level of access, the greater the chance for a large gender gap.

Table 4.6 lists the countries for which data is available that had relatively low gender equity ratios at the primary and secondary levels in the year 2000, along with an indication of the extent that ratios increased over the past ten years. By the year 2000, the great majority of countries had achieved a gender equity ratio at the primary level in excess of .90 or nine girls enrolled for every ten boys; the most glaring exception was Afghanistan, where the ratio was only .14, a sharp decline from .55 in the year 1990. Most of the other exceptions were in Africa. Similarly at the secondary level, the great majority of countries had achieved a gender equity ratio in excess of .90; nine of the 12 exceptions are in Africa.

Quality

The concept of education quality has several meanings—improvements in inputs such as textbooks, workbooks, and other instructional materials; improvement in teaching practice such as a greater involvement of students as active learners; and improvements in outputs as measured by student performance on tests. Among the various indicators of the quality of inputs, one that is frequently cited is the average student–teacher ratio. The general public tends to believe a lower student–teacher ratio leads to a higher quality of interaction between teachers and students. In fact, empirical studies of classroom interaction raise questions about this popular assumption. In the range

Table 4.6   Countries with Comparatively Low Gender Ratios in 2000

Country	Primary gender ratio 2000	Change from 1990 (%)	Country	Secondary gender ratio 2000	Change from 1990 (%)
Afghanistan	0.14	−40.8	Grenada	0.48	ND
Chad	0.63	18.7	Cambodia	0.56	13.0
Guinea-Bissau	0.67	12.3	Djibouti	0.62	−3.2
Central African Rep.	0.68	4.6	Equatorial Guinea	0.62	ND
Benin	0.68	18.9	Burkina Faso	0.65	11.7
Ethiopia	0.69	1.1	Ethiopia	0.66	−13.1
Burkina Faso	0.71	8.1	Gambia, The	0.71	22.0
Guinea	0.72	24.4	Eritrea	0.71	ND
Djibouti	0.76	4.8	India	0.71	11.5
Cote d'Ivoire	0.77	5.8	Burundi	0.77	19.7
Burundi	0.80	−3.6	Ghana	0.82	18.4
Iraq	0.82	−2.9	Angola	0.82	17.0
Eritrea	0.83	ND	Kenya	0.91	16.2
India	0.83	7.4	Guatemala	0.92	5.5
Cameroon	0.87	1.0	Iran, Islamic Rep.	0.93	20.3
Comoros	0.87	14.8	Egypt, Arab Rep.	0.94	12.3
Cambodia	0.88	7.5	Bolivia	0.96	10.8
Ghana	0.91	8.2	Austria	0.96	2.7
Gambia, The	0.92	23.8	Azerbaijan	0.97	−3.0
Guatemala	0.92	4.0	Italy	0.97	−2.4
Algeria	0.92	7.6	Kazakhstan	0.98	−5.1
Egypt, Arab Rep.	0.93	8.5	Bulgaria	0.98	−6.5
Congo, Rep.	0.93	5.0	Indonesia	0.98	15.4
Brazil	0.94	0.2	Germany	0.99	1.4
Grenada	0.95	ND	El Salvador	0.99	−6.7

Note: ND = No data

of 20 to 40 students per teacher, differences in class size may not affect quality of interaction. Classes have to be very small (perhaps less than 15 students) for rich individualized interaction to take place. On the other hand, average class sizes in excess of 40 are likely to lead to lower quality interaction.

Of the 81 cases for which data are available, the primary education student–teacher ratio stayed essentially the same in the majority of countries, possibly reflecting conformity to a national standard. The average student–teacher ratio in 2000 was 35, with 32 countries having an average as low as 20, and 51 with an average below 30. However, 34 countries experienced an increase in the student–teacher ratios, and some of these increases were substantial. Table 4.7 presents the countries with the highest student–teacher ratios along with an indication of the change in this ratio over the past ten years. Most of the countries with high student–teacher ratios are in Africa, and in many cases their ratios have increased considerably over this ten-year period.

Unfortunately, there is insufficient cross-national data for other quality measures of interest such as quality of buildings, availability of textbooks, and student performance on tests.

Efficiency

Education efficiency refers to the likelihood that an education system will provide schooling for young people in a timeframe corresponding to the official time. Affecting this likelihood is first the

Table 4.7   Countries with Comparatively High Student–Teacher Ratios

Country	S/T Ratio 2000	Increase from 1990
Chad	71.2	5.4
Cameroon	62.7	11.6
Congo, Rep.	59.5	−5.7
Bangladesh	57.1	−5.9
Ethiopia	54.9	18.9
Equatorial Guinea	54.5	nd
Benin	53.5	17.4
Cambodia	52.9	20.4
Burundi	50.2	−16.7
Gabon	49.2	nd
Burkina Faso	47.4	−9.2
Cote d'Ivoire	46.1	9.8
Eritrea	44.8	7.1
Guinea	44.4	4.5
Guinea-Bissau	44.1	nd
Afghanistan	42.7	1.5
Bhutan	41.1	nd
India	40.1	9.9
Gambia, The	37.5	6.2
Comoros	36.9	0.4
Dominican Republic	36.0	−9.4
Djibouti	35.6	−7.1
Honduras	34.1	−0.8
Jamaica	33.6	−3.0
Ghana	33.0	3.9

admission of children to school, and then the promotion of children through the respective grade levels. A variety of measures has been developed to gauge the efficiency of education systems. Perhaps the most attractive measure is the primary completion ratio that focuses on the percentage of young people who complete their primary education (which may range from five to seven years depending on the system). For the 135 countries for which information is available, the average Primary Completion Rate is 74.5%, and for the 64 countries with a per capita income below $5,000 PPP, the average is 65.4%. The first column of Table 4.8 lists those countries with a Primary Completion Rate of 60% or less. Afghanistan tops the list with a Primary Completion Rate of 8%. Virtually all of the other countries in the table are from sub-Saharan Africa.

In general, countries with a low Primary Completion Rate in the year 2000 also had a low rate in 1990. However, as can be seen from the last column in Table 4.8, several of the featured countries lost considerable ground over this ten-year period: notably Qatar, the Republic of the Congo, Cameroon, Afghanistan, the Democratic Republic of the Congo, Madagascar, and Rwanda.

Table 4.8 also presents two additional indicators of efficiency that are often utilized by education managers. The second column lists the primary GER, the most widely used measure of access (discussed earlier in this chapter and featured in Table 4.1). Children need access to school in order to complete their education; for countries with a per capita income below $5,000 PPP, this measure has a correlation of .660 with the Primary Completion Rate. The third column shows the percentage of primary level children who repeat in a year. In certain systems, often those with a Francophone heritage, the school system tends to hold relatively large numbers at each grade level before allowing them to move forward. Where repetition rates are high, many children drop out; thus the repetition rate has a correlation of $-.707$ with the percentage of children entering a school who complete grade five.[7]

Relevance

Relevance refers to the utility of what is taught in schools for survival and success in the world outside of school. Education seeks to

Table 4.8   Countries with Relatively Inefficient Education Systems

Country	Gross enrollment ratio 2000	Repetition rate 2000	Primary completion rate 1990	Primary completion rate 2000	Completion rate difference
Afghanistan	15.1	ND	22	8	−14
Central African Republic	75.3	ND	28	19	−9
Chad	73.4	25.5	19	19	0
Niger	35.8	10.2	18	20	2
Mali	54.0	17.5	11	23	12
Ethiopia	60.5	7.4	22	24	2
Burkina Faso	43.6	17.6	19	25	6
Madagascar	103.1	30.1	34	26	−8
Rwanda	116.9	36.1	34	28	−6
Djibouti	39.8	14.3	32	30	−2
Guinea-Bissau	69.7	24.0	16	31	15
Sierra Leone	ND	ND	ND	32	ND
Comoros	85.9	28.0	35	33	−2
Guinea	67.0	20.3	16	34	18
Eritrea	56.7	19.4	22	35	13
Sudan	58.2	11.3	ND	35	ND
Mozambique	91.1	22.7	30	36	6
Benin	97.0	19.9	23	39	16
Congo, Dem. Rep.	ND	ND	48	40	−8
Cote d'Ivoire	77.8	24.3	44	40	−4
Haiti	ND	ND	28	40	12
Senegal	74.1	13.9	45	41	−4
Burundi	65.7	24.5	46	43	−3
Cameroon	106.2	24.5	57	43	−14
Congo, Rep.	84.2	24.9	61	44	−17
Qatar	106.2	ND	74	44	−30
Equatorial Guinea	129.9	40.5	ND	46	ND
Mauritania	85.4	15.2	34	46	12
Malawi	ND	ND	30	50	20

Note: Completion rate difference calculated by Primary completion rate 2000 minus Primary completion rate 1990. ND = no data.

prepare young people for their multiple adult roles as parents, citizens, and breadwinners. Unfortunately, the only available indicator of relevance is in the economic sphere. This data focuses on the proportion of the age cohort employed. For a meaningful indicator of the relevance of education, it would be important to specify difference in employment rates according to education experience. While such data is available for a few countries, for comparisons across a large number of countries over time the only available data is on gross employment rates (by age group), and even this data is limited: only 42 countries have data for the two periods of 1990 (+ or − one year) and 1998 (+ or − one year). This data presents a dismal picture. In 31 of 42 countries where data is available for both periods, youth unemployment is up. In the following countries the level of unemployment in 1998 was in excess of 20%: Barbados, Belgium, Bulgaria, Colombia, Ecuador, Finland, France, Greece, Italy, Morocco, Puerto Rico, Spain, Sri Lanka, Suriname, Trinidad and Tobago, Uruguay, and Venezuela.

Missing Data

Any effort at taking stock of educational performance across many settings is inevitably constrained by the availability of information. One shortcoming is that international bodies to date have not promoted the measurement of many important education concepts including quality and relevance. This report card is thus inadequate in these areas. Secondly, for a substantial number of countries, data is not available at all or is only available for a subset of the common indicators. Indeed, many of the countries that fail to report critical information appear to be the countries with the weakest education systems. Liberia, for one example, provides information on only a fraction of the indicators discussed in this review. Finally, observers rightly point out that the reliability of much of the data presented in this review is suspect. For these various reasons, readers may wish to think of this report card as more of a methodological exercise than a true portrayal of the state of education improvement in the world. While recognizing the limitations of available data, we nevertheless suspect that an education system that appears deficient on several of the available indicators discussed above is a troubled system. Thus we believe the education systems listed in Table 4.9 below are likely to have significant weaknesses. At the same time, others that are in trouble are not even able to collect the necessary information to enable a statistical analysis of their difficulties.

THE REPORT CARD

We have reviewed several indicators of education improvement over the 1990s. Many countries have shown improvement in all or most

Table 4.9   Report Card of Education Improvement

Countries that appear to be realizing substantial educational improvement	*Countries unable to realize educational improvement*	*Countries with insufficient data but that do not appear to be realizing substantial educational improvement*
Algeria	Afghanistan	Kazakhstan
Bangladesh	Azerbaijan	Kiribati
Belarus	Benin	Korea, DPR
Bolivia	Burkina Faso	Kyrgyz Republic
Brazil	Burundi	Liberia
Cape Verde	Chad	Libya
China	Cambodia	Marshall Islands
Colombia	Cameroon	Micronesia, Fed. St.
Costa Rica	Comoros	Myanmar
Croatia	Cote d'Ivoire	Palau
Czech Republic	Central African Republic	Seychelles
Egypt	Congo, Rep.	Somalia
El Salvador	Djibouti	Tonga
Gabon	Equatorial Guinea	Turkmenistan
Gambia*	Eritrea	Uzbekistan
Haiti*	Ethiopia	West Bank/Gaza
Hungary	Guinea	
Jordan	Guinea Bissau	
Kuwait	Ghana	
Lao PDR	Iraq	
Latvia	India	
Lithuania	Moldova	
Macedonia, FYR		
Malawi*		
Mali*		
Mauritania*		
Mauritius		
Mexico		
Morocco		
Namibia		
Nicaragua		
Pakistan*		
Paraguay		
Serbia and Montenegro		
South Africa		
Swaziland		
Tanzania		
Togo*		
Tunisia		
Uganda*		

*These improving countries started the 90s with relatively low access rates, and thus still by 2000 were not reaching a substantial proportion of their young people.

areas. Others have faltered in a few. In the listing in Table 4.9, those countries that experienced the most difficulties in education improvement over the 1990s are listed—evidencing decline in at least two areas—alongside those that experienced the most improvement. It should be remembered, of course, that a number of countries did not report adequate data for inclusion in this exercise, and there is reason to suspect that many of these "no data" countries are experiencing considerable difficulties. (Those countries lacking formal data but for which informal data suggests difficulties are also listed in Table 4.9.)

Education contributes to economic and political development, and development contributes to education. Hence there are multiple benefits from education improvement. Unfortunately, a number of countries experienced difficulties over the 1990s. Table 4.9 lists 22 countries that reported inadequate performance in at least two of the areas considered in this chapter. It should be noted that 16 of these 22 low-mark countries are in sub-Saharan Africa. Table 4.9 also lists 42 countries that have evidenced sustained improvement over the decade. These countries are in all of the regions of the world including 12 from sub-Saharan Africa. There has been much progress in education development in the recent decade, but also much disappointment. The challenge to do better is evident.

NOTES

1. See UNDP, *Human Development Report*, 2002, for one assessment. Also see Kevin Watkins, 2000, *The Oxfam Education Report*, London: Oxfam Publications, 2000.

2. Despite our best efforts, there are numerous data gaps. The most widely available data for circa 140 countries is on access, but even this information is only relatively complete for computing gross as contrasted to net enrollment rates. For most other indicators, there is available data for a smaller number of countries. One of the great obstacles to a comprehensive report is the fact that the countries that are facing the biggest sociopolitical and educational challenges are the same countries that have difficulty in collecting and reporting appropriate information.

3. The distinctive virtue of the methodology introduced here is that it stresses multiple criteria of improvement. There is a recent trend in interna-

tional development agency thinking to stress the sole criterion of the primary completion rate, on the questionable assumption that this single indicator takes account of access, quality, and efficiency.

4. As these correlations are presented as descriptive statistics for the full "population" of nations, inferential statistical indicators of their levels of significance are not required; generally speaking, a correlation above plus or minus .10 indicates a meaningful relation and correlations above .25 suggest stronger relations.

5. This analysis also took a preliminary look at the relation of decentralization to education access and equity as well as education improvement. Our initial finding is that for the sample of all nations, those that in 1990 had more decentralized structures tended to have greater access and equity. However, these relations were reversed for the subsample of developing countries. On the other hand, for the total sample, decentralized societies were less likely over the 1990s to show an improvement in access and equity. But for the subsample of developing societies, decentralized societies were more likely to increase access at the secondary level and to reduce gender inequity. This is a complicated picture that encourages further investigation.

6. According to the World Bank Database, India in 1990 had a GER of 97.2%, which rose to 98.8% in 2000; these numbers are not consistent with those reported by other sources such as Oxfam.

7. A measure featured in *The Oxfam Educational Report* (Watkins, 2000) is the percentage of entrants to a school system who complete grade 5, a grade by which most children are able to read, write, and do basic arithmetic. This measure is moderately correlated with the repetition rate ($r = -.515$) and with the Primary Completion Rate ($r = .331$).

Part 2

TOOLS AND PROCESSES

CHAPTER 5

Assessing the State of the System

After the decision to initiate reform, the first step in the rational planning process is likely to be assessment, an attempt to understand the condition of the education system as a whole or the part of the system that is to be addressed. Assessments are known by several names—sector assessment or sector analysis in the language of the United States Agency for International Development (USAID) and the World Bank, or comprehensive or situational analysis, in the United Nations Children's Fund's (UNICEF) language. Though these approaches vary somewhat in the particulars, the purpose of all such assessment activities is to understand and document the status and context of the education system in preparation for planned change. In order to simplify referencing, we use the term *education system assessment.*

Education system assessments are useful in several ways. They provide a baseline of data against which future performance can be measured. With a baseline, it is possible to ask at a later point: Is the system improving? Is the reform having any impact? In addition, assessments can provide a comprehensive and "systemic" perspective on a national education system. Based on a good understanding of the whole, change initiatives can be designed to focus on the areas of greatest need. Without such a perspective, there is a danger of focusing on the most visible, short-term problems rather than more important systemic issues. Moreover, reformers lacking a systemic perspective may miss important linkages among components of the education system, or with the larger context in which education takes place. Thus, for example, a curriculum initiative designed without a comprehensive view of the entire system runs the risk of focusing only on curriculum development, textbook production, and distribution, and thus missing the critical linkage to teacher use of the new materials. Do teachers understand the new curriculum? Are they willing and able to use the new materials? If teachers are not considered, the new curriculum may be not implemented as intended, and the reform may not achieve its objectives. Finally, assessment provides the opportunity to look at the context in which policy will be introduced and the likely parameters of processes that may used to develop, implement, and institutionalize change.

THREE QUESTIONS

Education system assessment would appear to be the relatively straightforward technical task of answering questions such as: What's the status of the education system? What are the problem areas and priorities? While easy to understand in general terms, addressing these questions in a comprehensive and useful way is a challenging technical, conceptual, logistical, and political task. As we have argued, it is important to pay explicit attention to the process by which assessment is carried out, perhaps as much as answering the questions posed. And so, we suggest three questions to ask in thinking about education system assessment:

1. What information is needed?
2. What process should be used to obtain, make sense of, and communicate that information?
3. To what extent should the assessment process start the change process?

While we have talked in general terms about the importance of process, why is process so important in assessment? First of all, assessment can play a more, or less, central role in the change process, depending on how it is carried out. The process of change, for example, can begin with assessment or it can wait until afterwards. A more participatory assessment process can engender among stakeholders a common understanding and "ownership" of the problems to be addressed. Less participatory approaches are less likely to do so. Also, the process of education system assessment can be more or less educational for those who will plan and implement the reform initiatives. Assessment can serve a capacity-building role, or not, again depending on how it is done.

Even the question "What information is needed?" is not as straightforward as one might think. Time, space, and the attention of decision makers are limited. A lifetime or more could be spent studying an education system, trying to understand what's going on. Assessments are finite, and so a selection of the most important information is needed. But the relative importance of different kinds of information depends, in large part, on what one hopes to do and on one's values. An assessment aimed at developing a sectoral strategy would be most concerned with macro-system data. However, if that assessment were part of a reform aimed at increasing student achievement, the assessment would likely need to include information at the classroom level, data on instructional processes, teacher behavior and attitudes, the culture of teaching and learning, and the like. Such information, and the methods appropriate for collection and analysis, differs substantially from overall estimates of enrollment rates, for example, used in planning for increases in access.

It is quite likely that the relative importance of different kinds of information depends on other factors, such as how one understands the process of change (top-down versus bottom-up), where one sits in the system (outside, center, middle management, periphery, community), what one's goals are (quality, equity, efficiency, etc.), and how much trust one has that decision makers will represent one's interests. The answers to these questions are likely to vary across stakeholders in the system. For these reasons, we argue that a well-designed education system assessment strategy needs to think explicitly about the ways in which it will integrate substance (the "what" one needs to know) with process (the "how") for the assessment to be useful and to be used.

FOUR MODELS OF ASSESSMENT

In order to suggest some of the options for both substance and process, we provide an overview of four models of education system assessment, each with its own assumptions and strategies, advantages and disadvantages. Description and comparison of several models provides a richer set of options for thinking about and designing change processes, we feel, than does elaboration of a single "best" strategy. Ultimately, the decision makers in each context will decide how to proceed. A range of strategies provides the policy maker with options, each in the context of a coherent model of the assessment process.

The first approach is the *sector assessment model* used by the United States Agency for International Development (USAID) and others in carrying out education system assessments. Sector assessment was developed over several decades of work by international development educators working in and on education systems in developing countries. The approach is well summarized in the *Education and Human Resources Sector Assessment Manual*, developed by Mary Pigozzi and Victor Cieutat (1988) of the Improving the Efficiency of Education Systems Project, material we rely heavily on here. Sector assessment places most emphasis on developing good, data-informed answers to questions about the status of the system. Sector assessment focuses almost exclusively on the "what" part of the process.

The second model, the *Education Reform Support* (ERS) approach formalized by Crouch and Healey (1997), is described as "an integrated approach to supporting education reform efforts in developing countries" (p. v). To a much greater degree than sector assessment, education sector reform takes a political, process-oriented approach to education change, integrating the "what" and the "how" of assessment. Its rationale?

> The major binding constraint to successful education development in poor countries is neither the need to transfer more funds nor a lack of education technology and know-how. That is, we contend that in most instances, countries can make sufficient progress by better using whatever internal or external funds and pedagogical technology already exist, but that in order to [do] so, they need far-reaching modifications in the way they approach both policy formation and system-wide management. (Crouch & Healy, 1997, p. v)

The third model we refer to as the *informed dialogue* approach, and it is taken from the book of that title by Reimers and McGinn (1997).[1]

The "hypotheses" that make up the informed dialogue approach were derived from the researchers' experience, in particular their reflections on the "failure" of research to inform education policies in a series of developing country cases. Based on this failure, Reimers and McGinn (1997) worked to develop an approach that

> recogniz[es] the limitations of their own expertise to define which way education systems should go, and . . . see[s] themselves . . . in a dynamic process of dialogue with others whose interactions define what education systems do and fail to do. (p. 190)

Reform is a process whose outcome is determined not solely by policy makers or their plans, but by the actions of numerous actors in the system as well as a variety of internal and external forces. Reform is best carried out as a process of "dialogue" among stakeholders who use data and analysis to "inform" their positions and choices.

The fourth model was developed by the Improving Educational Quality Project (IEQ) (2002) and will be called the *IEQ Model*. The IEQ model is explicitly bottom-up, working to "strengthen the host country's capacity to systematically examine local conditions of teaching and learning—and to use the resulting knowledge as a basis for reforming national policy and local practice" (Improving Educational Quality, 2002, p. 6). The project itself was funded by USAID and used technical assistance to foster an indigenous research, analysis, and policy formation process, in organizations closely associated with schools, the critical institution, IEQ reasoned, in quality improvement efforts.

It should be noted that education system assessment is the sole focus of only the first model. In other models, assessment is more closely integrated into the larger processes of education change. Though certainly not exhaustive, these four models represent distinctly different approaches to education system assessment. Hopefully, the discussion will suggest some of the important decisions that need to be made in planning reform.

It should also be remembered that in addition to models of explicit and planned assessment, there is a fifth model of change in which no new assessment is carried out. In this approach, decision makers plan reform on the basis of their current goals and their current understanding of the education system, its problems, and opportunities. Uninformed by new information, this fifth model is perhaps the most traditional and common one in use worldwide.[2]

Sector Assessment[3]

Pigozzi and Cieutat (1988) define sector assessment as a "detailed analysis of the goals and objectives, status, plans, needs, constraints and priority target areas with rank ordered recommendations for actions in a national education system" designed "to encourage the use of relevant and current information for planning, policy formulation, and resource allocation that will improve efficiency throughout the entire education sector" (p. 2-2). Sector analyses are commissioned by government and/or external agencies and are typically carried out by teams of experts, contracted as consultants, locally and usually internationally. The immediate beneficiaries are host governments, the ultimate beneficiaries, students and other stakeholders. External assistance agencies are often ancillary beneficiaries.

Sector analyses are useful in several ways. They provide baseline information to help clarify system efficiencies and inefficiencies, constraints, and subsector priorities. They synthesize information about an education system. They serve as a planning tool and as a way to coordinate assistance from external agencies. One important strength of a sector assessment lies in its systems perspective. Changes in one subsector are understood to affect other parts of the system. A systems approach thus describes each component of the education system as well as the complex linkages within and among subsectors and with the environment. The systems approach examines events in their environment and as a whole before examining components individually. Such a strategy is particularly useful in assessing complex, loosely coupled systems such as education where it is impossible to attribute particular results to specific inputs, where many "agents" are involved in implementation, and where control of those agents is limited.

As noted, sector assessments are typically carried out by teams of experts with extensive knowledge of the different education specialties. Often hired by external agencies for their technical expertise and objectivity (as opposed to local knowledge or stake in the outcome), expert analysts typically work intensively over a relatively short period of time to review background documents, analyze and synthesize existing data, and interview important actors with particular knowledge of the system. The result is typically a major technical report with substantial documentation, generally written in the language of the funding organization.

Organization of a Sector Assessment

Sector assessment reports are organized into a series of chapters. Table 5.1 summarizes a "typical" sector assessment, including brief parenthetical notes (Pigozzi & Cieutat, 1988). This typical sector assessment report begins with three introductory chapters: an overview synthesis; an economic and financial analysis; and a discussion of the history, structure, and management capacity of the system. The opening synthesis chapter is particularly important for the majority of readers, who will not read the entire report. It provides an overview of the whole report, the economic and managerial context. Of particular importance is a ranked listing of recommendations for the education sector as a whole, synthesized from the individual subsector chapters.

The report then discusses each subsector in turn, generally including Pre-primary Education, Primary Education, Secondary Education, Teacher Training, Higher Education, Vocational and Technical Education, and Nonformal Education. Each chapter consists of two general sections, a section discussing the status of the subsector and an analysis section. The status portion describes the historical setting of the subsector, national goals and strategies relevant to the subsector, structural organization of the subsector, and its "programs" or activities. This is where the report presents detailed information on administration, students, teachers, curriculum, examinations, facilities and equipment, costs and financing, and quality of instruction.

The analysis section examines these data in terms of needs (gaps), plans (current activities aimed at filling gaps), constraints (problems that prevent filling of gaps), issues (matters to be resolved), and conclusions (summary statements about the subsector). Issues are further examined in light of external efficiency (relevance of school to employment or higher levels of schooling), internal efficiency (effectiveness

Table 5.1   Contents of "Typical" Sector Assessment

I.   Synthesis (overview of status, needs, constraints, conclusions, and ranked recommendations for the entire education sector within national and economic context; more than a summary, casts findings in larger context and uses them to identify priority areas for investment and intervention)

II. Economic and Financial Analysis (overview of economic conditions affecting the education sector and a review of funds reasonably expected to be available for expenditure in sector; sets context for subsequent discussion; covers four areas: macroeconomic conditions and trends, governmental fiscal capacity, manpower supply and demand, and unit and cycle costs within the major levels of education)

III. History, Structure, and Management Capacity of the System (briefly describes historical evolution of the education system, organizational structure and decision-making processes in education sector, and management of education, defined as ability to direct and implement activities in sector)

IV. Subsectors
     A. Preprimary Education
         i.   Status of Subsector
              1. Historical Setting
              2. National Goals and Strategies
              3. Structure
              4. Program
                  a. Administration
                  b. Students
                  c. Teachers
                  d. Curriculum
                  e. Examinations
                  f. Facilities and Equipment
                  g. Costs and Financing
                  h. Quality of Instruction
         ii. Preprimary Subsector
              1. Needs (deficiencies that need to be addressed)
              2. Plans (needs to be met according to current plans)
              3. Constraints (restrictions that will limit achievement of objectives)
              4. Issues (points to be decided)
                  a. External Efficiency (relevance of education or training program to subsequent activities of participants)
                  b. Internal Efficiency (how effectively part of education system uses available resources to achieve certain educational outcomes)
                  b. Access and Equity (access—availability of places to those who qualify to participate; equity—extent to which available educational opportunities are accessible regardless of characteristics that cannot easily be altered, location, gender, language spoken, ethnic group membership)
                  d. Administration and Supervision (management of subsector and quality control of activities)
                  e. Costs and Financing (costs: funds required to accomplish given task; financing: sources of funds)
              5. Conclusions (inference about major issues facing subsector)

Table 5.1   (Continued)

    iii. Recommendations/Policy Options (counsel for action/choices)
       1. First Priority
       2. Second Priority
       3. Third Priority

B. Primary Education
  i. Status of Subsector
    1. Historical Setting
    2. National Goals and Strategies
    3. Structure
    4. Program
      a. Administration
      b. Students
      c. Teachers
      d. Curriculum
      e. Examinations
      f. Facilities and Equipment
      g. Costs and Financing
      h. Quality of Instruction
  ii. Preprimary Subsector
    1. Needs (deficiencies that need to be addressed)
    2. Plans (needs intended to be met according to current plans)
    3. Constraints (restrictions that will limit achievement of objectives)
    4. Issues (points to be decided)
      a. External Efficiency (relevance of education or training program to subsequent activities of participants)
      b. Internal Efficiency (how effectively part of education system uses available resources to achieve certain educational outcomes)
      c. Access and Equity (access—availability of places to those who qualify to participate; equity—extent to which available educational opportunities are accessible regardless of characteristics that cannot easily be altered, location, gender, language spoken, ethnic group membership)
      d. Administration and Supervision (management of subsector and quality control of activities)
      e. Costs and Financing (costs: funds required to accomplish given task; financing: sources of funds)
    5. Conclusions (inference about major issues facing subsector)
  iii. Recommendations/Policy Options (counsel for action/choices)
    1. First Priority
    2. Second Priority
    3. Third Priority

C. Secondary Education
  See Preprimary
D. Teacher Training Education
  See Preprimary
E. Higher Education
  See Preprimary

Table 5.1   Contents of "Typical" Sector Assessment (Continued)

    F. Vocational and Technical Education
       See Preprimary
    G. Nonformal Education
       See Preprimary
V. Special Studies (any special studies needed)

VI. Background Documents Reviewed (comprehensive list)

Annexes

      List of acronyms
      Technical documentation
      Officials consulted
      Scope of work (for assessment team)
      Other supporting material

with which inputs are transformed into outcomes), access and equity (availability of schooling to eligible children; extent of variation across noncognitive student characteristics such as gender or ethnicity), administration and supervision, and costs and financing. Each subsector chapter ends with recommendations, ranked in relative priority.

Advantages and Disadvantages of the Sector Assessment
Approach

In comparison with the "no assessment" and intervention-specific approaches, the sector assessment model represents a considerable improvement in terms of systematic planning and even implementation. Sector assessment looks at the entire formal education system; it considers the relationships among components of the system, including the economic and administrative context. It looks at inputs and outcomes of the different subsectors, collects and presents a comprehensive picture of information about the system, synthesizes that information into an informed appraisal of the state of the system, and states priorities for the system in rank order. Generally drawing on the considerable comparative and technical expertise of consultants and the best available macro data on the education system, sector assessment provides a strong technical base for planning.

However, by placing so much emphasis on the substance of the assessment, the "what" component, sector assessment typically pays little attention to the implications of its own process for acceptance, adoption, or implementation of its recommendations. As a result, it misses opportunities to promote the changes it identifies as needed.

Education Reform Support (ERS)[4]

In presenting their model of reform, Crouch and Healey (1997) define ERS:

> ERS is . . . an operational framework for developing policy-analytical and policy-dialectal abilities, and institutional capacities, leading to demand-driven, sustainable, indigenous education policy reform. (p. vi)

Their model is based on three related premises, which differ qualitatively from those implicit in the sector analysis model: first is the idea that education development in poor countries is constrained primarily not by a deficiency of funds, technology, or know-how, but by the need for "far-reaching modifications in the way they approach both policy formulation and system-wide management" (Crouch & Healey, 1997, p. v). Meaningful change is blocked by powerful political forces, essentially vested interests. (The reader will find considerable resonance with the decentralization-sectoral reform model discussed in chapter 2.)

Second is the belief that technical analysis alone cannot solve the problems:

> information systems, databases, and models; training in public policy and cost-benefit analysis; training in management, budgeting, and planning; and so forth . . . while necessary, are not sufficient. The constraints to policy improvement are ideological, attitudinal, and political-economic as much as—if not more than—they are analytical or cognitive in origin. (Crouch & Healey, 1997, p. v)

Finally is the idea that reform requires informed *domestic* pressure to be effective:

> donor leverage of various kinds is largely insufficient and inappropriate. The pressure has to come from within (i.e., it must be both indigenous

and permanent), which means that until powerful national groups are mobilized and have the means at their disposal to exert positive policy pressure, little will happen in the way of thoughtful reform. (Crouch & Healey, 1997, p. v)

As a result, their approach aims to

integrate traditional public policy analysis (using known information and analytical techniques) with public policy dialogue, advocacy awareness, and political salesmanship, and to build indigenous institutional capacity that can strategically use this integration for purposes of effecting purposeful education reform. (Crouch & Healey, 1997, p. v)

ERS, in short, sees itself and reform primarily as political processes, albeit processes informed by data. Reform is led by politically powerful, technically minded policy activists, who act in the public interest to instigate change. To do this, ERS uses a framework, a set of principles and tools to plan for use of data collection, assessment, analysis, dialogue, and communication to bring about sustainable reform. The process aims to recognize and strategize around the political forces associated with reform. It seeks to develop analytic capacity among advocates for effective policy change and to empower a broad range of stakeholders to apply informed pressure in the political process. It actively promotes the use of information and analysis in policy debate, and works to institutionalize an improved policy-making process through formation and support of coalitions, networks, and core groups of policy activists. ERS works actively to promote disagreement, and thus debate, over education issues, and then to infuse debate with technical analysis.

The ERS Process

Crouch and Healey identify seven steps as part of the broad ERS process.

1. Assessment of education issues and political economy;
2. Development of (or support of existing) reform support infrastructure (usually including but broader than government alone);

3. Development of core group (including well-connected or powerful individuals interested in reform, committed to the public interest, and willing to think in technical terms);
4. Development, use, and training in specific technical tools for analysis;
5. Creation of demand for technical analysis;
6. Holding of seminars, symposia, workshops to present and debate policy issues;
7. Development of capability in drafting policy and legislation; extension to expertise in program management and policy implementation.

An ERS project is developed through ten steps:

1. Assess the political economy.
2. List and understand the key substantive reform issues.
3. List and understand the key process issues blocking reform.
4. List and understand the actors and stakeholders.
5. Understand the tools and techniques that can be used.
6. Relate substantive issues to process issues.
7. Assess the relationships of actors with each other and with issues.
8. Associate actors with tools and techniques.
9. Develop concrete action steps, levels of effort, etc.
10. Develop a monitoring and assessment strategy.

In this process, assessment takes place at the outset and, to a lesser extent, throughout the process. During design, analytic tools are used to identify technical needs, as well as substantive and process issues. The assessment involves understanding both substantive (and technical) perspectives as well as process and institutional needs. The design also includes explicit strategizing for building political support for reform. Implementation consists of ongoing strategizing and capacity building using information, analytic, and communication techniques.

Tools and techniques include:

- information gathering (case studies, focus groups, socioeconomic surveys, education management information system (EMIS) and school statistics, consumer and attitude surveys);
- research and analysis (simulations, statistical and econometric analyses, budgeting, planning, qualitative research, market research, traditional policy analysis);
- communication (policy dialogue, "boardroom" techniques, negotiation, policy dialogue, policy advocacy, social marketing, social advertising, and mass education campaigns).

And so, in contrast to sector assessment, the ERS model places a great emphasis on process, particularly the political process. Rather than trying to maintain an "objective" distance between technical analysis and politics, ERS works to make strong technical analysis an integral part of the political process. Assessment in this model is much more closely integrated with policy formation and implementation. Assessment includes analysis of the political-economic context as well as an explicitly political analysis of stakeholders and influential political leaders in and affecting education. ERS recognizes the politics of reform and provides a structured way to promote reform in a political context. It explicitly incorporates planners and implementers in assessment, analysis, and planning. It promotes demand for and utilization of data and technical analysis, and seeks to empower and institutionalize technical and strategic-political expertise.

At the same time, with its concern for process and engagement with the political dimensions of reform, ERS is less explicitly comprehensive in its approach. The process is placed in the hands of local policy makers. Certainly, everyone would agree that policy decisions should be made by those affected, or at least their legitimate authorities. One wonders, however, whether national policy makers will be able to step sufficiently out of their experience and interests to develop as "objective" an assessment as external experts with experience in similar activities in different contexts.

In addition, the ERS approach places a great deal of power and responsibility in the hands of those facilitating the ERS process. ERS is likely to be effective to the extent that those individuals are well-informed; well-intentioned; sensitive to the needs, interests, and dynamics of the host country; and able to carry out a complex set of analytic, political, and social responsibilities.

Informed Dialogue[5]

Informed dialogue is an approach, developed by Reimers and McGinn (1997), "intended to help the agent of education research define a context-specific strategy to create knowledge for educational change" (p. 175). The authors developed their approach as a result of their self-critical review of their many years of personal and institutional experience as researchers working to inform policy in poor countries. They begin their book with acknowledgment of failure in several instances to convince policy makers to use research findings in making decisions. The authors came to understand this failure as a problem with the conceptualization of research and policy and the roles of researchers and policy makers. The persistent view of research and policy as separate, sequential domains leads, they argue, to the production of research that is both less useful and less used than it might be. Their approach takes a strategy of structuring opportunities for informed dialogue, between external advisors, internal "knowledge agents," policy makers, and a wide range of other stakeholders both within and outside the formal education system.

The assumptions of classical models of change might be parodied as: education change is a result of good research read by wise policy makers who make technically good decisions implemented by faithful implementers. Unfortunately, as is well known, good research often offers little of direct use to policy makers, who rarely have time to read lengthy reports. Instead, policy makers typically make decisions by applying available, feasible solutions to pressing political problems. A better way to see education change, the authors argue, is as a process of organizational learning. "Dialogue" is the essential process necessary for organizational learning:

> We understand dialogue to be a disciplined participation [among stakeholders and actors in an education system] in an exploration of strengths and weaknesses of a collective project. Research is a powerful tool to provide information which can support this dialogue. Planning for the

future is an almost natural consequence of this dialogue. (Reimers &
McGinn, 1997, p. 119)

The authors come to this view through a constructivist perspective:

> Instead of living in a clockwork universe built (by God) for all time,
> we participate with God in a process of creation, of construction of new
> realities. Truth is not a static quality waiting to be discovered but some-
> thing that we bring into existence through our actions. . . . Science pro-
> vides the means for collective action to build society not by indicating
> the one and only path that all must follow, but by providing a means for
> people to share [their particular] knowledge and understanding and to
> build a common pathway. (Reimers & McGinn, 1997, p. 69)

The Informed Dialogue Process

The authors describe their model in terms of nine "situations, or
moments, of action." Moments represent opportunities for informed
dialogue. These moments need not be sequential; there is frequent stepping back, jumping ahead, or doubling up.

Moment 1: Define the change process—Moment 1 involves finding out
about the occasion of change—what is the problem, how is it understood, why is it being addressed and why now, where in the policy
cycle is the change located, how did the change agent come to be
involved, what is the purpose and function of the change process. Some
aspects of the change definition include:

> *Diagnosis of problems.* What problems are there? What is the nature
> and extent of problems? What is the status of the system? What
> are its strengths and weaknesses?
> *Analysis of problems.* What are the causes of the problems?
> *Responses to problems.* What will work to address the problem?
> How can we address the problem?
> *Monitoring of implementation of programs.* How is a program being
> implemented? Is it working as expected?
> *Examine effectiveness and efficiency of programs.* What was the
> impact of an intervention?

In clarifying these issues, it is helpful to develop a "map" of the problem, how it is understood and explained, and how different stakeholders see its solution. In mapping the solutions, it is important to include the assumptions that stakeholders bring to their analysis. Once named, these assumptions can be examined, discussed, acknowledged, and possibly revised in light of new information.

Moment 2: Define the stakeholders—Early in the change process, it is important to identify and understand the full range of stakeholders. Stakeholders are defined as those who have power to influence the change process, at either policy design or implementation stages, and those with both formal authority and informal power, inside and outside the education system. One reason for defining stakeholders is that many problems within education systems originate or must be solved by those outside the system. Dialogue with business; nongovernmental organizations (NGOs); political, cultural, and religious leaders; and local authorities can build support for reform. Another reason of course is to develop "ownership" of the assessment process and its proposals for change by those who will implement or receive the resulting program. Again, a mapping process is useful, especially if informed by knowledge of the beliefs, interests, past experience, intentions, and expectations of stakeholders as well as their organizations and paths of influence.

Moment 3: Define the current and relevant flows in the policy stream—In contrast to linear stages models of the policy process, Reimers and McGinn (1997) see policy formation as the product of flows of policy questions or issues, policy answers, and ongoing programs. This discussion is reminiscent of Porter's (1997) model of the policy process, discussed in chapter 3, as a result of convergence of three streams—problems, solutions, and politics. Understanding the problems, available solutions, the politics, and programs in a system helps clarify opportunities for change and potential linkages among critical components of the process.

Moment 4: Define what dialogues go on and should go on among key stakeholders—Dialogue, carried out by teams of stakeholders and system actors, is aimed at facilitating individual learning, and development of a shared vision for change. Changing classroom teaching practices, for example, might require dialogue among teachers; between teachers and principals, principals and supervisors; among staff at the Ministry of Education (MOE); and among trainers. Defining these teams appropriately is essential to successful dialogue. The composition of teams is important in building relationships and developing consensus across groups of differing perspectives and developing effective action plans with broad credibility and odds of success.

Moment 5: Empower groups for dialogue—Once teams are constituted, they must be helped to develop the interpersonal and group process conditions conducive to dialogue. (The substantive contents of dialogue are, of course, the education issues that led to the change process.) Facilitation or other approaches to team building are usually necessary to overcome natural organizational barriers to communication, build trust, and develop ways to "agree to disagree." Indeed, the outcome of dialogue is not necessarily consensus:

> The goal of team discussions should not necessarily be to reach consensus on a uniform view of problems and alternatives. This would prove very difficult in groups with diverse views and values. Instead, the goal should be to build coalitions and negotiate basic understandings so that all key stakeholders can support a change program even if they do it for different reasons or with reference to different value systems and goals. (Reimers & McGinn, 1997, p. 183)

Effective and ongoing management of dialogue teams is essential to the success of informed dialogue. When successful, it begins the process of organizational learning.

Moment 6: Establish rules for knowledge-based dialogue— Dialogue is a strategy for developing knowledge and "building coalitions around a change program." It does this by hosting conversation about both formal knowledge (research) and personal knowledge related to the education issues in question and facilitating discussion, even confrontation, around differing values and priorities among team participants. The process is a delicate one, requiring careful management, a clear set of rules agreed to by all participants, and substantial attention to interpersonal processes. The authors suggest that teams make more progress if they concentrate on intermediate objectives and problems, rather than attempting to reach consensus on overarching goals and values, or on the details of a program. Again, the purpose is not to achieve consensus on the larger values and ultimate endpoints but to agree on next and subsequent (but not ultimate) important steps.

Moment 7: Design operations to generate knowledge—Dialogue requires that appropriate research-based knowledge be introduced when needed, and in accessible format, to address a particular problem. In presenting research, careful attention must be paid to the needs of the clients, and the ways in which they make sense of research in light of existing knowledge and experience. Like most human beings, policy makers tend to believe research to the extent that it is either consistent with what they already know or serves a useful purpose for them. Changing what people already know is difficult and rarely accomplished by data alone.

Moment 8: Balance technical, conceptual, and process knowledge— Effective dialogue requires technical skills (ability to design and carry out scientifically credible research), conceptual skills (ability to analyze and map complex problems and develop innovative solutions), and process skills (ability to lead and work with other people, facilitate teams, manage conflict). The careful selection and preparation of facilitators and team leaders is important.

Moment 9: Prepare a reporting and dissemination plan—Dissemination is not the end of dialogue, but a critical step in the process. A careful plan needs to be developed to bring the findings of individual teams to larger and larger groups of stakeholders in a consultative and iterative manner that builds support for a plan of action. Again, accessible format and presentation of data are important along with careful structuring of opportunities in the larger arenas for reflection and dialogue.

Like ERS, informed dialogue places assessment in the context of a larger process of change. Also like ERS, informed dialogue sees the role of external advisors as one of facilitating change through actors within the system. Great emphasis is placed on process and interpersonal relations as well as technique, politics, and data. Informed dialogue suggests that questions about the assessment process are critical: Who leads the assessment? Who participates? Who decides the issues to be studied, the data to be collected, the analyses to be carried out, the interpretations and recommendations? The approach draws on the particular knowledge and viewpoints that participants bring in an explicit effort to help them develop a deeper understanding of the situation of the education system but also of the way the system looks to other stakeholders.

INFORMED DIALOGUE IN POST–CIVIL WAR EL SALVADOR

In the early 1990s, El Salvador was emerging from a debilitating 12-year civil war. Funding agencies, including USAID, were focusing their efforts on rebuilding education and fostering peace. In this context, the Harvard Institute for International Development was engaged to conduct a sector assessment.

A team of international consultants, headed by Fernando Reimers, decided that a conventional approach to assessment would not be effective. In the extremely polarized and politicized environment after the signing of the peace accord, all information was political. Trust was very low, boding poorly for any sustained national effort.

In this context, Reimers and team devised a dialogue strategy. First, data collection teams for each subsector (primary, secondary, nonformal, etc.) were constituted of one member from the Left, one member from the Right, and one international consultant. Teams were tasked with gathering as much information as possible and synthesizing it into a status of the subsector report, much like a conventional sector assessment conducted primarily by international consultants. Teams were instructed to come to agreement about the meaning of data when possible but to present controversies where there was disagreement.

The results of data collection were shared with the public in a series of consultations around the country. Initial results were presented, questions answered, the meaning explored in a public context. Reports were then revised on the basis of the consultations.

Recommendations were then prepared, and priorities developed by the teams for each subsector, then among the entire assessment group, and then shared, again in public fora throughout the country.

Finally, a plan of action was developed, presented again to the public, by members of both sides in the former conflict. Broad public support for both substance and process led to adoption of an ambitious plan for rehabilitation of the education system.

Assessment participants found to their surprise that despite profound disagreements about the overall goals of the system, they could agree on many immediate and intermediate steps.

Source: Reimers & McGinn, 1997

Thus, informed dialogue emphasizes a more facilitative and transparent role for the "external change (or knowledge) agent" than does ERS. Informed dialogue sees its role as explicitly educational, fostering organizational learning and an empathic understanding of the perspectives of others:

> The knowledge agent should keep in mind that educational change will be the outcome of changes in what some people in the educational system do. What people do is based on their perception of reality, not on reality itself. Therefore, it is necessary to understand those perceptions and to integrate new knowledge in a process which can alter those perceptions. We call this learning. (Reimers & McGinn, 1997, p. 178)

Such information is not easily obtained from existing documents and data, but requires a more intensive and context-sensitive approach to assessment, a more ethnographic methodology, a trained, empathic ear, and a highly skilled group of facilitators.

As with ERS, however, one worries, with so much emphasis on group process and participatory decision making, is informed dialogue not in danger of missing a potentially larger understanding of the system that an experienced outsider might bring, a perspective that might be missed by individuals involved, invested, and raised in a system? External consultants can certainly take part in the dialogue, but in a group decision-making mode, the degree of impact is likely to depend greatly on interpersonal skills and the dynamics and composition of the team. It would also seem that the process of dialogue might require so much time and energy that the technical details might suffer.

Improving Educational Quality (IEQ)[6]

Unlike the other approaches discussed here, IEQ's strategy was developed in the process of implementing a single project, albeit in a number of countries over a 10-year period of time. IEQ is included here because, unlike many education development projects, IEQ (2002) was explicit in its articulation of the education change process. Its purpose:

> The IEQ process provides a framework for helping education systems respond to the demands of universal access while maintaining a focus on quality. The balance is achieved by strengthening the host country's capacity to systematically examine local conditions of teaching and learning—and to use the resulting knowledge as a basis for reforming national policy and local practice. IEQ can be viewed both as a process and an outcome—a process because it examines what happens in learning environments and an outcome because it produces evidence to support change. (p. 6)

The IEQ Process

On the rationale that education quality, however understood,[7] is truly manifested only in the schools, IEQ "begins and ends in the classroom." Local conditions and needs, articulated by national and local educators and observed in classrooms and schools, become the focal point for each country's research. Preset projects are not imported. Instead a collaborative partnership is established with a national education research body, in a university, a curriculum development unit, etc. The selection of issues to be addressed, research design, instrumentation, data collection, and analysis and reporting plans grows out of dialogue among IEQ core staff and host country research team members.

Each country team selects a major national reform as the focal point for research and action. *Assessment* is the entry point into a cycle of assessment, analysis and assimilation, and action. Each country team conducts in-depth studies at the classroom level, first, to see how the reform is being implemented. Are textbooks arriving in the classroom as planned, for example? How are the teachers using textbooks? Do the children take their textbooks home to study? The intent is to create a locally valid and validated knowledge base of factors affecting teaching and learning, both positively and negatively. Teaching and learning are assessed using a variety of measures to capture a full range of perspectives on what's going on in schools.

The assessment phase is followed by an *analysis and assimilation* phase, during which the assessment data is examined, discussed, and absorbed. Workshops and seminars are held to provide training in quantitative techniques of data collection and analysis (construction of surveys, maintenance of large datasets) and qualitative methods (classroom observation, analysis of answers to open-ended questions). Quantitative data are examined in light of findings from classroom observations and interviews, and vice versa. The meaning, importance, and implications of findings are discussed widely among team members, across hierarchical lines within the education system, as well as with stakeholders outside the formal hierarchy—business, NGOs, community leaders, and so forth. Follow-up questions are posed. If textbooks scheduled to arrive in classrooms are not observed, for example, where are they?

In carrying out this research, international research consultants do not do the work, but assist host country researchers in analyzing the data and presenting findings. Host country researchers take the lead in deciding the best strategies for dissemination and policy leverage, sharing what they learn and answering questions about the value, validity, reliability, and policy implications of their findings. As the research findings make their way through the system, dialogue takes place about the pros and cons of different strategies for dealing with the problems identified.

At the end of the cycle, *action* steps and policies are devised to address the problems identified, and new assessments undertaken to see whether specific reform interventions are achieving the goals of improved teaching and learning. Findings are then shared to permit reflection, dialogue, and generation of new options for policy and practice.

Assessment, in the IEQ formulation, plays a particular role. Rather than providing a comprehensive understanding of a system of education, assessment focus on teaching and learning at the level of classroom and school and on a particular reform, identified in each country. The process of change is conceptualized as bottom up (or perhaps as an inverted hierarchy with the school at the top and the administrative structure as support). The effectiveness of education policy and management is thus assessed from the perspective of the teacher and pupil.

This approach to assessment is recursive, with each new cycle informed by results of the previous research cycle. Being led by national researchers, in partnership with international technical advisors, the IEQ approach is especially useful in training researchers, developing an appreciation of research among policy makers and a wide range of stakeholders, understanding the implementation of policies and programs in schools, and the nature and conditions of classroom practice.

Concerns and Value of the IEQ Process

As in any assessment, the quality of assessment and analysis depends on the capacities of researchers. IEQ's emphasis on classroom research may run the risk of relying on investigators with too local a perspective. More serious are questions about the extent to which classroom-based information and proposals for change will reach the center and be taken seriously. Experience is not encouraging in this regard. Vested interests and even the natural resistance of the status quo tend not to be persuaded by technical or even moral arguments unaccompanied by political pressure. A bottom-up strategy is likely to be effective in changing the system only to the extent that it engages the interest of powerful groups and individuals within government, the larger society, and beyond.

However, an important contribution of the IEQ approach, we feel, is its insistence that classroom practice is the core of education, and its elaboration of "backward mapping" approach to improving education quality (see discussion of backward mapping in chapter 9). In working to gain a systemic perspective, few education system assessments look closely at—much less get into—actual classrooms or schools.

COMPARING APPROACHES

This review has highlighted a number of issues to be considered in designing an education system assessment. All four models consider a systematic review of the education system, with the possible exception of IEQ, as a necessary starting point for planning change. They differ in the extent to which they are concerned with a comprehensive systems perspective versus a more problem-based approach. The models differ in the extent to which they emphasis process. All models are concerned with the use of information found; some explicitly organize the utilization of information by making assessment part of a larger process of education change. The more process-oriented approaches tend to be more concerned with implementation, with "ownership" of the policy issues uncovered, and with capacity building as important by-products of the assessment process. Only the IEQ approach places classroom instruction at the center of assessment; the other models consider schools, but in a less central way.

Tables 5.2–5.4 summarize the issues raised in this chapter in a series of questions, considered in categories corresponding to the central insights of the different models. Depending on the needs of a system, an assessment plan might be designed differently according to the extent to which it fostered: a systems approach to assessment (Table 5.2), informed participation (Table 5.3), organizational and individual learning and an implementation perspective (Table 5.4). Each of these tables examines the four models in terms of a series of specific good practices.

A Systems Approach

The larger intent of assessment, and its role in the reform process, is to provide a careful and comprehensive examination of current conditions across the system. A systems approach helps to clarify the interrelationships among parts of the system, and the need to address multiple aspects of a system to produce change. Of the assessment strategies examined, sector assessment places most emphasis on a systems perspective. Other assessment approaches may look at the system, but are not chartered to do so, as suggested in Table 5.2.

Informed Participation

As discussed, stakeholder participation in assessment may range from very little to quite extensive. Table 5.3 details some of the good

Table 5.2   Does the Assessment Strategy Adopt a Systems Approach?

Does/Is the approach to assessment:	No assessment (tradition, hunches)	Sector assessment	Education reform support	Informed dialogue	Improving educational quality
Consider the whole system?	Generally no	Yes	Depending on demand & facilitation	Depending on demand & facilitation	Generally no
Consider relationships among components?	No	Yes	"	"	"
Place the education system in economic, historical, & administrative context?	No	Yes	"	"	"
Examine inputs and outcomes for each subsector?	No	Yes	Depending on demand & facilitation	Depending on demand & facilitation	No
Comprehensive in collecting & presenting data about entire system?	No	Yes, albeit data of a certain kind	"	"	No
Synthesize findings into an overall appraisal of the state of the system?	No	Yes	"	"	"
Rank priorities for action steps?	Yes	Yes	Yes	Depending on facilitation	Depending on facilitation
Base analysis on comparative experience in other potentially informative contexts?	No	Yes	Depending on facilitation	Depending on facilitation	Depending on facilitation

practices associated with informed participation in terms of the approaches examined here. ERS, Informed Dialogue, and the IEQ approach all provide structured ways of informed participation.

Organizational and Individual Capacity Building

Assessment is a highly technical exercise: the skills involved would greatly enhance a ministry's policy-making and planning expertise. The occasion of assessment provides a good opportunity to develop

Table 5.3   Does the Assessment Strategy Include an Explicit Strategy for Informed Participation?

Does/Is the approach to assessment:	No assessment (tradition, hunches)	Sector assessment	Education reform support	Informed dialogue	Improving educational quality
Involve planners and implementers in analysis and planning?	Not particularly	Not particularly	Yes	Yes	Depending on how far up initiatives from bottom get
Increase awareness and "ownership" of problems in the system, thus leading to acceptance/adoption of reform?	No	Not particularly	Yes	Very much	Yes, at levels involved
Give responsibility for deciding priorities to a few external experts, a few local experts or leaders, or broader groups of stakeholders?	Local leaders/ status quo	External experts/local leaders	Broader groups of stakeholders	Even broader range of stakeholder groups	Broader range of stakeholders (depends how far up initiatives from bottom get)
Use a transparent process to decide priorities?	No	Somewhat	Somewhat	Very much	Very much
Help develop a political strategy to win acceptance/adoption of reform or new policies?	Implicit	No	Yes (process of persuasion)	Yes (transparent process)	Yes, but unclear how far "up" ideas get
Provide a strategy for engaging and sustaining the interest of the status quo in change or rely on good will or technical arguments alone?	Is planned by status quo	Relies on technical arguments	Strategizes to engage and change status quo	Engages status quo through participatory process	Largely reliant on good will
Provide a structured way of informing choices of priorities with data?	No	Provides technical info, but no process	Yes	Yes	Yes
Provide a strategy for dealing with disagreement?	No	No	Yes	Yes	Yes
Form coalitions around action plans?	N/A	No	Yes	Yes	Yes
Favor decisions based on data, power or authority, or informed negotiation?	Power/ authority	Data, no process (so use of data left to policies)	Informed negotiation	Informed negotiation	Data, with broader participation in assessment
Plan for institutionalization of its process?	No	No	Yes	Maybe	Yes

those skills among individuals and the organization as a whole. Table 5.4 elaborates the extent to which each of the approaches is likely to enhance the acquisition of data collection and analytic skills associated with a comprehensive assessment.

Implementation Perspective

The identification of problems and solutions is much easier than successful implementation of effective strategies, especially in complex, dynamic, highly political environments, over time, and particularly when the fate of reform depends on the cooperation of thousands of people over whom policy makers have (relatively) little influence. In such contexts, we feel, policy makers and planners need as much information as possible to enable them to plan with "initial intelligence" and use the influence they have to manage implementation with "ongoing intelligence." (Warwick, 1982). The more intelligence assessment can provide, the better. Table 5.4 considers the four approaches in this light.

Effective Conditions

Different approaches are likely to be effective in different contexts. Sector assessment works best when the problems facing a system are primarily technical in nature, with little political controversy. ERS works best when enlightened, technically able policy activists are available, and when entrenched, vested interests block reform. Informed dialogue is effective when participation and consensus building are as important as the technical quality of data, and when skilled, unbiased facilitators are available. The IEQ approach works best when dealing with issues of classroom quality, when a primary goal is to enhance the capacity of indigenous policy research organizations, and when those with power in the system are likely to be convinced by good ideas.

SUMMARY: ASSESSMENT AS COLLECTIVE LEARNING

By describing four approaches to assessment, we have tried to emphasize several important points about the change process. First of all,

Table 5.4   Does the Assessment Strategy Promote Organizational and Individual Learning and Adopt an Implementation Perspective?

Does/Is the approach to assessment:	No assessment (tradition, hunches)	Sector assessment	Education reform support	Informed dialogue	Improving educational quality
Organizational and Individual Learning					
Increase capacity of planners and implementers?	No	Depending on who does assessment	Yes	Yes	Yes
Have locals or expatriates carry out the assessment? (She who does learns.)	Local status quo; no formal assessment	Often expatriates, sometimes local individuals, rarely local institutions	Locals, with facilitation	Locals, with facilitation	Locals with facilitation
Ask what capacities need to be developed? (to initiate education/training process)	No	Not particularly	Yes	Yes	Yes
Implementation Perspective					
Collect information useful in planning implementation?	No	Not directly	Yes	Yes	Very much
See change process as mostly technical, political, or both?	Political	Technical	Both	Both	Technical but participatory
Likely to be informed about the macro and micro contexts of reform?	Yes	No	Yes, through participation of local policy activists	Yes, through participation of local policy activists	Yes, through participation of local policy activists
Organize assessment as a single, initial step or an iterative process?	No assessment done	Single initial step	Iterative	Iterative	Very iterative
See as underlying metaphor identifying deficits to fill, developing capacities, removing barriers, addressing technical problems	?	Identifying deficits, addressing technical problems	Removing barriers, developing capacities, addressing political problems, addressing technical problems	Developing capacities, removing barriers, addressing technical problems, addressing political problems	Developing capacities, addressing technical problems
Highly dependent on facilitator skills in analysis, politics, group process?	No	Particularly analysis	Yes: politics, group process, analysis	Yes: group process, analysis, politics	Somewhat: group process, analysis

there is no *single* way to make policy or plan for reform, or no overarching best way. Different strategies have advantages and disadvantages, and approaches can be adapted to the needs of the system. At the same time, there are better and worse ways of doing assessment. Assessment strategies are better, in our view, when they gather more information, engender more participation by stakeholders, ground recommendations in sound analysis, and develop a greater consensus and ownership about the priority problems facing a system and the best ways to approach them.

Assessment is not simply a matter of information, though information is essential. Assessment is a process, and not a neutral one. External advisors are important actors, and consideration should be give to their role, which may vary from essentially doing the assessment (deciding the questions, gathering and interpreting data, developing answers, and ranking priorities) in the least participatory of sector analysis approaches to facilitating and advising a dialogue process among indigenous stakeholders, as seen in the ERS, informed dialogue, and IEQs strategies. Assessment can focus only on systematic collection and analysis of information, or it can also include a systematic analysis—based on an understanding of context and the inside knowledge of important stakeholders—of the processes most likely to lead to the institutionalization of good practice.

At its worst, assessment uses resources needed elsewhere to generate a document that just sits on ministry and donor shelves. All too often, assessment is used to select and justify courses of action from among a few "usual suspects" of policy options. At its best, however, assessment leads to a new understanding of the system. The best assessment, we would argue, initiates the process of reform, and helps to develop understanding, ownership, and capacity on the part of a broad range of stakeholders.

ANNEX: DATA REQUIREMENTS FOR SECTOR ASSESSMENT

Administration

- Organization (chart depicting location of subsector within ministry or ministries and detailed administrative structure, including functions and staffing of each unit)

- Supervisory structure (how inspection is conducted, by whom, how frequently)
- Management personnel qualifications and capabilities
- Supply and demand of management personnel
- Communication links throughout the subsector
- School directors' qualifications (headmasters, principals, deans, presidents, etc.)
- Teacher appointment, review, salary, and promotion policies
- Sources of policy decisions
- Costs for managing the system
- Projections of future management needs

Students

- Enrollments (by grade or level; by program type; by gender; by region; by location [urban or rural]; by type of school [public or private])
- Age distribution for each grade level
- Percentage of the primary school age group in primary school (net enrollment)
- Children in primary school as a percentage of the primary school age group (gross enrollment—may be more than 100%)
- Admission criteria
- Cohort flow data (information on groups of students who begin the same grade together)
- Progression rates (rates at which cohorts progress from grade to grade)
- Repetition rates by grade
- Dropout rates by grade
- Graduation rates and numbers
- Progression rates of graduates to further training or occupations
- Enrollment projections

Teachers

- Numbers of grade or level; program type; gender; region; location (urban or rural); type of school (public or private); and by nationality or local/expatriate status

- Distribution by formal training (academic and pedagogical) and by experience
- Distribution by subject specialization
- Definitions of qualified, unqualified, and underqualified
- Salary schedule
- Attrition rates
- Age distribution for each grade or level
- Projections of future teacher requirements by subject, location, and qualifications
- Teacher supply (annual production and/or intake by level)
- Student/teacher ratios
- Number of trained teachers not engaged

Curriculum

- Scope and sequence of curriculum
- Whether it is national, regional, institutional, or program specific
- By whom it was designed and when
- Instructional materials required by grade or level
- Instructional materials actually available by grade or level
- Teaching methods
- Language of instruction by grade or level
- Relevance of curriculum context to students' subsequent activities

Examinations

- Form of the examination by grade or level and type of program (e.g., multiple choice, essay, applied skills)
- Prerequisites for taking examinations
- Numbers and proportions of students enrolled at each level taking the examination
- Pass rates by level, gender, region, and location (urban or rural)
- Who designs, grades, and sets pass rates for the examinations
- Purposes served by the examinations (e.g., entry to next level of schooling, evaluation of teacher or school performance, determination of areas for curricular improvement)

Facilities and Equipment

- Number of schools or institutions by level, program type, region, and location (urban or rural)
- Number of classrooms by level, program type, region, and location (urban or rural)
- Distribution and sizes of schools or institutions by level, program type, region, and location (urban or rural)
- Distribution of class size by level, program type, region, and location (urban or rural)
- Distribution of facilities by age, usable condition, and by utilization (single or double session)
- Necessary renovation or maintenance expenditures (amounts required and by whom to be paid)
- Support equipment and special facilities (e.g., libraries or laboratories)

Costs and Financing

- Costs per student year by program or curriculum
- Costs per graduate by program or curriculum
- Sources of financing by program or curriculum
- Sources and types of financing for central government, region, local community, school, families, and students
- Role of external assistance agencies in financing educational activities, both for capital and recurrent costs
- Financial commitments to this subsector in relation to other subsectors and the entire education sector expenditures

Quality of Instruction

- Type and predominance of pedagogical methods used
- Availability of instructional materials such as textbooks, by subject, by classroom, and by student
- Student/teacher interaction levels
- Availability of supplies and equipment (paper, pencils, chalk, blackboards)

- Amount of the school day actually devoted to learning tasks (time on task)
- Approximate number of school days teachers are present
- Approximate number of school days children attend class

(Pigozzi & Cieutat, 1988)

NOTES

1. Reimers and McGinn (1997) characterize their approach as "policy dialog with participation and organizational learning" (p. 70). We use "informed dialogue" as shorthand for the more descriptive term.

2. A sixth model carries out assessments, but limits their scope to aspects of direct relevance to a particular problem area or intervention. An example might be of an assessment carried out in preparation for curriculum revision. Such assessments are useful in preparation for targeted interventions, but are less useful in preparing for systemic reform.

3. We are indebted throughout this section to Pigozzi and Cieutat, 1988, *Education and Human Resources Sector Assessment Manual.*

4. For the information in this section, we are indebted to Crouch and Healey, 1997, volumes 1–6.

5. We are indebted in this section to Reimers and McGinn, 1997, *Informed Dialogue.*

6. The Improving Educational Quality Project (IEQ) is a USAID-funded education project, begun in 1991 and funded through 2002, in more than 10 countries.

7. There is no single definition of quality (Adams, 1993). Quality is understood, variously, in terms of inputs (highly trained teachers, for example), processes (high-quality pedagogical methods), content (high-quality curriculum), outputs (high achievement test scores), or outcomes (high rates of employment).

Chapter 6

Thinking about Education Goals

The assessment process highlights the major challenges facing educators, whether at the national level or particular local settings. In the face of these challenges, deciding where to begin, and how to muster collective will and direction, can be difficult. With too many problems as debilitating as too few, decision makers often decide to take on everything, and education plans end up looking like long wish lists. Many such wishes are never realized; education systems operate with finite resources. Only so much can be accomplished in a given time period, and thus educators must make difficult choices in the face of many challenges.

Often, the literature views choices in terms of two types: *choices among goals* and *choices among means*. The choice of goals is portrayed as a matter of preference, or a reflection of personal or social values. In contrast, the *choice of means* is dictated by more rational considerations such as benefits, costs, and likelihood of success. But in many ways, this distinction is too sharp. Discussion later in the chapter highlights, for example, situations where rational choices can be made between different goals, or at least in the timing of their pursuit. Moreover, choices, we feel, should be deeply informed by analysis of the current and past status of the education system in light of values and desired future states. Thus, choice of goals is not simply a matter of preference, nor is choice simply a rational exercise. The means by which ends are pursued have social, political, and economic implications. For many stakeholders in education systems, in fact, the means are of far greater salience. In addition, if for no other reason than to promote smooth implementation, the interests, values, and references of stakeholders need to come into play as decisions about means are made. Of course, the inadequacy of resources will ultimately limit the possibilities of choice—no system can do everything it desires. To be useful, goals must be prioritized and trade-offs made. Still, in the goal-setting process it is useful to first look beyond the limitations of current thinking, envisioning system goals beyond the means currently available. And so, we focus in this chapter on the first step in making choices—clarifying and prioritizing goals. The next chapter will look at means.

GOAL SETTING

The Three Tasks

In thinking about choice, it may be helpful to revisit the functions of goals. Goals serve several purposes in the reform process—to inspire and instigate coordinated action, to focus energy on a manageable number of targets, and to direct activities toward those targets. Goal setting thus involves three types of tasks:

- the *social conceptual* task of imagining possible future states, as unfettered as possible by current thinking or resources;
- the *technical* task of organizing coherent and achievable goals, strategies, and activities, given priority needs, the ways education systems work, and limited resources; and
- the *political* task of prioritizing goals and then generating and sustaining the political will to support the reforms.

Ultimately, education goal setting, a process we characterize as a *social conceptual task*, involves national decisions about the kind of society that is desired, what might be called the larger purposes of education. These decisions can be made through explicit and transparent processes, by coalitions of national elites, through more or less participatory approaches.[1] Chapter 1 discusses the processes by which the elites of six nations established the formative, or underlying, goal structure for education, its fundamental purposes. As suggested, subsequent formulations of education goals tend to remain resonant if not true to these formative models. However, during times of profound political and social change, the underlying goal structure may itself undergo deep transformation. "Transformational leadership" can also play a role in the deep transformation of the goals of an education system (see, for example, Burns, 2003), often by "reformation" of a system through a return to or reformulation of core societal values. Deep reform is assisted when, among other things, society achieves a sufficient consensus on the need for and direction of change. Leaders can play a critical role in helping develop this consensus, but sometimes agreement is reached without visible leadership. In reality, education goals are not always positive. In contexts of conflict, education goals often serve to exacerbate group tensions, where in the most severe case, education could offer a justification for genocide. Less dramatically, education goals tend to reflect both a nation's aspirations and fears, though the less "presentable" goals tend to be implicit, akin to the "theories-in-use" described in chapter 3.

The *technical task* of planning aims to achieve maximum efficiency with existing, and presumably finite, resources. Technical aspects of goal setting involve:

- prioritizing goals to ensure that the most important needs are met;
- operationalizing goals in unambiguous and measurable ways;
- organizing goals in terms of long-, medium-, and short-term impact;
- developing strategies to meet goals given available resources as well as what is known about education systems and their effective operation; and
- specifying activities to meet objectives defined by the strategies selected.

The technical task of planning also includes adequate provision for implementation, including sufficient funding as well as provision for the adequate guidance, support, and monitoring of implementers.

The *political task* of goal setting involves mobilization in at least five distinct points in the reform process, each of which requires new energy and different strategies:

- First, at the formative stage, mobilization of political will is necessary *to get the initiative or reform moving.* At this point, the critical political transaction is to get sufficient agreement among key stakeholders about the need for change and the broad outlines of that change for the initiative to move forward. At this initial point, details are often less useful than lofty but vague goals, which can enlist the support of as many stakeholders as possible.
- Second, mobilization is needed to *"get real,"* that is, to make hard decisions about trade-offs and priorities, costs, and possibilities. Inevitably, not all groups will get what they want, whether inadvertently or by design. Facing these trade-offs and managing organized disappointment, while continuing to move the reform forward, is challenging indeed.
- Third, mobilization is needed to *begin implementation.* As noted, political energy is often required to develop a plan—getting the initiative or reform on the agenda, carrying out analyses, developing a plan with sufficient detail, buy-in, and agreement—leaving little political energy for implementation. Without a new infusion of energy, however, implementation is likely to be hindered.
- Fourth, mobilization is needed *to continue implementation, while balancing commitment to essential goals and making necessary adjustments to the means.* As conditions change, other issues will come to the attention of policy makers and the public: maintaining commitment to the reform and to its core goals over the long haul is the essential challenge. Virtually all systemic reform requires years, and often decades, to be fully achieved; rarely is reform the project of a single administration or government. The reforms that survive are those able to maintain political support through different administrations, often by having developed powerful constituencies. Sometime during implementation, aspects of the means, perhaps even some of the goals, will require adjustment. The challenge is to balance updating the reform while not shifting course unduly.
- Finally, mobilization is needed to pause before adopting a new reform, *to garner lessons from the old initiatives and to build on the institutional capacity developed in the process of reform.* Organizations, particularly during a change of administration, tend

to seek bright new solutions rather than learning from the old ones. A new minister of education, perhaps from a former opposition party, is likely to throw out the old reforms, pointing to problems, in favor of a bold new approach, rather than continuing to build on what has been learned.

APPROACHES TO GOAL SETTING

Goal setting can be accomplished in different, not mutually exclusive, ways. Agreement on goals is made easier if the process is carried out in isolation of constraints, or if it never leads to agreement on priorities or necessary trade-offs, in other words, if everyone gets what they want. But such goals stand little likelihood of being achieved. In the end, resource constraints will come into play, and some groups will not get what they want, transparently as negotiated, or by default, as other priorities are acted on and funded, but as time and energy run out for others. This "something-for-everyone" approach to goal setting is undemocratic in the long run, we feel. It does, however, help start the process, and, in some contexts, may be necessary to build enough trust to move forward. In such cases, the trust generated during the initial agreement can be used to support subsequent agreements.

Goal setting is facilitated by a *grand vision*. Synoptic change in education (see discussion in the introduction) often accompanies or follows major social, political, or economic upheavals in the larger society. The achievement of majority rule in South Africa fostered a grand vision of the role for education in national transformation. Revolutionary movements tend to focus early on education and the development of, for example, "the new man." National independence also provides the opportunity for a grand revisiting of education, of its goals and contribution to society. Though synoptic change is unusual, organizational inertia in normal times may make it easier in some cases to make a series of major changes all at once rather than small ones over a longer period.

More frequently though, goals are introduced *incrementally*. The normal conditions of political life allow for small shifts in organizational goals and operating procedures rather than major adjustments. In such contexts, goals change incrementally over time rather than at once as part of a grand vision. Incremental changes can be introduced quietly as part of normal policy processes, that is, the budget process, or as part of external funding projects, as a coordinated effort on the part of political actors to shift the goals of education in a favorable direction. Incremental goal setting favors a technical, bureaucratic approach, which is appropriate to the extent that government represents the varying interests of society. At the same time, a savvy policy advocate can often introduce substantial change to a system by skillfully leveraging available means of influence.

Finally, education goal setting can be accomplished in explicitly structured *consultative policy processes* such as the post-peace accord sector assessment carried out in El Salvador (chapter 5), or the various discussions held in South Africa prior to and after majority rule in 1994. Consultative policy processes are not limited to dramatic changes in political context; most countries use some form of consultative process to discuss and announce major policy changes. (See Evans, 1994, for an interesting comparison of consultative processes in Francophone versus Anglophone education systems in Africa.)

TYPES OF GOALS

It may be helpful to consider goals in two dimensions, their *explicitness*, that is, the extent to which the goal is articulated or hidden, and what might be called their *seriousness*, the extent to which there is a real intent among policy makers to implement a goal, as evidenced by funding, preparation of appropriate regulations, inclusion in plans, or other behavioral indicators of organizational intent. Viewed as a two-by-two table, three types of goals can be identified (with a fourth cell that is not logically viable). Some goals (quadrant I) are articulated clearly but lack real support. It may be "politically correct" to assert such goals, or they may be included to generate political backing, but they lack real support and are unlikely to be implemented. Other goals are both stated, and real (see Figure 6.1). These are the goals that get attention in policy documents and plans. A third kind of goal is real but implicit. Real but implicit goals might include "system maintenance"

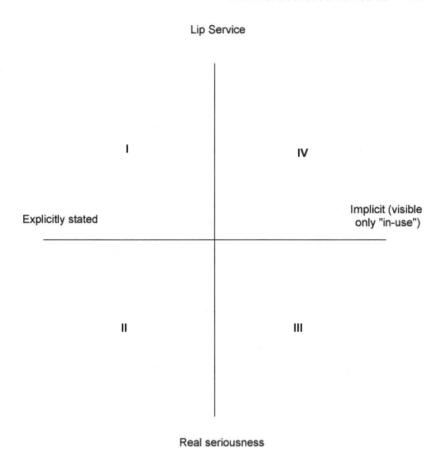

Figure 6.1   *Types of Education Goals*

goals such as the preservation of the social order and cultural values, or national goals such as building support for the state. Implicit but real goals may be widely shared but not discussed, or they may be such an integral part of the "culture" of a society and education system that system managers unconsciously work toward them with little awareness of what they are doing.

Finally, goals may vary in their focus. Windham (1991) distinguishes between the *outputs* of education systems, which can be thought of as the direct and intended products of schools, and the *outcomes* of education, or the larger effects of education in society. According to Windham (1991), "educational outcomes are determined

by many other factors than the nature and quantity of educational outputs, and the degree of determinacy of outputs to inputs is certainly
less than the determinacy of inputs to outputs" (p. 77). Outputs and
outcomes are produced by inputs and processes, as in one conventional
model of education production, summarized in Figure 6.2.

Beginning with this model, goals may, alternately, refer to:

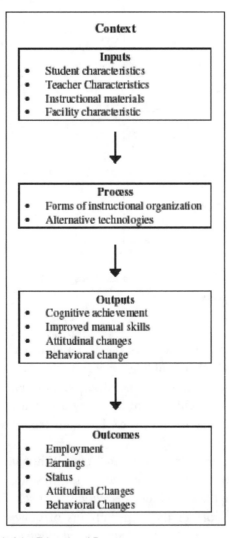

Figure 6.2 *Model of the Educational Process*

- *Societal outcomes* refer to the larger effects of education manifest in society, for example, employment, earnings, attitudinal changes, promotion of economic growth, or reinforcement of national unity. Goals directed at societal outcomes necessarily involve linkages with sectors other than education, to be discussed in Volume II.
- *System outputs* refer to the results of the education system, for example, increased rates of school completion, greater knowledge of mathematics and science. Outputs are largely under control of the education system, assuming it gets needed resources.
- *Instrumental goals* are those that are necessary or useful in achieving system outputs or societal outcomes, for example, increased internal efficiency, or improved education quality. Instrumental goals typically refer to the ways in which education systems work.
- *The embodiment of social values in education processes* is similar to instrumentalist goals, but generally represent social values of worth in their own right, for example, equity, critical thinking, respect for authority, conflict resolution, creation of social capital, etc. Education in this case serves primarily as a means to another end, for example, education for racial integration in the United States, or education for promoting civil society or democracy.

NATIONAL EDUCATION GOALS

In light of these various ways of understanding goals, it is interesting to compare explicit education goals around 1980 with those of 20 years later. A 1982 review of national education plans identified five generic rationales for government support of education and 34 specific expected outcomes from education. A similar set of plans was reviewed at the turn of the 21st century. (See Table 6.1.)

The most common rationales are rather familiar. Two are societal outcomes—nation building and human resource development; two are instrumental—efficiency and quality—and one embodies social values—socio-equity. The rationales and goals for education are quite consistent across the 20 years. Indeed, these goals are quite consistent with those from much, much earlier, as discussed in chapter 1. At the

Table 6.1   Comparison of Rationales for Education Expenditures

Lewin 1982	*28 National Reports published in 2001*
Nation-building rationales	Nation-building rationales
Develop and consolidate a national identity	Reinforce national unity***
Promulgate a national language	Acquire habits of hygiene and
Promulgate a national ideology	healthcare***
Promote self-sufficiency and self-reliance	Increase awareness and appreciation of
Reduce cultural and psychological	cultural/historical/linguistic identity*****
dependency	Promote loyalty to national religion*
Strengthen local institutions	Promote democracy*****
Develop individual potential fully	Promote indigenous language*
Localize expatriate manpower	Counter extremism and terrorism*
Ensure physical well-being and health	Modernize religious schools*
Manpower development rationales	Manpower development rationales
Increase the possession of general skills	Produce individuals to contribute toward
relevant to development	development*****
Increase the possession of skills relevant	Establish strong scientific and
to the modern sector	technological base**
Provide agricultural development	Prepare individuals for world of work****
knowledge and skills	Match manpower with labor market
Increase the prospects for self	demands*****
employment	Provide labor flexibility and mobility*
Extend literacy to increase productivity and	Promote economic growth****
innovation	Modernize agricultural technology**
Develop nonformal education programs	Eradicate illiteracy*****
Socio-equity rationales	Socio-equity rationales
Equalize educational opportunities and	Reduce gender inequalities*****
reduce regional disparities in access	Reduce regional inequalities***
Reduce income inequalities	Reduce urban/rural inequalities***
Reduce occupational differences between	Correct historical injustices**
groups resulting from educational	Provide free basic education*****
imbalances	Reduce income poverty
Provide basic education as a human right	
Improving efficiency of schooling	Improving efficiency of schooling
rationales	rationales
Reduce dropouts	
Reduce repetition rates	
Increase enrollments	
Improve cost effectiveness of teacher	
training	

Table 6.1   (Continued)

Lewin 1982	28 National Reports published in 2001
Improve efficiency of plant utilization	Decentralize system management***** Transition to transnational (EU) model of education**
Improving quality of schooling rationales	Improving quality of schooling rationales
Improve educational quality through curriculum development Improve quality through localizing examinations Improve teacher training Improve in-service professional development Improve resources available to teachers Enhance planning and research capabilities Increase private education standards	Update educational content***** Remove dogma and ideology** Universal minimum requirements* Improve teachers' social status***** Launch new teaching technologies* Improve infrastructure**** Improve teacher training***** Decrease student/teacher ratio***
	Technology rationales
	Keep pace with technological advances**** Avoid the digital divide* Use Internet as education resource*** Students can learn at own pace as self-learners** Develop workers to compete in information age*** Upgrade technological infrastructure***

*Refers to the number of references to a particular goal
Source: Lewin et al., 1982.

same time there are several interesting recent changes, reflective perhaps of the trends discussed in the introduction:

- The 2001 list places a greater stress on values in education including democracy, religiosity, and tolerance—but also the renewed stress on national unity and the (implicit) need to counter extremism and terrorism.
- The 2001 list has a much greater sense of urgency—for example, extend literacy is now replaced with eradicate illiteracy.
- The 2001 list is more specific in identifying inequalities that education is asked to address—gender, regional, rural–urban, poverty, and historical injustices.

- The 2001 list highlights a growing interest in technology both as an asset for learning and as a means for social development.
- Similarly, the 2001 list places more stress on indigenous higher education and research. Rather than remain customers of universities in the industrialized nations of the West, increasing numbers of new nations feel they can or should be creators and sellers of expertise.

STEPS IN GOAL SETTING

We suggest a four-step process of initial goal setting: structuring the process; envisioning and operationalizing desirable end states; mapping and prioritizing gaps between the current conditions and desired states; and prioritization. Then, in chapter 7, we finish the discussion of goals by turning to criteria for assessing trade-offs among means.

The remainder of this chapter discusses considerations in the initial goal-setting process; common goals by primary and secondary subsector; and some of the issues in operationalization and measurement of common concepts in education reform.

Step 1. Structuring the Process

As with other aspects of the policy process, we suggest that explicit attention be paid to the structuring of goal setting, in particular, who is involved in setting goals, how communication is organized among direct participants and with the larger public, what information is used in goal setting and how it is used, and how the task of goal setting is understood.

Step 2. Envisioning and Operationalizing Desirable End States

After a goal-setting process is structured, it is useful, in most contexts, to articulate as clearly as possible a vision of the desired end state of reform. To avoid the problem of "always fighting the last war," this vision of "what should be" is ideally developed with little reference to the current system. The idea is to create a rich and comprehensive vision of reform. In other contexts, notably highly politicized situations in which discussion of end states could lead to conflict instead of consensus, the envisioning process can begin with a focus on the current system and the next steps for improvement. Fresh visions can be stimulated by:

- new ideas from outside the education or national system;
- ideals—as expressed in international agreements and declarations, or national documents such as the constitution, even religious ideals taken seriously;
- examples from around the world—such and such a country achieved education for all, so can we;
- alternative discourse—visions of empowerment.

Some education systems are ready for major shifts in direction; others seek to work more effectively toward current goals. The goal-setting process tends to be less effective when goal setters:

- limit themselves to the first thoughts that come to mind;
- short-circuit their vision of goals with too early thoughts of feasibility;
- rely on external agendas and funding to set goals;
- fall back on the way things have always been done; or
- fail to seek out broader, deeper visions of change.

Step 3. Mapping Gaps between Desired and Current States

A third step involves specifying the differences between the current state of the system as revealed by assessment and the desired states developed through the visioning process. In order to do this, it is first useful to operationalize desired end states. Although broad goal statements are useful as inspiration, goals need to be translated into operational terms, often quantifiable targets. Later sections of this chapter discuss common goals in primary and secondary education and some of the measures used to operationalize them. Once identified, these gaps can be evaluated and prioritized according to the criteria discussed in chapter 7, and alternate strategies can be designed to close the gaps.

Step 4. Prioritization

Table 6.1 lists over 50 goals proposed by educators in various settings. The typical development plan proposed an average of 13 goals, too many to realistically achieve, in our estimation, and evidence of the pervasiveness of the *something-for-everyone* approach to goal setting. To help educators decide which of many goals to give primary attention to, at least for the short term, the following criteria might be used in prioritizing goals.

Importance

Perhaps most elusive, the relative importance of goals is a vital criterion for prioritizing goals. Stakeholders have different perspectives on the value of education. In the face of these different perspectives, one influential factor shaping the debate will be past priorities spelled out in major documents such as the constitution or the education charter, which highlight common themes acceptable to all. Within the framework of tradition, the different perspectives are likely to be promoted. Humanists may stress the importance of developing informed, sensitive children who think for themselves, while businessmen emphasize the development of skills directly applicable to the current industrial and commercial system. Politicians may favor the nurturance of political aptitudes, with a preference for cultivating the values of their particular political party. And religious leaders are likely to stress the importance of their religious persuasion. Although the ranking of relative importance is usually determined by the relative clout of those sitting at the table, decision-making tools exist that can build more rationality into choices.

Preconditions

Some goals precede others, either logically or as a precondition of subsequent goals. For example, education systems have generally worked first to open access, and then to improve quality. Improved quality may be necessary for increases in worker productivity, increased earnings, and economic growth. However, preconditions should be understood as context-dependent. Increased efficiency, for example, may be necessary to make room for quality improvements. A system may decide, as did Uganda in the 1990s, to take steps to improve the quality of the basic education system first, and then to expand access. The rationale was that it would be easier to expand a system of reasonably high quality than to improve the quality in a large, low-quality school system (see Christensen et al., 1997; Moulton et al., 2002).

Clarity of Operational Implications

While decision makers may agree on which particular goals to emphasize, they are less likely to share a common understanding of these goals. Indeed, our analysis suggests that securing agreement on fuzzy goals (rather than developing a shared concrete understanding of those goals) is a common approach to the political task of getting the initiative going. One example is education quality, a goal that nearly everyone will affirm. But what is education quality? Entering the lexicon of education planners in the 1960s, "quality" was used to rally educators to focus on what was happening *within* schools, as opposed to the larger system, where the energies of most planners had largely been concentrated. Immediately, administrators associated quality with what goes into schools rather than what takes places inside, arguing that the quality problem derived from a shortage of funds, antiquated buildings, and insufficient teachers.[2] Principals and teachers, professionals that they are, feel they know what needs to be done, provided they are given sufficient resources.[3]

Another group sought to focus the quality discussion on the goal of academic achievement, acknowledging that though schools had many purposes, the best focused on specific goals such as improving achievement scores. It was also argued that many education goals were diffuse and beyond evaluation, whereas academic achievement was specific and could be evaluated with reliable tests. Thus it was proposed that quality be equated with academic achievement.

In the meantime, quality had acquired other meanings. Quality can be seen as "value-added," that is the additional learning or knowledge that the school adds to the student. Students come to school with differing backgrounds that greatly affect what they are able to learn. While schools can do little to affect student background, they can affect what "value" schools "add." And so, value-added is a criterion on which schools ought to be judged. Quality can also be understood as selectivity. The more selective the institution, the higher the quality (Williams, 2002). Even so, these meanings may have left out the concerns of parents for a relevant education that teaches life skills or vocational skills, or an education that develops moral and spiritual values. A way out of this morass is to settle on more precise concepts. Rather than talk of education quality, one should talk about academic achievement, mastery of vocational skills, or instillation of values. Such an approach is likely to promote greater clarity (though perhaps reducing the possibilities for agreement around less precisely worded but valued terms such as *quality*).

As with education quality, there are different notions of efficiency in education. Some people focus on the speed of graduation, some focus on financial cost, others focus on fit with the labor market. Again it is important to develop a more operational list.

Likelihood of Impact

In setting priorities among goals, it is important to consider the likelihood of achieving progress. Some of the priorities discussed above have been given considerable attention by educators, and thus a number of means for gauging progress exist, including surveys and tests. But other priorities have received less attention, or simply are more intractable, and may not be associated with widely accepted measures. Progress in conveying values is one example. What are the values a school is expected to convey, and how can these be measured? The fact that these issues have gone unresolved in the past does not mean they are beyond resolution. But it may be unwise to devote substantial resources to a goal toward which progress cannot be assessed.

Allocations between Levels

We have argued that goal setting goes deeper if the envisioning process is guided by the question, "what should we do?" as opposed to, "what should we do with what we have?" Nonetheless, goal setters often start with existing resources and think within these parameters. In this way, intertwined with the decision on goals is often the emphasis, and the funding, allocated to different levels of education—primary and basic education, secondary education, higher education, early childhood education, nonformal and adult education. In more centralized systems, decisions on goals are likely made first for the system as a whole, and then later for specific levels. In a decentralized system, regions, states, and even individual schools and local communities may make their own decisions, or supplement state funds. Therefore any funding decision implicitly attaches value to different priorities.

And so, it is interesting to consider the relative emphasis placed on different levels of education for a sample of countries over the past three decades (see Table 6.2). Through the mid-1970s, many countries concentrated an extraordinary amount of funds on tertiary education relative to the other levels. Over time, various arguments were advanced by international organizations, for example, Education for All (EFA), in favor of increasing allocations for basic education. These arguments were differentially persuasive; the countries of Francophone sub-Saharan Africa, for example, were most reluctant to reduce support for secondary and tertiary education.

While today most countries affirm the importance of EFA, over the 1990s, a number of countries began to argue that a singular stress on basic education will relegate a nation to a peripheral position in the

Table 6.2   Trends in the Allocation of Education Resources by Level

Year	Primary education index	Secondary education index	Tertiary education index
1970	11.3	52.5	209.7
1975	13.5	37.3	170.4
1980	13.4	35.6	205.8
1985	13.8	29.4	148.4
1990	15.7	23.6	99.1
1995	15.2	21.9	92.7
2000	15.1	21.5	83.6

Note: Number of countries in averages varies from 50–80. The above indices were calculated as follows: (level of expense per student)/(per capita income)*100.
Source: World Bank (2004).

world economy. As a result, the coming years are expected to witness an increasing interest in secondary and tertiary education.

TOWARD A LIST OF EFA RELEVANT PRIORITIES

The next two sections consider some of the commonly discussed issues involved in selecting goals at the primary and secondary levels. As can be seen, this discourse emphasizes outputs and instrumental goals, with less explicit attention to outcomes or to the embodiment of social values in education processes. EFA places a strong emphasis on primary education, including a strong commitment to reaching the children of disadvantaged groups and providing, preferably in a school environment, the skills necessary to survive a changing world. Also, EFA seeks to foster an education experience that strengthens local communities and respects indigenous culture. In view of these commitments, the following is a list of priorities to guide EFA-related planning:

- *Equitable access of children to schools.* Access surely stands at the top of the EFA list. In no prior time has such a consistent concern been expressed for girls, disadvantaged children, homeless and street children, and other children at risk. Getting children to school can be viewed as a first step toward addressing many of their problems. The Education for All initiative rejects any compromise; access should be provided to all children, whatever their circumstances. Equitable access rather than equal access connotes that moral determination.
- *Children should acquire basic knowledge and skills.* Schools seek to help children through changing their mental and moral capabilities. Even when children do not earn impressive scores on abstract achievement tests, all children who attend school should significantly benefit from the experience.
- *Equitable provision of schooling*, taking full account of local circumstances. The provision of effective schooling will require different resources in different circumstances. Remote areas or communities whose parents are poorly educated require more attention than those at the center. Equity means providing each set-

ting with necessary resources to enable children to acquire mastery of basic skills.

- *Efficiency of schools and the school system* in realizing these priorities. Given the large number of children inadequately educated, wasting resources is inexcusable. Moreover, children will abandon formal education if schools are a waste of their time. Concerted effort should be devoted to energizing schools and school systems to these priorities as quickly as possible. A reasonable level of expenditures is one aspect of efficiency, keeping in mind that different contexts and teaching-learning processes may require different levels of expenditure.

- *Relevance of school experience.* The United Nations Children's Fund (UNICEF), in recent discussions of primary education, has proposed a survival skills approach to curriculum, which seeks to make the school a setting for learning skills with immediate applicability for survival, health, and well-being. These objectives are considered at least as high a priority as the standard academic curriculum of language skills and arithmetic.

- The richness of schools in conveying *local, national, and global values.* Relevant education is best conveyed in the language and symbols most familiar to the child. Another priority is to develop an education experience that reinforces local values and culture while at the same time broadening children's horizons to understand worlds beyond their immediate settings.

IS THERE AN INHERENT HIERARCHY
AMONG PRIORITIES?

The discussions surrounding the global EFA initiative argue for attacking issues of access, equity, and relevance first, as a matter of human rights; and taking up other issues in due course. Interesting questions for discussion include the relations between priorities, the order of priorities, and the reasoning behind the ordering.

As a first glance at these questions, it will be helpful to reflect on the nature of education systems. A system implies an organic linkage of components. Psychologists speak of needs that are hierarchically linked: lower needs such as for food and security have to be satisfied before intermediate and higher needs become germane (Maslow, 1970). Similarly, economists have discussed the need for certain increases in agricultural productivity as preconditions for industrial growth. Presumably the components of an education system, including its outcomes, have systemic links as well.

In the early 1960s, Beeby (1961) proposed a sequence of stages in the development of education systems. For Beeby, the major determinant in the development of an education system was the availability and preparation of teachers. The skills of teachers set limits on the possible achievements of school systems. Teacher skills could be organized along a hierarchy of meaning, with better-educated and well-trained teachers able to foster deeper meaning-making among students, including students with a wide range of individual learning needs, and to use a diversity of instructional methods as appropriate.

The first stage, entitled the "home school stage" utilizes teachers who are ill-educated and untrained. At this stage, education is characterized by lack of organization, reliance on relatively meaningless symbols, and very low standards. Memorization is all important.

The second stage, "formalism," also relies on relatively ill-educated teachers, but provides them with some training. Schooling at the formalistic stage is highly organized. Education is organized around symbols with limited meaning. There is an emphasis on the right syllabus, the "three R's," rigid methods, and the "one best way." Typically systems at the formalistic stage rely on one textbook, external examinations, inspection, tight external discipline, and memorization. The emotional lives of children are largely ignored.

The third stage, "transition," utilizes better-educated and trained teachers. Transitional schools have roughly the same goals as in the formalistic stage, but goals are more efficiently achieved. There is greater emphasis on meaning, but understanding is still rather "thin" and formal. The syllabus and textbooks are less restrictive, but teachers hesitate to use greater freedom. Final leaving examinations often restrict experimentation. There is still little in the classroom to cater to the emotional and creative life of the child.

The fourth stage of "meaning" uses well-educated and well-trained teachers. Meaning and understanding are stressed in the education process. There is a somewhat wider curriculum, and a variety of content and methods are used. Individual differences are catered for through activity methods, problem solving and creativity, and internal tests. Discipline is relaxed and positive. The emotional and aesthetic life is emphasized as well as the intellectual. There are closer relations with communities, better buildings and equipment.

Understood in this way, policy makers working to improve their education systems would be advised to focus on different goals, depending on where most of their system is developmentally. Whether or not Beeby's model accurately represents a universal pattern of development, it raises the useful question of what goals come first. What are the foundational goals necessary to achieve higher-order goals?

The Cultural Nature of Conceptions of Progress

Guthrie (1990), in a thoughtful defense of traditional teaching, observes that Beeby's stages capture the essence of Western thinking that has guided teacher education reform and interpretations of their failures. Most reforms have sought to shift teaching from more traditional, formalistic modes toward more liberal, student-centered methods. Questioning this thinking, Guthrie asserts that rather than concentrating on student learning as the criterion variable against which quality of teaching is assessed, teaching styles themselves have become a desirable outcome. Guthrie questions whether the assumptions underlying the relationship between a student-centered teaching style and student learning are valid in all cultural contexts.

Focusing specifically on the Beeby typology, which Guthrie viewed as a good representation of these fallacies, Guthrie specifically charges that the logic of the stages is circular. The criterion of judgment is culture-bound, the association of an ability to inquire with inquiry teaching techniques is not a necessary one. Attempts to have students learn higher-level cognitive skills may be inappropriate in many contexts. Whether Guthrie is correct in the particulars of his critique, he, like Beeby, raises useful questions.

A GENERAL CONSENSUS

Despite the variety of goals and the many ways in which goals can be considered, there is a general consensus as to the issues, trade-offs, and complementarities among these basic goals.

Access as the fundamental priority. One link is between access and all others. It is impossible to provide a relevant education or to ensure that young people achieve mastery of various skills if these young people do not get to school. This obvious link is splashed throughout the World Declaration on Education for All. The first paragraph observes, "More than 100 million children, including at least 60 million girls, have no access to primary schooling." The Third Article expands on this theme, pointing out that greater access enables a school system to address issues of gender, rural, ethnic, and other disparities.

Internal efficiency and access. In systems where large numbers of children repeat, considerable teacher time and other resources are devoted to helping these children advance. With these resources unavailable for new pupils, many may be turned away, or receive less attention than they need to do well. The waste of teacher time and other resources make difficult demands on limited school budgets. Improvements in internal efficiency can free up some of these resources for other purposes such as acceptance of additional students, or improvements in curriculum and instruction.

Learning acquisition as an organizing principle. Schools should be purposeful organizations, seeking to convey specific skills, knowledge, and attitudes to their pupils. Unfortunately, in some systems, schools are little more than a place where teachers receive a paycheck with little systematic attention devoted to pupil learning. It may be particularly difficult to promote learning when learning objectives are not specified. Thus one common theme in current discussions of primary education is to establish clear learning goals, and to develop some means for assessing the progress of pupils in realizing those goals. Where the goals of education are made explicit, teachers find it easier to organize their work. School managers have a basis for developing or purchasing instructional materials and for evaluating the performance of schools. For some, assessment implies the development of national standards and a sophisticated examining process. Less complex alternatives are

possible, and likely preferable in many cases, as high-stakes accountability schemes may do more harm than good to marginal schools in
systems lacking a strong school support system.

Learning versus efficiency. Haddad (1979) has highlighted the link
between (certain) education standards and efficiency. Setting higher
standards tends to result in an increase in repetition and dropout.
"Lowering" standards tends to reduce these inefficiencies, but also
weakens a major objective of schooling. One issue is the meaning of
high standards. In some systems, quality is equated with a distant metropolitan standard. Schools with high standards teach in a metropolitan
language; children only advance if they pass exams designed in that
metropolitan center. The majority of children do not succeed in such
systems. As a result, few children are qualified for secondary and
higher education, and, perversely, it becomes feasible to lavish generous funds on these advanced institutions. But clearly the slavish attention to high (and foreign) standards deprives many children of the
opportunity to learn.

Over the past decade, a number of policy analysts have proposed
assessments that focus on the mastery levels of children in the final
years of primary education, along with links between school or teacher
incentives and good performance (Greaney & Kellaghan, 1996). Such
schemes may have the beneficial effect of motivating school managers
to bring all of their pupils up to the mastery level. Unfortunately, past
experience suggests another possible outcome of assessment and
accountability systems: school managers may fail their weaker students, so as not to lower the school's scores. An excessive focus on
mastery, particularly mastery according to an external standard, may
have unexpected consequences.

Both learning and efficiency are important priorities, and school systems will wish to strike a balance between the two. Where systems have
adequate knowledge of their success with respect to these competing
goals, it becomes possible to develop a long-run strategy that leads to
improvements in both. East Asian schools are particularly noteworthy
in this regard because East Asian nations have achieved full access with
dropout and repetition rates virtually zero. Yet primary-level children
in East Asian countries repeatedly outperform children from other
nations in international assessments of achievement. Moreover, stu-

dent–teacher ratios in East Asia tend to be substantially higher than in much of the developing world. In Japan, for example, the average primary classroom has 39 students, while Korea has 45 (Cummings & Altbach, 1997). Thanks to impressive pupil discipline and motivation, much of which derives from cultural traits and family upbringing, teachers are able to handle large numbers of students, another form of efficiency. Clearly it is possible, in a supportive context, to design approaches to education that are both efficient and achieve respectable learning targets.

Relevance and values education as important priorities. It is apparent that access, as well as retention, can be enhanced if parents and children see some utility in attending schools. Less clear are the features of schooling that promote a sense of worth. In urban areas, it is apparent that many children see primary education as a stepping stone to higher levels, so value in their eyes is measured in terms of their success in the academic curriculum. But for many other children in poor areas, an extended education career may be unlikely. Still, according to a mounting body of evidence, many children, parents, and communities who appear to lack interest in schooling are in fact highly engaged in schools that are physically accessible and safe, are flexible in accommodating the multiple demands on children's time, validate local values, and offer relevant learning experiences (Glassman & Millogo, 2003). Increasingly among many populations in the world, the value orientation of schools is of utmost importance.

PRIORITIES FOR SECONDARY EDUCATION

While EFA is the major preoccupation of donors involved in education development, the education plans of an increasing number of nations indicate a concern to develop secondary education. As noted in Table 6.1, these plans highlight such goals as the need to keep pace with technological advances and to avoid the digital disadvantage. They also stress preparing individuals for the world of work and for helping the nation establish a strong scientific and technological base. There are concerns to counter the expanding incidence of youth unemployment and associated social and political problems. Broadly, the emerging goals for secondary education appear to include the following.

Access. The successes of EFA, incomplete as they are, have resulted in steadily increasing numbers of primary completers. In the absence of a major expansion in secondary education, most of these children will not be able to continue into secondary school. Reductions in opportunities to study are likely to adversely affect the motivation of young people to do well in primary education. And so there are pressures from several angles to increase the capacity of secondary education.

Efficiency. Young people are eager to make sufficient progress in their studies to receive a recognized credential. Many systems have midpoint exams, for example at grades 9 to 11, that may lead to the termination of studies for those who do not do well. Yet in these same systems, there may be few labor market opportunities for those who fail or drop out of secondary education. Secondary dropouts are among the most discontented segments of the population and are prone to deviant social and political activity. Inefficient secondary education systems, and those that fail to link young people with employment and the larger civic culture, help breed instability, a topic to be discussed in more detail in Volume II.

Local Relevance. National economies are largely comprised of diverse local economies. A common national secondary curriculum serves a useful function of supplying higher education institutions with appropriately prepared candidates. However, it may not serve the students as well when they seek local employment. A student trained in the arts will not be very competitive in a local economy based on agriculture, mining, or fishing. Some economies may need young people trained in such areas as bookkeeping or technology, the kinds of skills that are sometimes deemphasized in secondary curricula. Thus one concern is to develop secondary education opportunities that fit local economies while still providing students and their families opportunities for advancement.

Global Skills. Among the more persuasive arguments for strengthening secondary education is the fear that a nation will be left out of the world economy. Nations such as China, India, and Vietnam have attracted significant foreign investment because of their ability to supply large numbers of trained workers to serve in such functions as data entry, typesetting, computer assembly, and other operative jobs that require a secondary-level education. In contrast, most African nations have insufficient numbers of trained workers to attract foreign investment. If, at the low-skill end, greater numbers of young people acquire skills needed in the global economy, foreign investment may increase, thus improving the national economy. At the higher end, technological and scientific competitiveness is grounded in a high-quality, and broad-based, secondary school system.

Secondary education has responded to these trends with substantial expansions in facilities at considerable cost, but with little adaptation to the traditional models of secondary education. It seems unlikely that secondary education can be expanded to meet the demand, especially if current models of provision remain the norm, and especially if the universal aspirations of EFA are also to be attained. In contrast with community approaches to primary education, there has been relatively little experimentation in alternative modes of providing secondary education.

OPERATIONALIZING OUTPUTS AND OUTCOMES

In deciding what to emphasize in an education reform program, it is important to understand the current state of education. Both qualitative and quantitative information is useful for developing a picture. Quantitative information has the merit of being more independently verifiable and more enabling of precise comparisons. Of course, numbers can be simultaneously precise and wrong—made up or based on incorrect or misleading assumptions.

The collection of information on education performance begins either at school or household level and can be used to examine impact at various levels: Does an intervention benefit individual children, communities, regions, and the nation? Much international discussion has focused on national-level performance, but even in nations with impressive averages, certain areas are likely to perform at much lower levels. Thus in the assessment of education programs, it is important to delve beneath the averages to examine education's impact on the full range of actors.

Table 6.3 summarizes several of the procedures frequently used to measure the relative success of schools, local education systems, and national systems in achieving common goals. More detailed discussions of indicators are available along with practical suggestions for their systematic development and for the collection of appropriate data

Table 6.3   Common Procedures for Measuring Attainment of Education Goals

Goals	Indicators	Types of Data	Measurements
Outputs			
Access	Gross enrollment ratio* Net enrollment ratio	School survey, Population census	Enrollment grades 1–6/ Population ages 6–12 Enrollment ages 6–12/ Population ages 6–12
Efficiency	School completion rate Primary completion rate	School Survey, Population census	School Attendance Gd. 5/ School Entrants** School Attendance Gd. 5/ Population Age 11
Quality or Learning acquisition	Academic achievement	Exam scores Achievement studies	Average achievement End of school year Average end of year— Average beginning of year
Equity	Equity gap Equity rate	All of above	Indicator group A (e.g., boys)—indicator group B (e.g., girls), Indicator group B/ indicator group A Indicator group B × 2/ indicator group A GINI Index
Value change	Respect, responsibility, loyalty, tolerance, loyalty, peace	Attitude survey	% holding attitude % holding attitude at end of schooling—% at beginning
Behavioral change	Improved attendance, less delinquency	School and government records	Change in rate between two periods
Outcomes			
Employment	Graduate employment	Tracer study	% Employed three months after graduation
Earnings	Average wages of grads	Wage survey	Average for those employed
Status	% of grads in agricultural jobs, % in white collar jobs, etc.	Employment survey or census	Distribution of occupational placement of graduates

*The number of grades and years include will depend on the expected number of years for basic education (e.g., 5, 6, or 8).
**Can be computed with same year data, but it is preferable to use cohort data over the indicated years.

(see, for example, Chapman and Walberg, 1992; Davis, 1980; Windham, 1991).

Indicators for measuring access. Access indicators require information both on the children who enroll in school and those who do not. Data on children in school can usually be supplied by a national ministry of education from its school census or by a national statistics bureau from a survey of parents and children. Data on all children of the relevant age necessarily comes from the census. Thus, two calculations are possible for access indicators: one involves data exclusively provided from the national census while the second includes education ministry data in the numerator and national census data in the denominator.[4]

Unfortunately, much data of interest is only available from ministry sources. Thus, all of the other indicators discussed below come from education ministry surveys from Egypt in the early 1990s.

RELEVANCE OF EGYPTIAN DATA ON ACCESS AND QUALITY OF PRIMARY EDUCATION

Although the Ministry of Education (MOE) has developed an extensive national database on education (collected from school records), a recent study has concluded that reliable enrollment ratios, especially by sex and region, are not available, mostly because of a deficient demographic database. In particular, in calculating net enrollment ratios, the MOE data on pupils by age introduce an additional element of error. This makes it difficult to monitor the extent of universality of primary education or to plan for complete access to primary education In addition, analyzing the determinants of access to education requires special surveys, and these are rare.

A data set derived form a large labor-market study carried out in 1988 (Fergany, 1991) was utilized to chart access to primary education in a number of regions of the country, differentiating between rural and urban areas and between villages and hamlets in the countryside. The estimates of school attendance ratios for the age group 6–11 produced two major conclusions:

- Low school attendance levels are far more characteristic of rural areas: Upper Egypt as a whole ranks first, and the hamlets of Upper Egypt second.
- The largest discrepancy in school attendance ratios among the regions considered is found in school attendance for girls.

A very approximate index of gross enrollment by governorate and by gender was also considered. The index expresses the relative pattern of gross enrollment in different governorates by relating the number of pupils in primary education (according to MOE statistics) for the school year 1991/1992 to total population, assuming equal rates of population growth across governorates since the 1986 census. Unfortunately, this index does not provide a breakdown according to rural/urban residence, let alone a differentiation between villages and hamlets, and it is limited to enrolment in MOE schools only. The border governorates are excluded due to their small population size, a factor that tends to exacerbate existing errors.

Though not originally designed for the purpose, the same 1988 data set was used to investigate determinants of access to education in the age group 6–11. Among the socioeconomic factors considered in this analysis, child labor—particularly work outside the households—is the most serious impediment to universal school attendance. Girls are clearly at a disadvantage, especially in the rural areas of Upper Egypt and West Delta governorates. The levels of education in the household and in the local community are major determinants of school attendance; by comparison, the economic levels of the household and of the community are relatively unimportant factors. There is hardly any solid information available on the quality of the output of primary education, much less its determinants.

Currently, the available information on pupil achievement is based on standard examination results, which generally fail to reflect the "real" output of education in terms of actual knowledge and the skills imparted to pupils.

Source: UNICEF, 1994

Indicators for measuring efficiency. Efficiency is another area for which a wide variety of indicators have been developed. Conventional indicators of *internal efficiency* draw on the engineering model focusing broadly on the amount of "wasted" time pupils spend in school, wastage being considered any time other than steady progression from admission to completion of a course of study. Internal efficiency measures are developed from data from recurring school surveys on enrollments, repetition, and dropout. In the best situations, this information is summarized in a cohort flow diagram, disaggregated by pupil age and gender. Cohort flows can be problematic in that many systems do not routinely collect and process data on an annual basis, thus making calculations difficult to complete. Moreover, few systems are able to track the movement of children in and out of schools in different geographic areas. Children who move between schools or who drop out and then return can distort measurements (Cuadra, 1990). These distortions have less impact at high levels of aggregation (nation or province) but are considerable at lower levels of the system, such as the local district or school. A recent study in Malawi, for example, found that substantial numbers of children in schools in the area surveyed changed schools at least once a year (IEQ/Malawi, 2003). Finally, enrollment says little about how much education students attain, and so, in recent years, educators have come to favor the primary-level completion rate.

Over the years, various financial indicators have also been proposed. A major limitation of efficiency indicators is the insufficiency and inaccuracy of data, especially for financial indicators, which are not discussed here. External efficiency refers to the extent to which a school system produces graduates that are needed and utilized by the labor market. Lacking clear definitions and standards for collection, analysis, and interpretation, measures of external efficiency are conceptually significant but operationally difficult. Indicators of external efficiency are somewhat rare in practice.

Learning acquisition. Recent policy discussions focus on "actual learning" as an outcome (Article 4 of the World Declaration on Education for All). Individual schools have always sought to determine how much children learn through various forms of tests. In all schools, teachers carry out periodic classroom assessment for purposes of evaluating student performance and, hopefully, adjusting their teaching.

In some school systems, teachers are also required to administer tests developed at the provincial or national level. The function of such tests is often ambiguous: Are tests used to select students for higher levels of education or credentials? Tests used primarily for selection are known as *high-stakes* tests, and generally provide little useful feedback for instruction (Capper, 1996). Questions inevitably arise about the reliability and utility of such tests, particularly relative to their high costs. These questions are particularly apropos for the primary level where young people have little experience with testing, and where many other factors can influence their performance.

Still, many nations require primary school graduates to take a leaving examination. In Sri Lanka, for example, such test results are used as a basis for awarding scholarships to needy students who wish to continue in school. Where tests are available they may be used for comparisons between districts or even schools. Thailand is one nation that uses results from a uniform national test to monitor education performance. Technicians of Thailand's highly advanced management information system can compute results at any level of aggregation from the nation to the school. Districts and even schools whose test results slip are required to explain their shortcomings, and the responsible officers in districts or schools that repeat weak performance may be subject to disciplinary action (Wheeler, Radenbush, & Pasigna, 1989).

While Thailand relies on national tests, Indonesia has developed provincial tests. Because of a strong sense of cultural difference across the provinces of Indonesia, a common national test is considered inappropriate. However, provincial testing groups draw on a nationwide item bank to develop local tests. At one point Japan used a national test for primary-level students, but abandoned it out of a fear that it was stimulating excessive competition and leading teachers to favor their best pupils at the expense of the rest.

Thus, educators differ widely on the appropriateness of measuring acquisition of the intended curriculum through external testing. Periodic donor discussions urge an expansion of external tests, even proposing development of international tests so that nations and donors can compare performance of national systems. Indeed, some developing countries have already participated in international assessments, and the results are promising. But conducting these tests is expensive, and there are few reports of the results of international assessments actually stimulating reform in developing countries (though they have certainly stimulated reform in the industrialized nations). Perhaps this will change.

Values, behavioral change, and relevance. Education plans place much emphasis on value formation and change, and the report cards for individual children often provide assessments of the attitudes and behavior of young people. In view of the considerable stress placed on these areas by education leaders, surprisingly little attention is devoted to value and behavioral change in discussions of goals. Certainly, measurement in these areas is considered difficult and unreliable. At the same time, external funders of education reform view such areas as too sensitive and discourage systematic attention to their success or failure. However, this view could change as international concern grows over the international implications of values taught in schools.

Achievement tests, on the one hand, necessarily assume a hierarchy of knowledge. The tester knows what a pupil needs to know, and uses the test to determine how well the pupil can comply with the tester's prescription. On the other hand, relevance assumes that the pupils (or their parents) know what should be learned. Most discussions of relevance are somewhat ad hoc, pointing to simple examples of irrelevant curricular materials (children are asked to spell train when they have never seen one, or describe a flower that does not grow in their area). Alternately, discussions make judgments about the skills children need to know. Participatory approaches to education seek to flatten the hierarchy by turning directly to parents and children to discover their rationale for seeking an education. An ideal approach would identify needs specific to each school. More broadly, marketing surveys, or even the addition of simple questions about the relevance of local education, could be included in periodic national censuses. Tabulations of such questions at the district level would help to indicate where education fits parents' perceptions of needs and where it does not. These results could inform interventions in areas of discontent.

Equality and equity. Educators tend to sharply distinguish between equality and equity. Whereas equality can be objectively accessed with an indicator of dispersion, equity, which implies a judgment of relative fairness, is not objectively assessed. Still, at a minimum, it is generally true that inequity is found where inequality is observed. A focus on inequality is especially important at the point of access and in the early years of socialization, for inequities introduced at early stages have the most lasting effects.

Regional and ethnic/racial differences. Table 6.3 provided several measures for equality of access. Currently, many education systems routinely provide statistics of relevant data by gender, by province or state, and sometimes by urban–rural location. In countries where ethnic/racial categories are a focus of policy, statistical breakdowns may also be established with these categories. In addition, more statistics focus on physical, mental, and learning disabilities. The more refined the categories, the more possibilities exist to learn about inequalities in access.

In addition to access, it is possible to focus on other aspects of the education process, ranging from equality in the provision of inputs to equality in achievement. Nielsen and Somerset (1992), for example, have conducted a careful examination of the distribution of schoolteachers in Indonesia, focusing on interprovincial, interdistrict, and lower-level disparities (see following box). Descriptive statistics such as the Gini Coefficient prove useful in summarizing these distributions.

SIZEABLE DISPARITIES IN TEACHER PLACEMENT BY LOCAL EDUCATION OFFICES IN INDONESIA

Overall, Indonesia makes generous provision for staffing its primary schools; the national teacher–class ratio is 1:14. The problems of primary-teacher provision in Indonesia are essentially problems of distribution rather than of supply. Although there is a plentiful supply of teachers overall, many of them are teaching in the wrong places. "Pockets of shortage" frequently exist alongside "pockets of oversupply."

Teacher distribution is executed and hence can be analyzed at four levels: from the national level to the provinces, the provinces to the regencies (*kabupaten/kotamadya*), the regencies to the districts (*keca-*

matan), and the districts to the schools. The higher levels are mainly responsible for distribution, while decisions on transfers are generally made at the lower levels.

An inter-quartile ratio (IQR) was used to determine the equality of distribution of each of these levels. Perfect equality among units would yield an index of 1.0, with higher levels indicating greater inequality. The following are the results by level:

Distribution Level	IQR	(n)
Nation to province	1.35	1
Province to regency	1.47	27
Regency to district	1.63	256
District to school	2.76	36

It is clear that processes at the central levels tend to distribute teachers more evenly than processes at the more local levels. In the 36 districts for which data were available, the most favored quarter of pupils have, on average, about 23–24 times as many teachers as the least favored quarter.

Source: Nielsen & Somerset, 1992

In the early stages of education expansion, education leaders sought to improve equality in the provision of education resources, arguing that the initiative rested within individual pupils to take the maximum advantage of these opportunities. In other words, those who tried would succeed. In more recent years though, educators are increasingly aware that not all individuals are equally prepared to perform at the highest levels. Thus some reformers have proposed that equality of opportunity should be equated with equality in the mastery of the curriculum as measured in skill and achievement tests. Comparative measures of the standard deviation of achievement scores in classes, schools, or districts are helpful in addressing these issues.

Equity. Equity, as we have noted, involves a judgment about the appropriateness or fairness of the provision of education opportunities. It is one matter to observe an unequal distribution, another to decide what a fair distribution is. The issue of teacher distribution provides a useful analysis. The Indonesia example in the previous box indicates that children in different schools have differential access to teachers. What is the preferred distribution to achieve perfect equality in the student–teacher ratios between schools? In fact, that is what the official formulas prescribe. If the regulations are followed, is equity achieved? Some would say that it is necessary to go beyond the official formulas, for the formulas only deal with the children in schools. What about those who are not in school? A more equitable approach might be to establish ratios between the total number of school-age youth in a local area (the potential demand for education) and the supply of teachers. It could even be argued that the system should make up for the historical pattern of discrimination by providing even more teachers to deprived areas than might be implied by a straight ratio of teachers to population. Windham (1991) raises similar questions. While many equity discussions focus on who gets into school, Windham proposes that the discussion extend to what happens in school: Do girls get the same access to textbooks as boys? Do as many girls as boys complete schools? Do they learn as much? Clearly, deciding on an indicator of equity is a subjective matter.

SUMMARY: THE SUBJECTIVE NATURE OF GOALS IN EDUCATION

The chapter has discussed several ways of understanding goals in education: explicit versus implicit goals, "serious" goals versus "lip service" goals. Goal setting, we have argued, is a subjective and collective process involving objective information, a process that begs for structured participation. Goal setting involves decisions as to the role of education in society, ultimately the kind of society people want, in what we have called a social conceptual task. Goal setting is also a technical process of using goals to maximize desirable aims with an efficiency of scarce resources. Goal setting is a political task as well, of inspiring and directing the political energies of a people. A four-step process was elaborated for goal setting: structuring of a process appropriate to the context and what it is that is to be done; an envisioning process; a mapping of gaps between what is desired and what is currently; and a prioritization of goals. The chapter elaborated goals commonly associated with primary and secondary education. The choice of goals is an important first step in planning education reform. Choice among goals is primarily a political process, but a process that can be informed by data and criteria. A second objective of this chapter was to review common procedures for measuring the attainment of goals. When goals and their attainment are clear, it is easier to select options for reform.

NOTES

1. We would argue that goal setting is both a social and a conceptual task, even when it is undertaken as a technical or bureaucratic exercise with a compliant population.

2. Indeed, this is a common theme in most education systems. Educators naturally focus on what material resources are needed in their schools. Calls for quality invariably lead to a call for more "stuff." And while most systems do need more resources, many systems, some would argue, fail to make full use of existing materials.

3. In many countries, lowering the student–teacher ratio became a symbol of this quality argument. Subsequent research has suggested that that these arguments may be misguided. At the aggregate level, and when gauged by student achievement, variation in student–teacher ratios between 15 and 40 are associated at best with marginal differences in education quality (Glass, 1981). At the classroom level, of course, teachers feel they do a much better job with smaller classes.

4. In virtually every situation where the two calculations have been compared, the national census calculation provides lower numbers. It could be inferred that there are systematic incentives for the education ministry to encourage inflation of the statistics. School officials may exaggerate enrollment numbers to impress their superiors or secure additional funding. It is difficult to determine how pervasive this bias is, but knowing that it exists encourages a healthy skepticism about official education statistics that are uncorroborated by second sources.

CHAPTER 7

Evaluating and Selecting Reform Options and Developing the Plan

To recap the process we have outlined, education assessment provides an analytic portrait of where the education system has come from and where it is—its status, problems, and financial, organization, and social resources.[1] Goals provide a statement of where the system should be and the direction it should take. Chapter 6 describes goal setting as a process of structured consultation, envisioning of desired states, mapping and operationalizing of gaps between actual and desired states, and prioritization. Ideally, this process has resulted in narrowing and sharpening the reforms the education system has decided to undertake and a corresponding focus of political energy. The next steps are:

- the *generation* of strategic options, designed to move the system from actual to desired states—based on the best available understanding of effective solutions to particular problems;
- the *evaluation* of options—based on the three criteria discussed in this chapter;
- the *selection* of strategic options, making of the policy decision, and communication of the decision; and finally
- the *elaboration* of program theory and *completion* of the plan.

Chapter 7 does not discuss strategic options in depth, as Volume II is devoted to a full discussion of reform options associated with the various goals of chapter 7. Still, it is useful to point out that the generation of strategic options—like the envisioning process—is best organized as a separate activity from the selection process. The objective in such an exercise is to generate as wide a range of strategic options as possible, especially new approaches to old problems. Too early a reference to constraints and the "how tos" tends to limit the collective imagination. Once options are generated, selection then considers the scarcity of resources and political energy and the inevitability of trade-offs. The actual choice of reform strategy from among several options depends on the context, the actors, and their decision-making processes.

First, we discuss three sets of criteria used to select among options, and then consider the differential relevance of these criteria for key education stakeholders. The chapter concludes with a brief discussion of the logframe, an analytic tool used to flesh out program theory linking larger goals to subgoals, objectives, outputs, and activities, each with indicators.

EVALUATING OPTIONS

The rational dimension of planning emphasizes the importance of evaluating options before deciding which ones fit a particular situation. Three distinctive sets of technical criteria might enter into the evaluation of reform options (Haddad & Demsky, 1994):

- *Desirability,* or the benefits expected from the different options;
- *Affordability,* or the costs associated with each option;
- *Feasibility,* or the likelihood that the option can be implemented and sustained.

Desirability: Benefits

The systemic nature of education means that any given component is likely to have multiple desirable effects or benefits. Moreover, much that happens in education is related to factors outside of the schools and beyond the control of school personnel. However, a reform is generally intended to improve a particular outcome, such as access or quality, which must improve for the policy to be considered successful. Each benefit has its distinctive measurements as discussed in chapter 6. Access can be measured by enrollment rates, for example, relevance by employment rates, learning by scores on achievement tests, efficiency by dropout and repetition rates, and values by attitudinal measures and/ or behavioral indicators of valued activities.

The critical question is not so much whether a particular option is beneficial but which options are *most beneficial*, given the state of the education system, goals, and the other available options. The answers, of course, involve judgments as to which problems are most serious, which goals are most valued, and what the future is likely to hold. Such an evaluation cannot be concluded on an objective basis. Invariably, some groups will benefit more than others, while others will lose from different options; hence the importance of a legitimate process for making final choices. At the same time, the future cannot be known with any certainty; the final effects of current initiatives cannot be known, and education outcomes are at least as affected by external events as they are by internal decisions.

However, choices can be informed. Different groups can specify what they value, and the benefits and later costs of different options can be described, often quantitatively, along those dimensions. Arguments can be made about which set of benefits and costs is preferable from the perspective of particular groups, or from core values of the larger society. Benefits can also be assessed from a strategic perspective: Which options are more likely to enable to system to achieve other important goals? Which goals serve as preconditions for subsequent goals? The result of the desirability assessment should be a prioritized list of options, if not for the system as a whole, at least for the stakeholder group represented.

Affordability: Costs

Reform interventions usually increase the cost of education operations. The actual measurement of costs is a complex matter taking into account such elements as capital and recurrent costs, direct and indirect costs, and public and private costs. The methodology for estimating these various costs is treated in a number of publications (see, in particular, Levin & McEwan, 2001). In estimating and discussing costs, it is always useful to break down costs by component, or ingredient. Calculations should be based on real costs, not on budgets, which are sometimes padded, or expenditures, which reflect other considerations in addition to cost.

Costs should be evaluated comparatively, and in light of the costs of *not* taking another possible course of action. For example, one strategy to increase girls' access is to reduce school fees, while another option provides families with financial incentives to keep their girls in school. In such a case, analysis of the fee reduction option should include an estimate of the likely *costs of not providing incentives*, and vice versa. Choice of one option means foregoing another. It is important to be as clear as possible about what is being foregone, and its estimated value. Discussion of costs, as well as benefits, should certainly include financial costs to the education system. But other important costs should be included, even when difficult to quantify, such as direct costs to families, loss of potential increases in productivity, or decreased self-esteem on the part of young women, to continue the example.

In addition, the costs of unintended consequences should be considered. Policy advocates and planners working to enact a reform tend to focus on sunny scenarios, in which the initiative proceeds according to plan. But in weighing different courses of action, it is advisable to consider less positive scenarios, in which things go wrong.

In most education systems, teacher salaries are the major recurrent cost. Buildings and facilities are the major capital cost. All other expenditures receive modest allocations (Mingat, 2001). While teachers is a high cost area, certain teacher interventions such as the recruitment of volunteer teachers from the community, or the use of peers and tutors to strengthen the instructional process, may be useful ways to cut down on the high cost associated with teaching (Mehrota & Buckland, 1998). The longer-term costs of such approaches should be weighed as well: Will volunteer teachers continue to teach year after year? To what extent will students be disadvantaged by having teachers with less training? Are current economies likely to lead to higher costs in the long run?

In considering costs, it is also useful to look beyond the financial aspects to other costs, in particular, costs in terms of politics, social capital, and so forth. As with benefits, it is critical to consider *costs to whom*, as costs and benefits accrue differentially to different groups of stakeholders. The result of these analyses should be a listing of costs, alongside each strategic option, possibly ranked in descending value of cost. It may also be useful, when possible, to attempt to combine costs and benefits into an indicator of net benefit.

Feasibility: Implementation

The third criterion often used in evaluating reforms is the feasibility or likelihood of implementation and, we would add, sustainability. In the optimistic past, it was often assumed that the mere promulgation of a reform ensured its implementation, but after decades of woeful experience, decision makers have come to appreciate that promulgation is only an initial step in reform (Nielsen & Cummings, 1997; Warwick and Reimers, 1995). In chapter 8, we discuss in considerable detail factors that influence implementation. Some tentative generalizations relating to implementation might include the following:

- The more complex a reform, the greater the difficulty of implementation;
- The more bureaus involved in the implementation of a reform, the greater the difficulty of implementation;
- The more highly placed the advocate of a reform, the more promising the chances of implementation;
- The greater the stability of the individuals involved in implementing a reform, the more promising the chances of implementation; and
- The more thorough the process of consultation with implementers and beneficiaries, the more promising the chances of implementation.

Needless to say, a core feature is the reform environment as discussed in the introduction and chapter 3. The process of implementation will differ between an *organizational* environment as contrasted with a *political* environment. Similarly, implementation of a *synoptic* reform will differ from that of an *incremental* reform.

Again, the product of this analysis should be a ranking of options in order of feasibility, with indications of the nature of potential difficulties, to enable decision makers to "choose their poison."

STAKEHOLDERS AND THEIR PREFERENCES

As is apparent, we feel the choice of strategic option depends largely on who is sitting at the table. Calculations of benefit, of cost, even of implementability, vary according to the perspectives of key stakeholders. Key stakeholders include the following.

National governments. National governments have been the most vigorous proponents of systematic education planning. Their concerns are typically to shape a system that fosters loyalty to the national leadership, supports national defense, and contributes to economic development. National governments command limited resources, so, on the one hand, they seek to distribute these resources in a rational and efficient manner among various programs, one of which is education. On the other hand, governments are political regimes, with values and agendas, and almost invariably, opposition. The tasks of maintaining legitimacy and holding onto power may favor, or hinder, rational, efficient allocation of resources. Because education ministers often serve for a shorter period of time than most reform cycles, ministers are under considerable pressure to produce results, quickly, to do something that is sensible, distinctive, and fast.

Funding agencies. Various multilateral and bilateral agencies have developed an interest in education, especially basic education. Most view education as a key element in economic progress, but each agency has its distinctive viewpoint. Some think girls' education is the key. Others believe more stress should be placed on vocational skills or on preschool education. Yet others urge improvements in the teaching of a particular language, local or metropolitan. Others are more interested in policy reform. These donors typically deal with the representatives of national governments, providing substantial financial assistance in exchange for recognition of their priorities in the national program. By favoring national governments, they implicitly erode the position of other actors. At the same time, the priorities of national governments in need of financial and technical assistance may be overshadowed by the goals of donors possessing those resources.

As discussed, sectoral investment strategies are an attempt to address such problems through the government's development of a policy and investment framework, based on its own analysis, priorities, and needs.

According to the rationale of sectoral planning, donors then fund different aspects of the program. Donor programs thus fit into the government's overall framework of goals and priorities, rather than determining them ad hoc through the funding of particular donor priorities. In practice, sectoral strategies do not yet seem to have led to a redefinition of donor–government relationships (Moulton et al., 2002), though the idea of government-led sectoral investment planning seems sound.

Local governments and communities. National governments are formed through the consolidation of local communities with their distinctive governments and traditions. Where national governments are strong, they seek to direct these local governments to promote the goals of the center. National governments may assert the right to appoint local officials, for example, thus potentially distancing local governments from their communities, or they may adopt curriculum that, implicitly or explicitly, works to build a national rather a local identity. Local government may be asked to contribute a certain share of the education budget as a condition for receiving central funds; cost sharing may tilt the focus of local governments toward efficiency. At the same time, local governments enjoy some discretion, the degree varying widely by nation and also within nations, by the relative assertiveness of the local unit, to promote their own priorities, which may include the perpetuation of a distinctive culture, or the perpetuation of a traditional political elite.

In some polities, notably those influenced by the Anglo tradition, the level of local discretion may be extensive, with local governments enjoying considerable autonomy to set their own priorities as well as the responsibility to collect their own funds. In these "decentralized" polities, local governments may become important foci for strategic planning. Decentralization initiatives sometimes result in greater responsibility and/or discretion on the part of local governments and communities. Sometimes local governments and communities have the resources and capacity to manage well in a decentralized context. In other cases, notably when central government uses decentralization to shift burdens away from itself, decentralization may simply mean the de facto withdrawal of central government, without a corresponding empowerment of local authorities.

Local governments may or may not represent the interests of local communities, and local communities may be more or less homogenous. Actors at central levels tend to conflate the interests of local actors, hearing perhaps a single voice instead of the cacophony of voices, as well as the systematic silences that characterize real communities. A similar distillation results when external observers equate the voices and perspectives of the elite leadership of a country with the will of the people. What is heard are the voices and perspectives of the elite, whose interests are likely to differ from those of many other citizens. Similarly, the voice of the village leadership is unlikely to adequately represent the perspectives of the local powerless.

Cultural and religious organizations. Before the rise of governmental interest in education, cultural and religious organizations were the main promoters of formal education. In many nations they continue to sponsor a significant proportion of schools, which they see as a vehicle for transmitting their particular values to children. Often cultural and religious organizations and their schools build close links with local communities to the point that the interests of the two are virtually indivisible. For example, the school and the church or mosque may be located on the same premises, using land donated by community members. Generally, national governments require these independent schools to follow a curriculum based on priorities determined by governmental authorities, who may or may not have consulted the independent schools in their formulation. At the same time, when the reach of government is weak, cultural/religious schools can be enormously influential, even political, and can play a determinative, if inadvertent, role in the education of the community.

Local, national, and international nongovernmental organizations (NGOs). While NGOs have always been involved in education, recent years have seen a tremendous increase in the number and extent of involvement of NGOs at all levels in education. In part, this may be due to increasing awareness of the limitations of government resources and capacity, and a consequent search for partners in the provision of education. Certainly, NGOs have shown remarkable success in *reaching* peripheral populations where government has been much less successful. In some cases, such as the Bangladesh Rural Advancement Committee (BRAC) in Bangladesh, the nongovernmental provision of basic education has approached the size of the government system. The liberalization of economies and government regulation in many countries has led to an expansion of civil society organizations, including NGOs. Such organizations promise an expanded civic space at both local and national levels, fostering greater, if differential, participation of citizens in national life. Based on belief in "the democratic wish" (see chapter 2) and a substantial distrust of the efficiency and honesty of government in many contexts, the international development community has provided NGOs with substantial support. This support has, at once, increased the activity and prominence of nongovernmental actors in education decision making and provision. But at the same time, it has often not served the interests of building government capacity. In considering the participation of NGOs, it is important to distinguish between local and national NGOs and international NGOs, funded by Western governments and citizens. A number of international NGOs are viewed more as donors than as equal partners with indigenous organizations. Still NGOs often do good work, work that government is often unable to do well. Thus, NGOs have complex, somewhat contradictory effects on developing education systems.

Teachers and principals. Despite being frontline actors in national education strategies, teachers and principals are rarely consulted in the development of these plans. On the one hand, teachers and principals are portrayed as "professionals," committed to the ambitious education goals of these plans. On the other hand, these educators are "workers" who prefer autonomy over their work routine and seek a fair wage, an opportunity to get ahead, a decent life. Reforms that stress efficiency at the risk of teachers' well-being are certain to be resisted. In many countries, teachers are organized in unions that are able to call strikes if they perceive that reforms threaten their interests. Teachers are generally provided training, mostly at the beginnings of their careers, but principals are far less likely to receive training for their management function. In general, neither teachers nor principals receive extensive professional support once they begin work. Nevertheless, most are highly committed to effective education and have many useful proposals for strengthening education quality. Many education reforms simply cannot succeed without the support of teachers and principals.

Employers. One of the most prominent rationales behind the commitment to education expansion is the cultivation of a more productive workforce. In preparing plans, governments sometime carry out studies of the needs of employers, but in most instances they do not set up a meaningful mechanism for consulting with employers. Similarly, in most local areas employers have little contact with schools. Thus gaps may emerge between the needs of employers and the education and training that occurs in schools. These problems are more evident at the secondary level, though they may have implications for primary education as well.

Disadvantaged social groups. Not to be forgotten are the various disadvantaged groups in society, many of whom have very little voice in education or other decisions affecting their members or their lives. Disadvantage may accrue to ethnic or linguistic "minorities," to rural children, to the poor, to the disabled, the displaced and refugees, often to girls, out-of-school youth, and so forth. Rarely are such groups involved in the process of dialogue that leads to education reforms.

The family. Primary education is surely intended, in part at least, to help the family in its duty of raising healthy, happy children, and teaching the skills and knowledge required for productive lives. While families may appreciate the value of formal education, they also may think of their children as resources for work in the home, family business, or farm or as assets to exchange in marriage. Parents may have reservations about what transpires in schools, about the timing of the school schedule, or about the safety or propriety of sending children, especially girls, to school. Often, parents have little opportunity to express these concerns or to influence the school program. Parents are often lumped together with the community, when in many particular instances, their interests and perspectives differ.

The child. Much education discussion tends to subsume the child in his or her family, positing a common interest. Yet in many families, the child is a resource to exploit more than to develop. And in other instances, the child may have no family or at best a limited family consisting of a single parent and/or siblings. Substantial proportions of children in southern Africa, for example, serve as heads of households, their parents having died of AIDS. While a child may not have the opportunity or ability to articulate his or her concerns, it should not be assumed that the parents (or for that matter the other actors noted here) always have the child's best interests at heart. Indeed, rights-based approaches to basic education adopted by the United Nations assign children, not families, the right to basic education, a right that is the legal obligation of government to secure.

Conventional processes of reform planning rarely incorporate all of these multiple stakeholders. Still, a number of countries strive to do so, especially in the process of assessing needs (chapter 5) and selecting reforms.

COMPARING REFORM OPTIONS: THE CASE OF SOMALIA

Education systems, whether national or local, frequently undergo some sort of reform. An unusual case is Somalia, which lacks an effective national government. Instead, Somalia consists of three major zones essentially independent with distinctive approaches to social organization. The Republic of Somaliland in the Northwest Zone has an elected government and a minimal system of public schools, whereas in the other areas most schools are established by NGOs, including religious organizations.

The presence of a functioning government and the reduction of ethnic strife in the Northwest have been accompanied by an impressive popular demand for schooling. In the past few years, a number of international assistance agencies including the United Nations Children's Fund (UNICEF) and the United States Agency for International Development (USAID) have sought to devise a pragmatic response. But where to start when the needs are so great, the prospects for long-term stability are so dim, and the likelihood of institutional development weak?

To take its first steps in this environment USAID sponsored a subsector assessment of Somalia education in 2003. USAID had modest funds available, which it sought to allocate for one or more education initiatives that could achieve visible results in a brief period. The assessment was charged with the task of conducting an overview of the system, identifying current strengths and gaps, and highlighting several interventions that had promise. The assessment team carried out most of the activities described in chapter 5 including the review of available documents and interviews with a wide spectrum of stakeholders. Based on this information, the team identified six options, and then drawing on the criteria of desirability, affordability, and feasibility, it outlined the advantages and disadvantages of these options. Table 7.1 below compares the options presented to USAID. Ultimately USAID chose the teacher training option, as it was no more costly than the other proposed reforms but seemed more easily implementable in a timely manner. Table 7.1 illustrates a presentation that might be used to highlight the pluses and minuses of alternative reform options.

THE ROLE OF PILOT STUDIES

Education systems can be very large and the publics they serve very diverse. Under such conditions, it may be difficult to devise a new reform that is equally applicable to all situations. It may be difficult, for example, to assess the costs, benefits, and implementability of a reform until it is tested in the field. Alternately, policy makers may hope to build support for an innovation by trying it out as a demonstration project. Or they may have interesting innovations they wish to introduce, but following the process of policy generation, they may lose courage. Will this new innovation be feasible in all of local areas? Will it have the same benefit/cost ratio in all situations? Maybe not.

Under such circumstances, one possible approach is to introduce the innovation in selected areas to see if how it works there, to gain some sense of the obstacles likely to be encountered during implementation. This pilot stage can be scheduled, for example, for a fixed period such as three years, and then a summative evaluation can be carried out.

One important consideration in implementing pilot studies is the receptivity of the community in the pilot sites. Parents will be unhappy if they suspect their children are being experimented with. Thus, in planning a pilot study, it is important to build in safeguards so that those in the pilot study do not experience negative consequences. Continuous monitoring of the academic progress of children is desirable to produce evidence for parents that things are going well. Or if there are problems, the project managers will have the necessary information to introduce modifications in the project and take immediate remedial actions to help any children who have suffered negative consequences.

Table 7.1 Comparing Potential Actions

	Capacity building for educational managers	Strengthen community education committees	Develop ICT with English focus	Induce females to take up teaching	Enhance scope of Koranic/Islamic schools	Expand nonformal education
Time to start	High priority of Somaliland MOE, requires 2–3 months for design and recruiting consultants	Requires careful design and groundwork; possibly 6 mos. Models are available which could reduce start-up time.	Requires careful design but analogues already in place so could begin in 3–4 months.	Working through STEC, could begin as early as Sept. 2003	Requires careful design, negotiations with interested schools. Many months at least.	Requires careful design and identification of effective partners
Relation to U.S. strengths	U.S. has considerable experience in training for management, policy analysis, exam preparation	U.S. has pioneered such projects in several African sites including Ethiopia, S. Sudan, and Francophone Africa. USG partners in Somalia have experience.	U.S. has relevant experience in Region (including Ethiopia, Somalia, Kenya, and elsewhere).	U.S. has relevant experience in Africa and other regions; also was active in teacher training in Somalia	Relatively little experience	U.S. has promoted nonformal approaches throughout the world.
Potential partners	UNESCO has initiated some activities; EC also interested	Many international and local NGOs encourage CECs and might become partners	African Education Trust has experience working with BBC; also Swedish government	UNESCO has initiated some activities; EC also has high interest	Not clear	Most donor and many agencies involved, though activities are usually small in scale.

Table 7.1 (Continued)

	Capacity building for educational managers	Strengthen community education committees	Develop ICT with English focus	Induce females to take up teaching	Enhance scope of Koranic/Islamic schools	Expand nonformal education
Time before initial impact	Within a year	Could take 2–3 years	Very soon	First graduates in Nov. 2003	Considerable	Requires at least two years to train
Educational impact	Immediate on efficiency; later on access, equity, quality	Potentially significant impact on access, equity, quality	Immediate on quality	Significant impact on quality, equity	Enhance access, equity	Enhance access, equity, relevance
Political/cultural impact	Primary impact is educational	Primary impact is educational and economic	Enhances receptiveness to Anglophone culture	Primary impact is educational	Opens dialogue between different pedagogies	Primary impact is educational
Sustainability	In the NWZ, MOE committed, modest turnover of top officials	CECs already widely prevalent throughout Somalia; involves redirection of their activities	Relatively cost-efficient	High priority of MOE in NWZ. Clear continuing demand for new teachers	Not clear	Not clear. However, noteworthy that MOE in NWZ has increased emphasis on nonformal ed.
Prospects for expansion	Could be replicated in NEZ, though no obvious beneficiaries in the CSZ	Could be replicated throughout Somalia with refinements in approach adjusted to political environments	Immediate impact across Somalia; could add other subjects	STEC could accept admits from other zones; later could set up branch campuses in other zones	Approach relevant throughout Somalia	A sound approach has extensive possibilities

One pitfall is to lavish substantially more resources and attention on the pilot project than will be available in similar locales if the innovation is taken to scale. Particularly well-resourced pilot projects may draw participants from outside the area, thus spoiling the test. At the same time, the pilot must be nurtured if it is to succeed, and some experimentation, and wasted resources, can be expected as the organization "learns to become effective" (Korten, 1980).

Assuming the pilot study shows promise, policy makers can then consider steps to expanding the innovation to new areas or what is sometimes referred to as "going to scale." With information from the pilot study, policy makers can plan an expansion that may lead to substantial cost savings through economies of scale. Alternately, they may find that many of the new areas lack the resources required to implement the innovation. Still, going to scale, like any complex institutional activity, involves more than replicating the specifications of a blueprint. Education systems are not mechanical systems, but closer perhaps to farms, where plants must be nurtured in a diversity of environments.

MAKING THE DECISION

So far, we have proposed a variety of strategic options and evaluated each in terms of desirability, affordability, and feasibility. At a minimum, such an analysis should lead to informed understanding of costs, benefits, and feasibility of different options. The actual decision is likely to be messier. Other factors such as the interests of particular stakeholders, the sudden availability of new funds either from an international donor or a local source, or simply the whim of a top official may enter into the decision-making process. These factors are likely to have an impact not only at the time of making the formative decision but later as the policy is implemented.

Still, a decision is made, through some mix of rational and political processes. Ideally, the use of a participatory and information-based approach to the evaluation and selection of options has raised awareness about the upcoming reform and generated ownership and excitement among a broad range of stakeholders.

Hopefully, the decision represents a true choice of direction and a genuine commitment to the reform on the part of the nation, as opposed to "something-for-everyone," a bureaucratic exercise, an unwelcome imposition by those in power, or externally driven reform. The political will represented by a genuine decision can go a long way to sustaining the initiative through the challenges of implementation and changing circumstance.

DEVELOPING THE PLAN

Once individual options are evaluated and decisions made, the plan is developed. Ideally, particular initiatives integrated into a coherent policy framework drawing on the analysis of the education system, consideration of its goals, and the outcomes of the goal setting and option evaluation processes. Overall goals need to be operationalized, strategies discussed, and the chain of activities and intermediate results leading to achievement of short, medium, and long-term goals explicated.

The logical framework, or logframe, first developed by USAID in the 1970s, is a useful device for project planning at this phase. Figure 7.1 gives an overview of a common approach to logframe analysis, borrowed from AusAID, the Australian bilateral development agency. The vertical axis describes what the project is trying to do, the causal logic, as well as critical assumptions and potentially influential factors outside managers' control. The horizontal axis describes how project objectives will be measured and how they will be verified. See the website or other resources for detailed guidance.

The final step is the costing of activities, the sequencing of activities, and the assigning of tasks. A monitoring plan will need to be developed, and evaluation plans tentatively drawn up. A number of management tools exist to help with these tasks, including PERT and GANTT. Volume II elaborates several examples.

SUMMARY: DEPARTURES

Not surprisingly, rational strategies sometimes get short shrift, often in an effort by some to push a particular initiative or strategy, or to avoid

Project description	Performance indicators	Means of verification	Assumptions
1. Goal: The broader development impact to which the project contributes - at a national and sectoral level.	10. Measures of the extent to which a sustainable contribution to the goal has been made. Used during evaluation.	11. Sources of information and methods used to collect and report it.	
2. Purpose: The development outcome expected at the end of the project. All components will contribute to this	12. Conditions at the end of the project indicating that the Purpose has been achieved and that benefits are sustainable. Used for project completion and evaluation.	13. Sources of information and methods used to collect and report it.	9. Assumptions concerning the purpose/goal linkage.
3. Component Objectives: The expected outcome of producing each component's outputs.	14. Measures of the extent to which component objectives have been achieved and lead to sustainable benefits. Used during review and evaluation.	15. Sources of information and methods used to collect and report it.	8. Assumptions concerning the component objective/purpose linkage.
4. Outputs: The direct measurable results (goods and services) of the project which are largely under project management's control	16. Measures of the quantity and quality of outputs and the timing of their delivery. Used during monitoring and review.	17. Sources of information and methods used to collect and report it.	7. Assumptions concerning the output/component objective linkage.
5. Activities: The tasks carried out to implement the project and deliver the identified outputs.	Implementation/work program targets. Used during monitoring.	Sources of information and methods used to collect and report it.	6. Assumptions concerning the activity/output linkage.

Figure 7.1   *Typical Logframe Structure*

conflict. As a result, reforms often include far more options than are affordable or feasible, because no manageable focus was negotiated. Options are often not ranked, for setting priorities would result in someone's loss. Activities are often costed, scheduled, and assigned first, before their contribution to larger objectives is carefully considered. Policies are often adopted before their desirability, affordability, and feasibility are assessed. Doing so results in wasted money, lost time and momentum, and a loss of political energy. Something, in an overambitious plan, will be not done.

Even so, few organizations or education offices consistently conform to these orderly, rational processes. Recognizing that, it is useful to consider the reasons for departures from the rational process and the consequences and to learn from them. One approach is to redouble one's efforts to get the organization to act rationally. Haddad and Demsky (1994) suggest several questions that might be asked: How was the decision made—did it go through all the stages of policy analysis? How radical a departure is the decision from current policy? How consistent is this decision with policies of other sectors? Is the policy diffusely articulated, or is it stated in a manner which is easily measurable? Does the policy seem operational or is its implementation implausible? Another approach is to try to work with the rationality of a complex organism, linking politics and people in new ways, yet to be systematically understood.

NOTE

1. Many planners find it useful to use systematic strategic planning framework, for example, a SWOT analysis of strengths, weaknesses, opportunities, and threats, to characterize the current state of the system.

Chapter 8

Planning Implementation and Monitoring

Implementation is where, as they say, the rubber hits the road. Allison estimates that only about 10% of the total effort required to bring about change in a complex system is completed up to the point where the policy decision is made (Allison, 1971). This leaves 90% of the work for implementation.

AN IMPLEMENTATION PERSPECTIVE

As we have argued, a poorly implemented plan may well have been a poor plan to begin with. Good planning does not end with formulation of an ideal program regardless of circumstances, but requires considerable understanding of the context, the situations and people involved in implementation, as well as thought about how the plan will be implemented and what difficulties the plan is likely to encounter. Moreover, because of changes in context, unanticipated outcomes of intervention, and "slippage" during implementation, planning is best not organized as a one-off operation at the beginning, but as an iterative and essential component of implementation. Implementation requires that program managers pay attention to the ongoing fit of intended and implemented plans. Program managers may need to take on some of the responsibilities of planning and policy making, and planners some of the ways of thinking of program managers.

As discussed in chapter 3, one of the weaknesses of stages models of planning is the gap between ends and means, between planning and implementation, that gives policy makers and planners little responsibility for implementation. Quite frequently, planners develop a plan that cannot be implemented or whose difficulties could have been foreseen. At the same time, assigning responsibility for such problems to the *people*—either implementers or planners—may keep reformers from noticing that it may be the *process*—a staged, hierarchical, overly optimistic model of planning and implementation—that is not working. In such circumstances, change agents learn little about designing a more effective process of planning for and implementing reform.

While not claiming that policy makers and planners are responsible for implementation failures, we do feel they have the responsibility:

- to assess implementability;
- to develop a realistic, informed, and legitimate implementation plan based on pessimistic as well as optimistic scenarios of change;
- to develop a considered strategy for dealing with implementation problems;
- to distinguish adaptive from maladaptive deviations from the plan; and
- to create a monitoring system that enables the system to learn—enhancing the capacity of implementers to implement (and to see beyond the particulars of their context) and the capacity of planners to plan.

Many plans fall victim to the great fallacy that, in Elmore's (1982) words, "decisions are . . . self-executing" (p. 22). Optimistic, hierarchical, stages models of planning are based on a series of assumptions and expectations that may not hold true in practice, several resonant with the dysfunctional "theories" discussed in chapter 3:

- That what is planned is what will happen;
- That policy makers have sufficient control over implementation (through organizational authority);
- That implementers can and will do what they are told to do;
- That planners and policy makers alone can assume full responsibility for the policy process; and
- That policy makers, planners, and others at the center/top of the organization know enough at the outset to plan for effective implementation.

Indeed, research and experience suggest that these assumptions may not hold much of the time. What is planned is often *not* what happens. Central planners and policy makers often have little control over implementers, and implementers frequently lack the capacity or perspective on the problems and solutions that would dispose them to acting as envisioned by the plan. Involvement of implementers in planning is sometimes essential to effective implementation. Central actors may never know the actual conditions of implementation, and good information on conditions of implementation is particularly scarce at planning stages.

Moreover, "command and control" approaches to organizational management tend to assume several additional "theories" related to implementation but likely to work at cross-purposes with reform:

- That discrepancies between the plan and implementation are necessarily counterproductive;
- That (as a result) implementers should be permitted as little discretion as possible;
- That people are at fault (and someone should be held accountable) when there are discrepancies between what is planned and what is implemented; and
- That tightening central control is the (best or only) way to move toward goals when implementation deviates.

Because of this, discrepancies from the plan *may* indicate needed accommodations to varied and changing conditions. In such cases, capable implementers need discretion to best move toward reform goals. Deviations from the plan may be no one's fault; holding the wrong people accountable in such circumstances may cause a negative reaction against the program. Tightening central control is only one response to discrepancies between implementation and plan, and not always an effective one.

STEPS IN PLANNING IMPLEMENTATION

For instructional purposes, this chapter organizes implementation planning into five steps.

Step 1. Assess implementability. It is useful to think forward through the process of implementation to gauge the extent and nature of "problems" that implementation of a particular plan is likely to encounter in a particular context. Assessing implementability allows planners and policy makers to select an appropriate approach to implementation and monitoring, and it lays the groundwork for development of implementation and monitoring plans.

Step 2. Decide the approach to implementation, monitoring, and the deviations from the plan. As in other parts of the reform process, policy makers can take several different approaches to implementation, monitoring, and "mistakes," each with trade-offs better fitting some circumstances than others. We argue that implementation and organizational learning are enhanced, ideally, by an approach that combines high levels of participation and support for implementers, appropriate levels of discretion, and correspondingly high levels of accountability for implementers and others. More common in practice is an approach that emphasizes compliance—accountability of implementers without corresponding support, participation, or discretion.

Step 3. Develop an implementation plan. The implementation plan should specify who needs to do what, when, of course. At the same time, implementation is enhanced when the plan anticipates potential problems during implementation, devises possible countermeasures for such problems, and maps critical but delicate transactions and political energies. Implementation planning is strengthened by a "backward mapping" approach. Learning is enhanced by mapping of program theory.

Step 4. Develop a monitoring plan. Related to the implementation plan, the monitoring plan specifies who will track what aspects of implementation, when and how. Linking implementation and monitoring plans to program theory allows planners and implementers to test hypotheses about program inputs, activities, and intermediate outcomes and to make adjustments during, rather than at the end of, implementation.

Step 5. Develop a strategy for dealing with discrepancies between implementation and plan. It is inevitable that there will be discrepancies between plan and implementation. Depending on the approach taken, the organization may establish criteria for assessing the "adaptability" of the discrepancy. Some discrepancies, we argue, are desirable, representing a positive move toward program goals in the context of a variable and changing environment. Such discrepancies provide the basis for innovation; in favorable circumstances, implementer discretion vastly extends the learning and adaptive capacity of an organization. Some discrepancies, of course, are undesirable, mistaken, or badly intended.

Step 1: Assess Implementability

Thinking about implementation forces one to think about one's theories of change—how exactly does change take place in a system? Typically, policy makers initiating a change automatically assume a top-down or "forward planning" approach (Elmore, 1982). Policy intent is defined, increasingly specific steps are detailed for implementers at different levels of the system, and the outcome is operationalized in measurable terms. In this conception of change, power is seen as residing primarily in formal authority, which flows primarily from the top. Implementers are responsible for enacting the provisions specified by the leadership.

A more realistic understanding of change, we believe, is one that sees authority as reciprocal—formal authority (and resources) flowing from the top or center as well as authority from the bottom up. Bottom-up authority is derived from the understanding and expertise of local actors in dealing with local conditions, their proximity to the problem, and, most importantly, their agency—those at the bottom are (typically) the ones who must bring about whatever change is to take place (Elmore, 1982). In this view, implementation is an ongoing process of negotiation among actors in different parts of the system. Policy makers and planners play an important but not definitive role: In Warwick's (1982) words, "Policy is important in establishing the parameters and directions of action, but it never determines the exact course of implementation. . . . Formal organization structures are significant but not deterministic in their impact" (p. 181).

Implementers themselves make de facto policy in the way they implement official policy, based on their understanding, capacity, and will. This is much the same as with classroom instructors, who teach an implemented curriculum based on their understanding, capacity, and views of the intended curriculum. Understanding implementation in this way, assessing implementability is a matter of predicting the nature, difficulty, and outcome of those negotiations or transactions. Because the outcome of negotiations cannot be known in advance, implementation is inherently unpredictable. Nonetheless, the factors that affect implementation are understood, and many potential difficulties can be anticipated.

In this section we draw heavily on Warwick's (1982) research on implementation, a comparative study of population policy implementation in eight developing countries. Warwick presents, we find, a compelling set of principles with which to assess implementability.

Conceptualization

Whether articulated or not, a plan or reform embodies a theory as to "how things work" and how some intervention will lead to improvements. In fact, we cannot know what will happen, but good theory can help make good guesses. "Theoretical" is often considered the opposite of practical, but in fact a good theory is very practical. A good theory can and should:

- point to areas of intervention likely to produce the desired results;
- correctly indicate how those results can be brought about; and
- warn of unintended consequences (Warwick, 1982).

Program theory may be context specific: The problem in Context X is that school fees raise the cost of educating girls too high for many families. As a result, (too) many families keep their girls at home. Eliminating school fees will reduce the costs of girls' attendance, and will lead to increased enrollment.

Because theory is always a guess, albeit an educated one, it is important to be critical about theories, in order to refine them and develop more accurate explanations. As discussed in chapter 3, it is particularly important to become aware of unconscious or implicit theories, for they limit awareness of alternative explanations and courses of action and lock one into old ways of thinking. If program theory is correct, the program has a chance for implementation. If program theory is wrong, implementation is unlikely to lead to the desired outcomes.

What Warwick calls the "initial intelligence" of a plan is the extent to which a program is based on an accurate understanding (or theory) of cause and effect as well as the extent to which the plan is organized so as to maximize implementation. "Ongoing intelligence" refers to the extent to which program theory remains accurate as conditions change. Obviously, ongoing intelligence cannot be assessed before implementation; however, the monitoring process can be organized to include periodic checks on the continuing "intelligence" of an intervention. To continue with the example, the opportunity costs of girls' schooling might increase if local economies provided increased opportunities for school-age girls to earn money. In such a changed situation, elimination of school fees might not have the desired effect, and ongoing intelligence would require a revision of intervention strategy.

Process

The process by which a policy, program, or reform is developed often has a great impact on its relative success during implementation. Implementation is smoothest if the reform is supported by powerful leaders in both national leadership and opinion-leading roles and by those responsible for program execution; if the policy, program, or reform is viewed as reasonably free of foreign influence; if the policy, program, or reform is adapted to local conditions; if it is worded using appropriate language; and if the issues it raises are not divisive. Implementation is more problematic when there is little or negative support by powerful leadership; when the reform is seen as unduly influenced by outsiders or outside agendas; when the program is not adapted to local conditions; when language is offensive; and when the issues or process are polarizing (Warwick, 1982).

Political Context

Regardless of how important and well-conceived and formulated a reform, it will be implemented in a political context. The reform must make sense in terms of political as well as technical rationality. Implementation is enhanced when there is commitment by top leadership, support from domestic interest groups, and when there are relatively low levels of external threat or environmental uncertainty. A certain degree of high-level commitment is desirable, but too much commitment raises stakes, thus increasing the political costs of failure. Implementation is more difficult when top-level commitment is too low or too high, when there is little domestic support, under conditions of uncertainty and threat, or when the population is polarized along ethnic, class, political, or religious lines.

As observed earlier, the stages of planning and of implementation each require mobilization of political energy and support. Often, the energy required to reach consensus on the plan dissipates after agreement is reached, leaving little energy for implementation. Implementation is greatly enhanced when the reform generates moderate to high levels of political energy and low levels of opposition.

Cultural Context

Reform is also implemented in a cultural context. Some initiatives have little effect on cultural context, while others are highly cultural. Implementation is enhanced when a program is compatible with tradition, when it is valued by local cultural interpreters, and when it does not play into cultural conflicts. Implementation is more problematic when a reform is incompatible with tradition, when it is devalued by cultural leaders, and when it increases cultural conflict.

Bureaucratic Context

Change initiatives are implemented by organizations, often including government agencies. Even with good theory and process and favorable political and cultural contexts, organizations can prevent successful implementation. Implementation is facilitated when the reform involves a small and manageable number of agencies; when the responsibilities of different parties are clear and unambiguously assigned; when there is a spirit of cooperation among implementing agencies and when their missions are compatible; and when implementing routines are feasible and available or readily developed. Implementation is hindered when too many implementing organizations are involved; when responsibilities and assignments are vague, overlapping, or leave gaps; when agencies compete or start with different missions and incompatible organizational cultures; and when administrative routines are difficult to develop or carry out.

Implementers

Implementers along with beneficiaries have the greatest impact on implementation, and are most difficult for central authorities to manage. Implementation is enhanced when implementers have the capacity and the will to carry out their assigned tasks; when tasks are clear and feasible, given other responsibilities; when the extent of innovation is manageable; when implementers' superiors value the program and support its implementation; when implementers themselves like the program and its methods; when morale is high; when their program responsibilities are compatible with community expectations; when there are incentives (not necessarily financial); and when there is compatibility between the requirements of the job and implementers' ideas of themselves. Implementation is weakened when implementers lack the knowledge or will to carry out their work; when the work is unclear or there are competing time commitments; when there are more innovations required than can be managed; when morale is low or when implementers dislike the program or its approaches; and when program responsibilities conflict with community norms and expectations or when self-identity is not congruent with the job.

Beneficiaries

Like implementers, beneficiaries are (obviously) essential to successful implementation. Implementation is easier when there is demand for the service; when the service is accessible, understandable, and low risk; when beneficiaries like the implementers, program, and delivery; when social and economic conditions remain favorable; when there is support from local interest groups and cultural leaders; and when the service and implementers enjoy a good reputation among beneficiaries. Implementation is more problematic when there is little demand; when the service is difficult to access, hard to understand, or risky; when beneficiaries dislike the program and delivery or implementers; when economic, political, or social conditions destabilize; when there is opposition from particular interest groups or religious and cultural leaders; or when the service providers or implementers are subject to gossip and rumor.

Using these principles, it is useful to take the first step, to assess implementability and to identify potential problem areas.

Step 2: Decide the Approach to Implementation, Monitoring, and Deviations from the Plan

In a prototypical bureaucratic organization, implementation is assumed to take place pretty much as envisioned, because of the hierarchical nature of the organization—implementers will implement the plan, because that is their duty. We have contrasted this command and control model with a model of reciprocal authority, in which local implementers have authority by virtue of their understanding of the context of implementation, their expertise at getting things done in those contexts, their proximity to the problem(s), and the fact that they are the ones who will most directly take steps (or not) that will affect the outcome. These two perspectives, although presented somewhat ideally, manifest themselves in quite different ways of approaching implementation, monitoring, and deviations from the plan. We believe that it is useful for policy leaders to make a conscious decision as to the approach they will take and to embody that decision, at all levels, in the approach the organization takes to deviations (see Step 5). How will the organization discern the difference between mistakes and useful adaptations? Will accountability be organized in such a way that encourages both innovation and responsibility? Will the system bear responsibility for implementation failures when appropriate, or will all responsibility fall on the backs of implementers?

These various elements come together in implementation. An interesting examination of policy implementation in the United States suggests that reform takes much, much longer than the project cycle, often

50 to 100 years. With such a time frame, sustaining commitment to implementation is critical indeed.

MAJOR POLICY REFORM IN THE UNITED STATES

Jackson (2004) carried out a study of seven moderately to highly successful U.S. education reforms of the past two centuries using parallel case histories and policy analysis. The focus of the study was on forces that propelled and resisted the reforms. Lessons were inferred about factors affecting the widespread adoption of reforms and were examined in the context of prior literature on reform. The reforms he examined were large reforms, sustained, though not without considerable difficulty in some cases, over generations. They mirror larger social changes in U.S. society, but were adopted and adapted in the particular context of U.S. schools. The reforms include: universal education, religion in education, progressive education, teacher preparation, special education, compensatory education, and multicultural education. Based on extensive analysis, Jackson draws ten lessons:

1. Successful reforms are stimulated and pushed along by several changing social contexts that pose problems or opportunities within society or the schools.
2. Ambitious changes, once initiated, are more likely to succeed than modest ones, although they take more effort and time.
3. Successful reforms offer multiple appeals for various stakeholders, often with different appeals for parents, educators, business leaders, citizens, and politicians.
4. A large corps of reform leaders is needed for nationwide success, highlighting the problems or opportunities, proposing the reform, and managing implementation, doing so throughout the states, districts, and individual schools.
5. Federal or state mandates, incentives, and monitoring usually accelerate reforms.
6. High costs do not necessarily thwart reforms, although they may preclude adoption by certain districts at given points in time.

7. Reliable and favorable information about the reform helps, including information on the problem or opportunity being addressed, the resources needed for the reform, approaches that facilitate implementation, and the effects of the reform.

8. A systems approach is helpful in planning and implementing reforms, giving consideration to interactions with schools' goals, structures, processes, and external relations with society.

9. Teacher capacity and motivation are important for carrying out classroom reforms.

10. Persistence is essential, often for 50 or 100 years, for difficulties and setbacks are inevitable.

Step 3. Develop an Implementation Plan

The implementation plan provides program managers with a guide to monitoring the implementation process. We suggest three sets of schedules and "maps."

Implementation Schedule

At a minimum, the implementation plan should detail *who* is responsible for carrying out *what activities, when.* Such a schedule permits program managers and others to monitor program activities. We suggest the implementation schedule be developed through backward mapping, at least in addition to the usual forward mapping approach.

As discussed, forward mapping involves specifying a policy goal, detailing a series of specific activities to be taken at increasingly "lower" levels of the system to reach that policy goal, then operationalizing a measurable outcome consistent with that goal at the end point. Monitoring most basically involves tracking the implementation of activities according to the plan. Evaluation might consist of measuring and comparing achieved goals with stated objectives (approaches to evaluation are discussed in the chapter on evaluation).

A number of implementation researchers have suggested that "bottom-up" strategies better plan for the dynamics of complex organizational change. Elmore (1982) captures the essence of bottom-up planning nicely in his discussion of "backward mapping." Backward mapping begins not with a statement of intent but, in Elmore's (1982) words,

> with a statement of the specific behavior at the lowest level of the implementation process that generates the need for a policy. Only after that behavior is described does the analysis presume to state an objective; the objective is first stated as a set of organizational operations and then as a set of effects, or outcomes, that will result from these operations. Having established a relatively precise target at the lowest level of the system, the analysis backs up through the structure of implementing agencies, asking at each level two questions: What is the ability of this unit to affect the behavior that is the target of the policy? And what resources does this unit require in order to have that effect? In the final stage of analysis the analyst or policy maker describes a policy that directs resources at the organizational units likely to have the greatest effect. (p. 21)

Backward mapping helps to anticipate problems that forward mapping may miss. A study of the effect of a large primary education project in Nepal found that millions of dollars in resources were provided to the school system but that children's achievement changed very little over the five years of the program (Khaniya & Williams, 2004). Closer consideration of the implementation process suggested that while new textbooks were prepared and distributed, school facilities repaired, teacher training improved, and so forth, there was no check to see if teachers knew how to implement the curriculum in ways likely to improve student learning. Evidence suggests that they may not have known how to use the materials to advantage. There was little change in the behavior of teaching; not surprisingly, student achievement failed to improve. Backward mapping may not have known how to address the problem, but it would not likely have overlooked it, starting as it does with the desired end behavior, and backing up to the various supports needed to achieve that end.

Map of Program Theory

Ideally, the implementation plan would specify the causal linkages between inputs, activities, intermediate outcomes, and larger outcomes.

Mapping program theory provides a rigorous check on the assumptions of a planned intervention. Many organizations are likely to resist such a check when a more or less comprehensive plan has already been developed and adopted. Still, would it not be cheaper to discover problems before actual implementation begins than afterwards? Mapping program theory also provides a way to test the hypotheses of the program: In the context of the "natural experiment" of the reform, do inputs and activities lead to the outcomes, as hypothesized? Finally, mapping provides a way to track implementation. Because program theory maps link inputs and activities to relatively immediate outcomes (which are then linked to larger and longer term outcomes), the failure of important early causal relationships can be caught early.

Figure 8.1 provides a simple example of program theory. At each

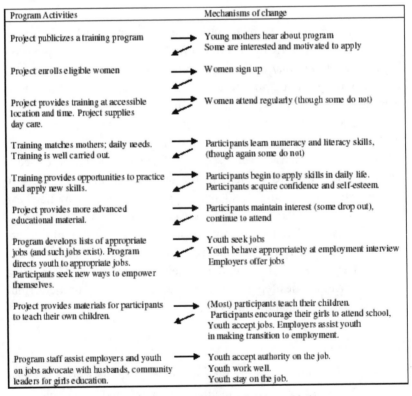

Program Activities	Mechanisms of change
Project publicizes a training program	Young mothers hear about program Some are interested and motivated to apply
Project enrolls eligible women	Women sign up
Project provides training at accessible location and time. Project supplies day care.	Women attend regularly (though some do not)
Training matches mothers; daily needs. Training is well carried out.	Participants learn numeracy and literacy skills, (though again some do not)
Training provides opportunities to practice and apply new skills.	Participants begin to apply skills in daily life. Participants acquire confidence and self-esteem.
Project provides more advanced educational material.	Participants maintain interest (some drop out), continue to attend
Program develops lists of appropriate jobs (and such jobs exist). Program directs youth to appropriate jobs. Participants seek new ways to empower themselves.	Youth seek jobs Youth behave appropriately at employment interview Employers offer jobs
Project provides materials for participants to teach their own children.	(Most) participants teach their children. Participants encourage their girls to attend school, Youth accept jobs. Employers assist youth in making transition to employment.
Program staff assist employers and youth on jobs advocate with husbands, community leaders for girls education.	Youth accept authority on the job. Youth work well. Youth stay on the job.

Figure 8.1 *Program Theory in a Literacy Program for Young Mothers*

point, managers can check to see if planned activities are being carried out and whether they are leading to desired consequences. A program theory map allows planner/managers to see where a program gets off track, hopefully in time to take effective corrective action. The map allows managers to see which hypothesized relationships do not hold and also to map unanticipated consequences. In this way, the organization can learn. More complicated initiatives would likely show mixed results: In some contexts, activities are likely to lead to the specified outcomes, pretty much as expected, whereas in other contexts, the same activities may lead to different results. Such relationships can also be mapped with the intervening variable, once identified.

Map Anticipated Trouble Spots

Finally, we suggest mapping potential trouble spots for the implementation process. It is likely that planners will be aware of a number of potentially difficult implementation transactions. Others are likely to surface during assessment of implementability, backward mapping of implementation scheduling, and specification of program hypotheses and theory. It is suggested that planners/managers imagine countermeasures for likely implementation glitches, according to both positive and negative scenarios.

Step 4: Develop a Monitoring Plan

Like the implementation plan, the monitoring plan specifies *who* will track *what aspects* of implementation *when* and *how*. The analyses developed earlier—implementation schedule, map of program theory, and map of anticipated trouble spots—can be used to track implementation and monitor progress toward program goals. Apart from the mechanics of monitoring, which are left to planners in each context, the monitoring plan needs to decide what it will monitor, at which points during implementation, who it will involve in the monitoring process, and how far up the questions go.

What to Monitor?

It is possible to describe a rough hierarchy of possibilities for monitoring, ranging from modest to more profound:

- Adherence to details of the plan—Have necessary inputs been delivered? Are program activities taking place as expected? Are different groups playing their expected roles? What accounts for any differences in delivery of inputs or carrying out of program activities?
- Specific cause and effect hypotheses—Are program activities leading to expected intermediate outcomes? What factors account for differences in the effect of program activities across locations or groups? What unintended consequences are arising? Under what conditions? Is the program making it through the anticipated trouble spots? Is the program managing the critical transitions and transactions?
- Larger program theory and reform goals—Is the reform, as a whole, reaching its larger goals? Are the intermediate outcomes leading, as expected, to the larger outcomes? How well does program theory hold? Does the program continue to fit the problem and context? How is the "ongoing intelligence" of "implementation? Is the reform moving toward a situation where "the operation was successful, but the patient died"?

Ideally, a monitoring system would provide implementers with information about the effects of their activities so that they could learn how best to implement the program at the grassroots level: What works, and what doesn't? What unintended consequences arise?

At an intermediate level, a monitoring system might provide implementers and policy makers with information about the consequences of other implementers' activities. Implementers typically see only their part of the system. It would be useful for them to see what works, and what does not, across the larger context. Policy makers, for their part, need to see the effects of activities in the variety of contexts of implementation.

At the policy level, a monitoring system would help planners and policy makers learn how to plan for the kinds of systemic change they are seeking to bring about: What policies are effective with whom? What sequences of activities are needed to achieve certain outcomes? What support is needed?

When to Monitor?

The timing of monitoring activities involves a delicate balance between looking to see how things are going, particularly during delicate and important transactions, and allowing implementation time to take place.

Who Should Monitor?

In a typical top-down change process, monitoring is carried out by those in charge or their delegates. In a more participatory process, actors at all levels of the system would take part in monitoring— planners, managers, implementers, and beneficiaries. Broader participation promises a much richer understanding of implementation and reform processes than is possible with a single group working at some distance from the actual locus of implementation. Such participation requires an appropriate structure.

Who Should Be Monitored?

Similarly, we would argue for monitoring all key groups in the reform, policy makers as well as implementers. Are implementers doing their job? Are officials maintaining financial and political support? Are beneficiaries acting as expected?

Step 5: Develop a Strategy for Dealing with Discrepancies between Implementation and Plan

It is a truism that the plan will not be implemented precisely as intended. The variables are how implementation will deviate, by how much, which deviations are adaptive (that is, move toward or away from the larger goals of the reform, or the nation), and which are counterproductive. We have argued that an organization's approach to mistakes is quite revealing. There are three tasks, it seems, all best thought through before implementation:

- Deciding criteria for assessing whether a deviation is an innovation, a failure, or insubordination;

- Accurately understanding the cause of the deviation; and
- Dealing effectively with the deviation.

Deciding Whether the Deviation Is an Innovation, a Failure, or Insubordination

Depending on the confidence an organization has in its plan and whether it has decided to adopt a strictly top-down approach or a more participatory strategy, it may be useful to identify criteria by which innovative discrepancies can be distinguished from those that are merely bad implementation or willful disruption. Corrective action will vary accordingly.

Accurately Understanding the Cause of the Failure

For corrective action to be effective, it is necessary to understand why implementation failed. In a hierarchical organization, it is easy to assign fault to implementers. Before doing so, however, it is worth asking whether implementers were able to carry out the specified activity: Did they have the resources, time, technical know-how, and discretion to do what was required? Did they understand their responsibilities and the timing and manner in which they were to be carried out? If so, implementers may deserve credit for the failure. At the same time, it is worth asking if policy makers may have played a role, however inadvertent.

In many cases, it is useful to see implementation failure as a more complex phenomenon. Solutions are likely to be more effective if they address a range of causality. Let us consider the case of student failure, for example. Who is to blame if a student does not acquire the expected curriculum within the prescribed time? The student, for not learning the material? The teacher, for not teaching so the student could learn? Past teachers, for not providing the student with adequate preparation? The school, for not providing an adequate learning environment? Curriculum developers, for not developing student-proof learning? Parents, for not providing a sufficiently supportive/demanding home? The school system, for not making sure teachers, curriculum, and school were equipped so that all children would learn? The government, for providing insufficient funds for all students to learn? The international community, for not pressuring/supporting all countries to ensure all children learn? After a certain point, it becomes difficult to discern who is responsible for what, or what to do about it. Most likely, student failure arises from a combination of factors. In the case of implementation failure, it is likely that implementers did not quite do their job, *and* that they were not as informed as they should have been about the details and importance of the activity.

Just as we have argued for broad participation in planning reform, we argue, ideally again, for broad participation in understanding and accepting responsibility for failure. Sometimes, the responsibility for failure is clear and can be located at a certain place. Often, the causality of implementation failure is complex.

Dealing Effectively with Failure

One reason to think clearly about the causes of implementation failure is to learn the right (that is, effective) points for intervention. If implementers are incorrectly blamed for a systemic failure, sanctioning implementers will do little to improve the situation. Provision of resources is a fine remedy only if their lack is the cause of the problem.

In the process of implementation, it may be necessary to adjust the balance among accountability, support, discretion, and participation. In some cases, it may be useful to institute greater measures of accountability. In others, the critical task may be that of providing additional support—technical, financial, human. In still other cases, implementers may need more, or less, discretion. Finally, the most important step may be the widening of participation or the defining or renegotiating of roles. Top-down organizations tend to emphasize accountability. Bottom-up approaches tend to emphasize participation and support. An appropriate balance, we would argue, is what is most important. An atmosphere of fear, in which everyone is afraid to make or admit mistakes, is not conducive to smooth implementation or organizational learning. Yet fear is the consequence of too heavy a reliance on accountability without corresponding support, discretion, and participation. A climate of permissiveness may result from an underreliance on accountability. If participation is low, those on the lower end of the hierarchy may question the legitimacy of plans from above and resist their implementation, overtly or covertly. Too much participation or participation poorly structured may result in little getting done. Too little support and implementers cannot do their job. Too much support and implementers look first to others for resources they may themselves have.

SUMMARY: IMPLEMENTATION AS LEARNING IN ACTION

This chapter has considered the planning of implementation and monitoring. It is an important subject indeed, particularly if, as Allison asserts, implementation represents 90% of the effort of guided change in a complex social system. As in other stages of the reform process, we have urged policy makers and planners to think carefully about their choices in planning implementation and monitoring. Stages models of policy reform see planning as a discrete stage preceding implementation, which, in practice, is carried out by different groups of people. We have argued that planners need to think about the implementability of their plans. Too little can be known at the outset of a reform and by those in the center to plan every detail of implementation. Rather than creating the perfect plan and enforcing compliance, we propose a more flexible arrangement, whereby implementers are provided with an appropriate balance of discretion, support, accountability, and participation; where monitoring is less a matter of adherence to a blueprint than an ongoing process of learning what works, when, where, and for whom, within broad goals legitimately decided. We have urged policy leaders and managers to be especially mindful of failure—to understand it fully and correctly, in all its complexity, to encourage it in the sense of experimentation and pursuit of innovation, and to take corrective steps, early, often, and with a broad range of participation.

CHAPTER 9

Evaluation and the Institutionalization of Reform

Evaluation is the phase in the reform process when the organization stops to assess how it is doing—how is the reform going, what changes need to be made to continue developing the reform, what effects the reform is having or has had, and what next and future steps should be undertaken. Most basically, evaluation compares "what is" with "what should be." Is the reform taking place as planned? Has the reform led to expected benefits?

By its nature, evaluation involves judgment and values. Judgments may be made on the basis of authority, intuition, tradition, or expert opinion, or they may rely on information collected on a more formal basis. We argue for an approach to evaluation that uses social science research methods to inform judgments made through legitimate political and organizational processes. The point is to inform decision making with more systematic and credible information, and to highlight the importance of focusing explicitly on the decision-making process as it relates to information collection, analysis, and utilization.

Weiss (1998) provides a useful definition of evaluation research: "evaluation is the systematic assessment of the operation and/or the outcomes of a program or policy,[1] compared to a set of explicit or implicit standards, as a means of contributing to the improvement of the program or policy" (p. 4). In unpacking her definition, she highlights:

- the use of *systematic inquiry* in evaluation research;
- the use of evaluation *to understand* how a program is being implemented—the *operation*, and/or the effects of the program—the *outcomes*;
- the use of *standards*, explicit or implicit, against which the operation or outcomes are judged; and

- the applied use of evaluation research, *to improve programs and policies.*

Systematic inquiry may be qualitative and/or quantitative in its data collection, analysis, and interpretation. Research may be carried out in a participatory manner or using a more traditional "objective" and detached approach. Standards may be measured by test scores, program goals, expected as well as unanticipated program effects or consequences, efficiency, cost effectiveness, justice, beauty even, community or national values.

FORMATIVE AND SUMMATIVE EVALUATION

One common distinction is between formative and summative evaluation. Formative evaluation is used to improve a program, summative evaluation to assess it. In their purest forms, the two "types" are quite different.

Formative evaluation is used to answer such questions as:

- How is the reform being carried out?
- What is actually happening in the reform? How does that compare with what is supposed to be happening?
- What changes should be made to better implement the reform?
- What, if any, unanticipated directions is the reform taking?

Summative evaluation is used to answer questions as:

- How well is the reform meeting its objectives? Are beneficiaries receiving the expected benefits?
- What are the actual effects of the reform? How do actual effects compare with intended effects?
- What unintended outcomes have resulted from the reform?
- What are the benefits of the reform, and how do benefits compare with costs?
- How effective are different aspects of the reform? How does their effectiveness compare with other similar programs? How effective overall is the reform?

- What aspects of the reform are more and less effective? Under what conditions is the reform more and less effective? Does the reform work better for some people than for others? Does it work differently in different contexts? How and why?
- What evidence is there to support continuing, expanding, scaling up, modifying, cutting back, or discontinuing different aspects of the reform?
- What changes does evidence suggest would make the reform more (effective/efficient/etc.)?
- What does evidence suggest are the next and future steps in working toward the goals of the reform?
- What can the organization learn from this program? More generally, what can be learned from this initiative?

In practice, evaluation is usually carried out at the end of a project cycle, and so there is a summative component to most evaluation—how well did it work? What were the effects? How effective was it? At the same time, most reform efforts continue in some shape or manner, and so there is a formative element as well to most evaluation—how can the reform be improved?

ARRIVING AT CREDIBLE ANSWERS

Credible answers to both types of questions are difficult to arrive at informally, especially when the program is complex, as most substantial reforms are, when its effects are difficult to see, when decisions are important and expensive, and when evidence is needed to support conclusions and convince stakeholders (Weiss, 1998). Notice that these questions are phrased in "positive" terms, that is, the questions can be answered with data. Data-based answers can be used to *inform* "normative" questions about values and preferences, for which there is no single answer (see discussion of convergent versus divergent questions in chapter 3). So, for example, evaluation can help answer such questions as, "What are the likely effects of continuing a program?" Evaluation cannot answer the question, "Should the program be continued?" However, evaluation can *inform* the decision-making process with likely trade-offs, costs and benefits of continuing a program or cancel-ing it.

While often used to answer questions about a project or program, evaluation is also used to understand the effects and effectiveness of policies, and, in our case, aspects of the reform and its process. Evalua-tion can play five critical roles in the process of reform:

- assessing what is being done
- examining the effects or consequences of what has been done
- comparing "what is" with "what should be"
- informing plans for what should be done next
- providing instructional material to an organization willing and able to learn.

Answering these seemingly sensible questions is often more difficult than it may seem: programs are complex, with multiple, often contra-dictory, purposes. Some of these purposes are clear; others are implicit. Still other purposes may be "politically incorrect" but, while difficult to articulate in a given organizational culture, nonetheless true. Many different groups of people are involved in a program, as decision mak-ers, managers, implementers, stakeholders, or as political opponents. Typically these different groups have different goals, competing ideas of what constitutes program effectiveness, even contradictory views of what is happening. In a complex organizational environment, the effects of a program are often subtle, equivocal, difficult to see and measure; the causes difficult to disentangle; and the effects long-term. To a project manager working overtime to implement a new program, evaluation may seem premature, even counterproductive, as it diverts resources from implementation and introduces a tone of judgment and accountability into what is often a delicate process of negotiation and implementation. In some cases, the evaluator may be seen as "pulling up the flowers to see if the roots are growing" before they have had opportunity to take root.

Wrong Reasons

Evaluations may be undertaken for the wrong reasons—to delay a decision (pending a "rigorous" evaluation), to avoid responsibility for a difficult decision (let the results of the evaluation point the way out of a quandary), to provide scientific legitimation to a decision already made, or even, in the case of known successes, as public relations. Funding agencies typically mandate some sort of evaluation as a condition of support. Not surprisingly, program personnel often see such evaluation as a "hoop" to jump through rather than tool for learning. In Weiss's (1998) words, "Evaluation . . . is a rational enterprise often undertaken for non-rational, or at least non-informational, reasons" (p. 23).

Social scientists have come to a much more sophisticated understanding of the utilization of research in policy in complex organizations. The naïve rationalistic belief that enlightened decision makers would put the findings of well-conducted research into direct practice has given way to a deeper understanding of the complexities of organizations, the constraints facing any one actor or group of actors in bringing about desirable change, and the multiple perspectives that diverse stakeholders and actors bring to even the simplest of truths. In influencing policy and practice, new information must contend with existing understandings, the ideologies and interests of a range of actors as well as with the history, culture, and customs of the institution (Weiss, 1995).

Organizational Learning

Even when evaluation is undertaken for informational purposes, results are not automatically utilized to improve policies and programs. The results of evaluation, as in most research, are typically equivocal and guarded, context specific or qualified. Conclusions are often difficult to apply in any direct or immediate way to a particular set of circumstances. More often, the results of research accrete into a slowly developing understanding of a situation. Optimistically, Weiss (1998) refers to this as a process of (gradual) "enlightenment." Others are less sanguine, seeing most encounters with new information as heavily conditioned by what the individual or organization already knows. Information that conforms to, essentially confirming, what the organization or individual "knows" is accepted. Disconfirming information tends to be rejected. Others see through a more political lens; ideas are adopted in a context of power, not enlightenment. In either case, research is often of little direct or immediate application.

Certainly, organizations can be rather poor learners. Few organizations, it seems, learn much from reports. A substantial body of research suggests that decades of evaluation have had relatively little impact on policy and practice in the United States, for example. Yet as Porter and Hicks (1997) discuss, policy is rarely acted upon unless the politics are favorable. Organizations are generally quite resistant to change. Information alone is rarely sufficient to bring about substantial organizational change. Evaluations tend to focus rationally on the problem and solution, eschewing, in the name of objectivity, the politics that might lead to change.

These issues of research utilization and organizational learning are particularly important in the case of education reform, because so little is known about how intentional change can be made to happen in education, and central planners can know so little at the planning stages about the actual conditions of implementation. An effective organization must be able to learn and make adjustments on an ongoing basis while maintaining central goals and an energizing vision.

Another reason for underutilization of evaluation research may be the dual function that evaluation serves—both accountability and learning. Learning is facilitated by an open stance, which is hindered by moves toward accountability (see also discussion in the chapter on implementation). All else being equal, we would suggest, an organization that treats mistakes as failure will tend to act more defensively, and learn less from evaluation, than an organization in which mistakes are treated as opportunities to learn. Yet evaluation is often called for in contexts of accountability, where effectiveness is a concern. It often seems that the organizations in greatest need of learning are most resistant. Moving a defensive organization toward a learning stance, while maintaining the organization's viability, especially in a politicized context, requires unusually strong leadership. Often, change is foisted upon a less than willing organization.

Evaluation can focus on more superficial aspects of a reform and its organizational context, or on deeper, more fundamental aspects. Consider the difference between an evaluation that asks simply whether or not a project was successful according to specified criteria, with an evaluation that continues beyond assessment of effectiveness to ask what broader factors in the organization and its modes of operation foster effectiveness, and which are associated with failure. The approach that an organization takes to evaluation reveals as much as anything about the extent to which that organization is willing and able to learn in a systematic way about the effects of its efforts and how they can be improved. Certainly, some organizational conditions are more supportive of organizational learning than others.

The remainder of this chapter synthesizes existing material into a general methodology for carrying out evaluation. The discussion is organized in a series of steps. Like the planning process in general, these steps are not as distinct or as linear in practice as they are presented on paper. Nonetheless, a linear stage format is helpful as a learning and memory aid. It helps to organize thinking and direct energies toward the next necessary steps. As previously, we emphasize multiple ways of carrying out a particular policy task and the trade-offs associated with different choices. And so, we take pains to avoid presenting material as if there were one best way. Nonetheless, there are some important principles that cut across many of the choices of reform and evaluation strategy.[2]

Evaluation is a form of research, about which hundreds of books have been written. While it is beyond the scope of this book to discuss the details of methodology in a comprehensive way, we do provide an overview of important issues, aimed at those involved in evaluation, whether as evaluators or decision makers. Dealing effectively with these methodological issues according to established standards of social science research will help ensure that the evaluation provides credible and defensible answers to the questions it poses. That being said, there is considerable debate among evaluation specialists as to what constitutes credible evidence and rigorous and appropriate methodology. One approach to resolving such differences is to present one particular methodology either as the only valid approach or as the only approach discussed. Again, our strategy is more ecumenical. We believe that the differing approaches provide policy makers and other stakeholders with a range of choices of models to best fit their needs. Still, evaluation research is a highly specialized field requiring substantial expertise. Adding the dimensions of multiple models, approaches, and choices adds considerable complexity to an already complex undertaking. The payoff is potentially greater utilization of information in the reform process on the part of those in the education system, and thus more effective reform.

Like the rest of the book, this chapter is aimed at both planner/evaluators and policy/decision makers. It is intended to provide both with a common vocabulary and reference point for discussing questions of process and value. The intent is to provide a framework for planning and a series of design choices, according to the philosophy and conditions facing policy leaders, managers, and stakeholders in particular contexts.

EVALUATING THE EFFECTS OF REFORM

Evaluation is an integral part of the reform process. Our approach to evaluation considers the task in six steps:[3]

1. (Re)consideration of "evaluability" of the reform
2. Focusing of evaluation and agreement on major parameters
3. Development of evaluation and research plan
4. Collection, analysis, and interpretation of data
5. Communication of findings and steps to promote utilization of results and organizational learning
6. New planning–implementation–evaluation cycle

Again, these steps are seen as necessary elements of a process that typically involves considerable looping back. Initial findings in data collection and analysis, for example, may lead to revision of the evaluation plan. Data analysis may suggest important overlooked information and so, the evaluation plan will need revision, and so forth.

Step 1: (Re)consideration of "Evaluability" of the Reform

Before planning *how* to do an evaluation, it is important to revisit the question of *whether* to do one: Are conditions favorable for effective evaluation? As discussed earlier, evaluation is undertaken for a variety of reasons, only some of which are informational in nature. Not every situation is suitable for evaluation, or worth the cost in time, money, or aggravation. A colleague of ours calls this the "evaluability" of an evaluation task (see Jackson, 2003). In assessing evaluability, it is important to determine, for example, whether the *sponsors*—those who request and, generally, fund the evaluation—are serious about evaluation, which is likely to include negative as well as positive findings. Are they willing to accept negative as well as positive findings, or will they insist on a particular outcome? Is there sufficient political support for an evaluation and acceptably low levels of opposition? Is there in fact a coherent program to evaluate? Is there reasonable agreement among key actors and stakeholders about the goals and objectives of the program? Is the program sufficiently developed and stable for its effects to be examined? Are sufficient resources available to conduct the evaluation, in terms of time, money, access to information? Are expectations realistic? Will the sponsor want more information than the evaluator can provide? Will stakeholders or sponsors want more definitiveness than is likely possible? Is there an expectation that the evaluator will take a stand that s/he or they cannot or will not assume, either an impartial position or an advocacy role? (Stecher & Davis, 1987)

Under certain conditions, it is worth reconsidering the decision to evaluate: If a reform has not sufficiently matured and has little stability, there is little value in trying to assess it. What is the point of evaluating a program or policy that is likely to be different tomorrow? Similarly, there is little utility in attempting to evaluate a reform if there is no agreement among those involved in the reform process about what the reform is trying to achieve. In order to compare "what is" with "what should be," there needs to be substantial agreement as to "what should be" is. Evaluation is unlikely to be effective if there is strong opposition to the evaluation. And finally, evaluation should be reconsidered if there are overly tight constraints on what issues can be examined, if evaluators do not have sufficient autonomy, or if available resources—funding, staff, and time—are insufficient to the task (Weiss, 1998).

Basically, we see four questions:

- Are there sufficient legitimate reasons for evaluation?
- Is the reform sufficiently coherent in goals and practice that it can be evaluated?

- Will the organization provide sufficient autonomy and protection?
- Are there sufficient funds, staff, and time?

Step 1 Checklist: Assessing Evaluability

_____ Does the client appear to want an honest evaluation that will identify both strengths and possible weaknesses?

_____ Do at least several stakeholders support conducting an evaluation?

• Program funder?	• Others?
• Intermediaries?	• Program participants?
• Potential client's bosses?	• Community leaders?
• Program designers?	• Interested scholars?
• Program director?	• Others?

_____ Are no more than a few stakeholders strongly opposed to conducting an evaluation at this point in time?

_____ Is there at least moderate agreement among these stakeholders about the objectives of the program?

_____ Have the program objectives remained fairly consistent for awhile?

_____ Is there a real program being implemented or operated?

_____ Is the program being implemented in a fairly predictable manner or operating fairly stably?

_____ Is there one or a few coherent program theories explaining how the program operations are expected to affect the program objectives?

_____ Does the client have some good priority questions for the evaluation?

_____ What designs would be most appropriate to answer the main questions of interest and are they feasible (experimental, quasi-experimental, single group compared with norms, survey, case study, ethnography, other)?

_____ What information on the contexts, participants, program inputs, program operations, outcomes, and finances would be necessary to address the main questions and is it feasible to secure the information in a timely manner?

_____ Will the program director, managers, and staff be able to devote the time needed for any roles they will play in the evaluations?

_____ Can needed human subjects clearance be secured in a timely manner?

_____ Can the needed anonymity/confidentiality be achieved?

_____ Is there enough time, money, and technical expertise to do at least a moderately good job of the evaluation? (Source: Jackson, 2003)

Step 2: Focusing of Evaluation and Agreement on Major Parameters

If the reform and context suggest reasonable evaluability, the next step involves "focusing" the evaluation, clarifying what is to be evaluated and how. Agreement needs to be reached on the major "parameters" of the process, that is:

- the major goals of the evaluation,
- the types of consultative and technical procedures to be used, and
- the nature and scope of interaction among those involved in the evaluation (Stecher & Davis, 1987).

Focusing involves negotiating boundaries and developing a structure for the evaluation process. These agreements will form the basis for development of the evaluation plan in Step 3. Once a decision has been reached to evaluate, there is a natural desire to get started immediately. Sponsors will have legitimate questions, and the conscientious evaluator will want to get started, using those questions. Instead, experience suggests the importance of first developing as complete as possible an understanding of the task, context, and questions from a range of perspectives, then structuring the evaluation process carefully through negotiations among key stakeholders. This suggests two broad focusing steps: understanding existing beliefs, expectations, organization, and politics about evaluation and about the reform, and learning as much as possible about the program or reform (Stecher & Davis, 1987).

Context of Evaluation: Belief, Expectations, Organization,
Politics

In beginning an evaluation, it is useful to try to understand as much as possible of the beliefs and expectations that important individuals hold as well as the organization and politics that led to the evaluation. What are the beliefs of sponsors and key decision makers about evaluation in general, and the expectations for this evaluation process and the reform? Who wants the evaluation carried out? Why? What are likely to be the most important uses and audiences for the evaluation? What are plans for use of the results (Herman, Morris, & Fitz-Gibbon, 1987)? What is actually meant by evaluation? What methods of inquiry, kinds of data, and methods of reporting do key players see as legitimate? What methods of inquiry, data, and reporting mechanisms do they turn to in practice? How do key players and major stakeholder groups feel about this reform? How do different groups differ? What questions do they want answered? What questions do they not want posed? What concerns do they have about the reform? And about the evaluation? How invested are different groups in a particular outcome for the evaluation, and what outcome would they like to see?

At this stage, evaluators are seeking to understand what informal political constraints there are likely to be on the evaluation process and to sharpen their understanding of needs and wishes of policy leaders and other stakeholder groups vis-à-vis the evaluation.

Information about the Program

The second aspect of focusing is to gain as complete as possible an initial understanding of the reform, both as espoused and as implemented. Understanding the program prior to, or as part of, the planning process is useful to gain an informed sense of the issues at play and formulate good questions. Later, this understanding helps the evaluator assess the importance and context of data, interpret evidence meaningfully, make sound recommendations, and prepare reporting so as to maximize chances for utilization (Weiss, 1998).

Understanding the program involves at least six broad sets of questions:

- What are the purposes of the reform—formal and informal, really and for show?
- What is the plan for the reform—its nature, primary activities, geographic scope, beginning, and expected end?
- How can the reform that is actually implemented be characterized?
- Who is carrying out the reform? Who has a stake? Who is affected? Who is affected but unlikely to be heard? Which parts of the organization are more and less receptive to change?
- How is the reform supposed to work? What is the program theory?
- What issues in the reform need evaluating? What issues are coming up soon? Which issues have traction?

A variety of information can be collected from sponsors, observation, and available material, including project documents, background papers, progress reports on the reform itself, previous evaluations, and material on similar reforms. Information on the *reform as planned* is likely to be relatively accessible: What are the primary activities of the reform? Where is the reform taking place? Who is participating, as staff and as beneficiaries?

Information on the *reform as implemented* is more difficult. Even at this initial stage, it is useful to learn as much as possible about the actual reform. Necessarily, most of the details will wait until the evaluation is formally begun.

It is important to identify stakeholders, beneficiaries, and according to Guba and Lincoln (1989), victims. Who, beyond the initial group, has an interest in the outcome of the evaluation? Who else might need to be consulted in developing the evaluation plan? What useful information might other stakeholders, beneficiaries, and victims possess (Stecher & Davis, 1987)?

It is also important to develop as complete and as clear an understanding as possible of what the program is trying to accomplish, in terms of both espoused and hidden goals. Official goals and those of the sponsor are a useful starting point (though poor places to stop). Formal goals are often written, frequently in idealistic yet ambiguous language.

Vague formulations often serve to permit agreement on a program of action under a broad set of goals, while masking underlying differences in the particulars. Staff may be working at cross-purposes. Indeed, in a large organization implementing a complex reform, cross-purposes should be expected. In seeking to clarify program goals, evaluation can bring such discrepancies to the surface, challenging any accommodations various players have made to differences on important but difficult issues.

Program staff are likely to convey a different, more accurate portrait of the real reform than will official documents. Discussions with managers and field personnel can help evaluators distinguish between active goals and objectives of the reform—those receiving funding, staff time, and energy—and goals and objectives only receiving lip service. The implicit and explicit knowledge of program personnel is essential, and typically not documented. Similarly, talking with a variety of stakeholders, beneficiaries, and victims provides a broad understanding of the various perspectives on the purposes of the reform. It is typical for goals to be multiple, somewhat contradictory, and variable, depending on the standpoint of the individual being asked.

It is useful to see how goals may have evolved since their initial formulation and how original conditions may have shifted. Original goals may look quite different if the environment, staff, or political climate have changed. It is also useful to consider what other social, political, or economic functions the reform may serve in addition to its formal goals. Some of these functions may be necessary "system maintenance" goals (Weiss, 1998). Others may suggest the real reasons for the reform, for which the formal instrumental objectives serve as legitimatory cover.

In addition to specifying what the reform is trying to accomplish, it is most useful to try to explicate the reform's theory of change, how the reform expects to achieve its objectives and goals (see also discussion in implementation chapter). In particular, it is useful to surface and chart the chain of linkages among reform activities, assumptions, expected intermediate consequences, and subsequent outcomes. In this way it is possible to see what is planned and has been carried out (reform activities), and to compare expected consequences with what actually happened. This permits the tracking of reform activities, the testing (and if necessary revision) of key assumptions about causal relationships, and the tracking of intermediate outcomes. The evaluator can see where the reform has worked well, and where it got off track—either through poor theory or poor implementation (Weiss, 1998). Diagramming program theory can also point to the kinds of information needed. During the actual evaluation, unintended consequences can be charted alongside those intended, and the further consequences of unintended consequences documented as well. Ideally, evaluation will illustrate both consequences of the reform, intended and accidental, and the mechanisms by which these consequences resulted. This provides the opportunity for organizational learning as planners and policy makers reexamine their theories in light of the evaluation data.

During this broad survey, a number of potential evaluation issues are likely to have arisen. Wise evaluators will have catalogued these issues in preparation for negotiations over the parameters of the evaluation, to follow.

Evaluation Parameters

Having examined the reform in some detail, the evaluators now need to come to agreement with sponsors about the critical decisions affecting the evaluation. Once agreement is reached, evaluators can then develop the technical details of the evaluation plan. Before that, however, agreement needs to be reached on the following aspects of the evaluation.

Issues to Be Addressed/Questions to Be Answered. What are the primary questions driving the evaluation? Few if any evaluations can address all potential issues. Consensus as to the critical issues to be addressed is essential. One can use a number of criteria to rank priorities: importance to policy leaders, importance to the reform, political salience, academic interest, importance to beneficiaries, importance to disenfranchised, importance to those most willing and able to bring about change.

At this point, the evaluation also needs to consider how far it intends to probe in examining the reform.

1. Is the evaluation going to limit itself, for example, to achievement of reform goals, or will it look beyond the stated goals to all effects, negative as well as positive, unanticipated as well as expected? Will the evaluation look only at the reform, or will it

look to the organizational context as well? A ranking of questions might be developed, as follows, from less to more systemic and intrusive:

- Did the reform achieve its goals? How did it realize those goals?
- What unintended effects did the reform have? How?
- What factors in the organization account for effects (positive and negative, anticipated and unexpected)?
- What aspects of the organization does evidence suggest be changed in order to better achieve desired goals?

2. Will the evaluation focus only on implementation staff or will it consider managers as well? Decision makers and policy leaders? Will problems be seen only as "theirs," or will "we" have to change as well?

3. How will the evaluation approach political controversies?
   - Sidestep politics and claim only to provide "technical input"
   - Take one side, with or without admitting to existence of another
   - Work to resolve the controversy
   - Establish a process for dialogue and focus on more immediate action plans around which agreement is easier

4. Will the evaluation focus only on "single-loop" learning or will it consider "double-loop" learning as well? (See discussion in chapter 3.) Essentially, organizations as well as individuals tend to rely on known diagnoses of the problem and familiar remedies. When a familiar solution fails to solve the problem, the natural tendency is to try it again, but harder, without questioning the "diagnosis." It is wise, however, to consider the adage, "When you only have a hammer, every problem looks like a nail." A true evaluation needs to question both the diagnosis and the remedy.

Appropriate Evaluation Model. Selection of an appropriate approach to evaluation depends on the key questions and on the function and emphasis of the evaluation: for example, to understand, scientifically, the effects of the reform? To assess effects in light of goals? To empower stakeholders? To inform decisions? And so forth (see also

Herman et al., 1987; Stecher & Davis, 1987; Stufflebeam, Madaus, & Kellaghan, 2000). Some of the models in common use include:

- *Experimental.* The purpose is to provide scientifically credible evidence of the effects of a reform/program/intervention. Experimental evaluation asks: What were the effects of the reform/program/intervention? Can they be generalized?
- *Evaluation research.* The purpose is to add to knowledge about relationships among inputs, processes, outcomes, for different contexts and populations. Evaluation research asks: What were the effects of the intervention? Can they be generalized?
- *Goal-oriented.* The purpose is to understand the extent to which a program achieved its stated goals and objectives. Goal-oriented research asks: What were the goals of the reform? How successful was the reform in achieving them?
- *Goal-free.* The purpose is to understand all the consequences of the reform/program. What were all the effects of the intervention (good and bad, intended and unintended)?
- *Decision-focused.* The purpose is to provide decision makers with information on specific decisions (choices of programs, scale up/cut back) or systematic information for management and operation. Decision-focused evaluation asks: What decisions and decision makers need support? What information can inform those decisions?
- *User-oriented.* The purpose is to provide program "users" with information useful in their work. User-oriented evaluation asks: Who in the organization needs information? What information do they need?
- *Responsive.* The purpose is to facilitate efforts to understand the program from multiple perspectives (Stecher & Davis, 1987). Responsive evaluation asks: Who are the stakeholders? How do they see the reform?
- *Empowerment.* The purpose is to empower stakeholders. Empowerment evaluation asks: What are the forces of oppression? How can evaluation raise critical consciousness?

Appropriate Mix of Formative and Summative Components. To what extent is the evaluation intending to inform development of the reform, to measure the effects of the reform once implemented, or both?

Roles of Different Parties. Who is to be involved in what phases of the evaluation and how? Other than qualitative or quantitative approach to data collection and analysis, participation, more than any other aspect of evaluation, defines differences across models. The most technical approaches tend not to discuss the issue of participation.

Among the most potentially contentious issues rarely discussed in technical approaches to evaluation is *who participates* and *how*. Figure 9.1 presents a schema for thinking about the range of possible participants in an evaluation activity. It is assumed that the evaluators and sponsors will be involved in making decisions about the evaluation. In traditional hierarchical design, the sponsors and evaluator make all important decisions, and the evaluators would carry out research *on* or *about* those lower in the hierarchy, using the sponsors' questions. More

		Evaluator	Sponsors & funders	Policy-makers	Top program staff	Other program staff; Beneficiaries; Other stakeholders; Victims; Communities
	As sources of data					
	Developing recommendations					
	Analyzing & interpreting data					
Toward participation	Collecting data					
	Formulating questions					
	As evaluators					
	In deciding parameters					

Toward ultimate beneficiaries

Figure 9.1   *Mapping Participation in Evaluation of Reform*

participatory approaches would add groups from "lower" in the organization to the decision-making and evaluating processes and add those higher in the organization to the groups being studied. The more participatory the approach, the more groups lower in the traditional hierarchy would take part as evaluators and decision makers.

Less participatory approaches, which might be described as *evaluator controlled*, permit a more objective, detached stance on the part of researcher and are most appropriate when the primary purpose of the research is to determine effects of an intervention independently from the perspectives of implementers and other stakeholders. Complex data collection, analytic and presentation techniques are easier to use with evaluator-controlled approaches, and the evaluation task is easier to define and coordinate. Evaluator-controlled approaches are less useful, however, for generating broad "ownership" of the evaluation and its recommendations, less able to draw on the tacit knowledge of implementers and other stakeholders, and less useful for understanding "process" from the perspectives of those involved. They tend to focus only on the questions actors the "top" of the system.

The most participatory approach would involve all groups both as active evaluators, albeit with different roles and responsibilities, and as sources of data. In participatory models, evaluators carry out their work *for* and *with* implementers and other stakeholders. Participatory approaches are better able to develop broad ownership of an evaluation task, and to generate political energy to carry out recommendations. They can draw on the knowledge of a broad range of participants and stakeholders in the reform, and they are innately more democratic. They are also more difficult to define and manage, and, arguably, less technically acute. Perhaps the clearest distinction is a perspective of research "on or about" participants in the reform versus that of "for and with" them. Despite preferences for greater participation, we would argue that different purposes can be served by different approaches.

Methods, Data, and Reporting (see Step 3). What data collection and analytic strategies are appropriate to address the questions, legitimate and convincing to sponsors and other key actors and within the resources of evaluators? What styles of reporting should be used? What is the timeline for completing the evaluation and its major components?

Resources. What budget, staff, equipment, and supplies are devoted to the evaluation? What time is needed from nonevaluation staff? What access is needed? What can be accomplished with available resources?

Strategies for Handling Disagreements and Requests for Changes to Report. Though difficult to bring up at the beginning of a new evaluation, it is useful to establish a process for dealing with disagreements about the findings and substance of the report and for dealing with changes requested by the sponsor.

Dissemination/Advocacy. Reports alone are rarely effective at leveraging organizational learning and change. A more explicit, personal, intentional, and political strategy is usually needed. Such a strategy might include involvement of practitioners and other stakeholders and beneficiaries in the research; selection of (some) strategic research questions; advocacy documents in interesting formats accessible to different audiences; a variety of public forums to discuss issues in the reform; plans for the use of media and other means of conveying information and debate. Experience suggests that advocacy and dissemination are more effective when discussed and planned from the outset.

Step 3: Development of Evaluation and Research Plan

After reaching agreement on the parameters, the evaluators develop a detailed evaluation and research plan. Such a plan needs to:

- Select most appropriate methodology for this evaluation
- Plan design and analytic strategy
- Think about validity and reliability
- Plan data collection methods
- Plan sampling
- Pilot procedures
- Structure participation
- Plan dissemination

As elsewhere, these steps should not be understood as necessarily sequential. Evaluators are likely to move back and forth among steps, as they weigh feasibility, emerging findings, and so forth. As many books have been written about research design, a comprehensive discussion is beyond the scope of this chapter. However, a brief overview is useful to highlight some key points.

Appropriate Methodology

From a pragmatic perspective, the best methodology is the one that best answers the research questions. One major decision will revolve around the use of a quantitative or qualitative approach to data collection and analysis, or elements of both. (It should be remembered that the terms *quantitative* or *qualitative* methods refer to broad approaches to research rather than specific methods of data collection and analysis, of which there are many.) There are advantages and disadvantages to each methodology in terms of the kinds of questions better answered.[4]

Quantitative research is generally more appropriate for confirmatory analyses, and examining phenomena at many sites. Quantitative data allows precision and permits a precise estimation of probability. Quantitative methods are useful when the phenomenon is large, many, very small, or too subtle for direct observation, and of course, when appropriate measures exist. Quantitative analysis permits comparison, generalization, and highly specialized analysis leading to an "untangling" of complex effects. Done well, it can allow the researcher to see with few preconceptions. Quantitative research is less useful when important variables and processes are poorly understood. It is poor at portraying the perspectives of those being observed, at capturing distinctions too subtle to measure, observing nonquantifiable phenomena or relationships. Quantitative research tends to impose the vocabulary, categories, and meanings of those who design and carry out the research on those who are being studied. Done poorly, it can easily be used to confirm a researcher's biases.

Qualitative research is more appropriate when the nature of the phenomenon is poorly understood, when the researcher does not know what to measure, or when the key variables and processes are poorly understood. Qualitative research is good at getting at context, and capturing an emic perspective (participants' view). Qualitative research can lead to deep insights into the meaning of phenomena. Done well, it can allow the researcher to see with few preconceptions. Qualitative research is less useful when generalizability or comparability is important across time periods, sites, or individuals. Qualitative research is less precise. It is limited by the observer's capacities. Done poorly, it can easily be used to confirm a researcher's biases.

Mixed methods (quantitative and qualitative) have the potential, infrequently realized, to utilize the best of both approaches: the richness and insight of qualitative research with the precision and generalizability of quantitative research. Qualitative research could be used, it would seem, to understand the phenomenon well enough to measure and analyze it with the "rigor" of quantitative methods. There is always the danger that qualitative researchers will simply find their expectations confirmed and learn little, or that quantitative researchers will "fish" for statistical significance with little theoretical foundation. Some researchers claim the approaches are philosophically incompatible. Given researchers' expertise, one or the other approach usually gets short shrift.

Design and Analytic Strategy

Having decided on a broad set of issues to be addressed and on a general methodological approach, research design begins to plan the details, wherein, as they say, lies the devil (or is it god?). Research design must specify:

- What individuals or units will be studied
- How they will be selected (discussed following under "Sampling")
- When they will be studied (Before and after the intervention? During? Several times before, during, and after?)
- What variables in quantitative research will be studied; what themes in qualitative research
- How data will be collected

- What methods will be used to analyze data and how, exactly, the research questions will be answered
- What steps will be taken to ensure confidence that the observed differences, relationships, or patterns in outcomes resulted from the intervention and not some other factor

In addition, confirmatory quantitative research requires that the expected relationships among variables be specified in advance of data collection and that those hypothesized relationships be grounded in theory and past research. (Exploratory quantitative research allows the researcher to look more broadly for relationships. However, conclusions drawn from exploratory research are less convincing to critics than research in which research-derived theory and a priori-specified hypotheses are tested.)

Careful research design works to make certain that the answers to the research questions are convincing, especially to skeptics. (It is easy to convince believers.) If certain positive outcomes are associated with a reform, how confident can the skeptic be that those outcomes were the result of some component of the reform and not some outside factor or some external event that probably would have taken place with or without the reform? Experimental design allows the most confidence that the intervention *caused* the observed results. At the same time, experimental design is unnatural by definition, and inappropriate for observing phenomena in their natural settings.

The true randomized experiment is regarded as providing the strongest evidence for a true effect, for it rules out competing explanations for observed differences in outcomes between experimental and control groups. As such, true experiments are the classical ideal in traditional research. Experiments address most of the problems raised above. Randomized experiments are used to test the efficacy and safety of new drug treatments, for example, for the confidence they provide. The essential requirement for a true experiment is that individuals/sites are selected in the same way and then randomly assigned before treatment to experimental (or treatment) and control groups. The two groups are then typically measured on the outcome and other relevant characteristics before treatment, sometimes several times to ensure "stability" of pretreatment conditions. The treatment is then administered to the treatment group, but not the control group. Finally, the outcome is measured again after treatment (and sometimes during) and the results compared statistically, to see if the groups differ, on average, and to a large enough extent to conclude that the treatment was the cause. Random assignment and a large enough sample size provide confidence that the only systematic difference between the two groups is the treatment/intervention.

Classical experimental design is of very little use in examining major reform efforts, for it is difficult, and possible unethical, to assign individuals or sites to treatment/experimental and control groups. Such control is impossible in most reforms, which take place with naturally occurring groups, whose composition is rarely random, and which is often related to the outcome. Indeed, the experimental control that provides confidence in attributing causality creates an artificiality that is of limited use in modeling the effects of reform in real-world settings. In such cases, however, it is still useful to try to identify control groups that are as similar as possible to the groups experiencing the intervention, especially in ways that are expected to affect the outcome. It is useful to measure important characteristics of the members of two groups, when possible, as well as the status of the outcome before and after intervention for both treatment and control groups.

In cases where secondary data are available for comparable groups exposed and not exposed to the "treatment," random samples can be drawn to simulate random assignment, and statistical controls used to make statistical adjustment.

In fact, in most cases of research on education reform, it is necessary to use the best design possible, and then employ *statistical controls* to adjust for differences across groups that are not attributable to the intervention or reform. For example, one might want to compare the effectiveness of school lunches versus school breakfasts on children's growth. Unfortunately, let us say, the program has already begun (thus ruling our random assignment), and pupils receiving breakfast are in grade 2, while the pupils receiving lunch are in grade 5. Because of developmental differences by age, it would make little sense to compare outcomes directly. Instead, the researcher would want to control for these differences, perhaps with an initial height-for-weight score, or perhaps through some other measure. Similarly, if one wanted to compare the effects of an instructional program on high- and low-income children's learning achievement, it would be wise to control for initial achievement, as substantial research suggests that achievement is highly correlated with income and other measures of family socio-economic status. Without statistical control, it would be difficult to distinguish the effects of the program from the "prior effects" of family income. The weakness with using statistical control is that it is effective only to the extent that the necessary variables are known, measurable, and well-measured. In the real world, these conditions are not as common as one might wish.

Education reforms may be best examined as "natural experiments," in which thoughtful measurement of relevant variables allows the researcher to make a convincing if not airtight case for the observed effects. Whatever the design taken, the best quantitative researchers plan as much of the research as possible at the outset, identifying data and naming variables, specifying hypotheses, and detailing data collection and analytic procedures. In this way, quantitative research seeks truth by extensive background preparation and adherence to rigorous procedures.

It is useful to understand possible challenges to conclusions drawn on the basis of less ideal research designs. In fact, we would argue the importance of understanding the strengths and weaknesses of all research designs. Table 9.1 summarizes some of the questions that arise when using less than ideal research designs.

Other factors that may falsely account for improved outcomes include:

- *Selection*—program recipients were different from others from the beginning, therefore making it difficult to attribute differences in outcomes to the intervention or the initial differences. This is a common problem with examining school effects, because children

Table 9.1   Questions Arising from (Less Than Ideal) Research Design

Research design	Disadvantages/Issues or questions that arise	Ways to improve credibility
	Non-informational designs	
Reliance on custom, habit, tradition	No evidence that custom, etc. is most effective/ efficient; Does it meet current conditions?	Research systematically
Reliance on preferences/ practices of one's "own" people	No evidence of effective- ness, efficiency, etc.	Research systematically
Reliance on hierarchy	No evidence of greater effectiveness/efficiency; Gives more weight to power/position than to other values	Research systematically
	Subjective designs	
Self evaluation (by staff, or beneficiaries)	Valuable information from people who know program from ground level. But questions arise: Does their "stake" bias them toward positive results? Can they see the program clearly and objectively? Do their goals correspond to pro- gram goals? Can they see the "big picture"?	Use data obtained but sup- plement and verify with other viewpoints and more objective means
Expert judgment, connois- seur	Benefits of expertise and knowledge; but open to questions about objectivity and bias, even if informed	Multiple experts; May be better at process than at outcomes (Weiss)
One-group designs—one program/reform, no comparison groups		
After Only—outcomes measured only after inter- vention	Difficult to know if there was any positive change in outcome	More data (before-during- after or before-during- during-after); Dose- response (compares some individuals/sites, who get more of the dose with oth- ers, who get less); Time series (before-before- during-during-after-after); Add comparison groups as similar as possible to group receiving treatment

Table 9.1   (Continued)

Research design	Advantages/Issues or questions that arise	Ways to improve credibility
One-group designs—one program/reform, no comparison groups		
Outcomes measured before and after	Outside events or natural maturation may have caused changes in outcome, not the intervention	More data (before-during-after or before-during-during-after); Dose-response (compares some individuals/sites, who get more of the dose with others, who get less); Time series (before-before-during-during-after-after); Add comparison groups as similar as possible to group receiving treatment
Time series (gives confidence in stability of status before and status after intervention, may show growth during intervention)	Outside events may have caused the change	Add comparison groups
Comparison-Group Designs (control groups if randomly selected and randomly assigned to treatment and control groups; comparison groups if logically selected or matched on important characteristics, etc.)		
After only with comparison group	Difficult to know whether observed differences were pre-existing or were effect of reform or program	Measure outcomes before and after; see if groups are similar in other characteristics
Before and after with comparison group	Are comparison groups really same as treatment groups? Is enough known about causality to identify factors to match groups? (Maybe outcomes are caused in part by other factors that differ between groups); Maybe some outside events caused the observed differences	Use best controls and matching possible; Use several comparison groups; See if groups are similar in other characteristics; Use statistical controls; Compare multiple time series (to see if outside events affected one group and not others)
Multiple time series	Was it something else that caused any observed differences in outcomes?	

who attend some schools are different, in unmeasured but important ways, from children who attend others.

- *Attrition*—those who leave one group are different than those who
  leave another; or those who leave are different than those who stay
  (almost by definition); what was a representative group at the outset is no longer representative of the larger population one wants
  to understand.

- *Outside effects*—those in comparison and control groups may have
  been exposed to different external events that affected the outcomes, thereby making it difficult to know whether observed differences were a result of the intervention or the external events.

- *Maturation*—many natural processes involve development;
  observed differences may be a result of growth rather than the
  intervention.

- *Testing*—those who take a pretest may learn from the pretest as
  well as or instead of the treatment.

- *Instrumentation*—use of different instruments to measure outcomes before and after treatment make it difficult to know whether
  observed differences are a result of the treatment or of different
  instruments.

Qualitative researchers, for their part, tend to approach their subject
more loosely, by design. They do less advance planning, believing that
complex situations and people are better understood with fewer preconceptions and prior specification of research strategies. Qualitative
design is sometimes described as "emergent," evolving in response to
insights and questions that emerge during the process of research. If the
researcher knew enough to specify procedures, a qualitative researcher
might argue, he or she would not need to do the research. The point of
research is to find out what is not known and to generate new theory,
and to do that, an open mind is essential.

While there are many different kinds of qualitative research, qualitative approaches tend to share certain characteristics and assumptions.
They tend to observe people and interactions in natural settings. Sites
are analyzed holistically rather than through isolation and control.
Qualitative researchers try not to anticipate what they will find, but

they do seek to identify as clearly as possible at the outset the preconceptions they have about their research. Speaking of "the researcher as the instrument," qualitative researchers may try to identify with respondents, so as to better capture and portray their view of the world, as contrasted with quantitative researchers, who work to maintain detachment and objectivity. Qualitative research often involves developing a relationship between researcher and researched.

Still, good qualitative research does not involve simply hanging out and writing about whatever comes to mind. The best qualitative research gives careful thought to design: specifying the researcher's own preconceptions, carefully selecting those who will be studied, explicating hypotheses from the data and systematically testing them with new information, nurturing relationships with informants, and so forth. The essential trick in qualitative research, it seems to us, is to accurately see what is being observed from the perspective of those being observed, and to avoid too easy confirmation of the researcher's preconceptions. A colleague refers to this last approach as "exampling," whereby a researcher uses qualitative research to find "examples" of his/her hypotheses rather than seeking or even seeing contrary evidence. For this reason, some qualitative researchers suggest that researchers actively seek disconfirming evidence for their beliefs. Like quantitative research, qualitative research design must specify who will be examined, what themes and when, as well as what methods and instruments will be used for data collection, how data will be analyzed and the research questions answered, and what steps will be taken to ensure confidence in findings.

Data Collection

Data collection, of course, is closely related to research design. One of the critical early tasks facing evaluators is operationalizing reform concepts into concrete measures. Data may be obtained from multiple sources and through many means, including surveys; formal, informal, structured, semistructured, and open-ended interviews; observation; participant observation; mapping; document review; examination of existing records; experiments; polls; questionnaires; tests; and so forth.

Data may be obtained from:

- individuals served or affected by the reform—their knowledge, attitudes, skills, behavior, values, etc.
- organizations involved in or affected by the reform—processes, or outputs
- systems—characteristics of systems, levels and distribution and changes in desirable characteristics, etc.
- institutions and societies—national and international statistics

Quantitative data tend to be numerical, ideally interval or ratio in scale so that meaningful mathematical calculations can be carried out on them. Quantitative data are generally collected using standard instruments, whether from observations, interviews, records, or surveys. The same information is collected from each individual/site in the same way so that observations are as comparable as possible. Data collection is much easier when well-designed surveys contain existing data, or when established, well-developed instruments are available for use. Development of valid, reliable data collection instruments is a major undertaking, and the decision to do so should be balanced with assessments of the kind and quality of available data. All data have their potential limitations. Existing data may be of poor quality, especially, for example, if drawing on school records from many sites, where those who collect and report data, teachers and principals, have little training and possibly little incentive to be perfectly accurate. Self-report data are subject to the biases of individuals reporting. Observed data may be the best, but are subject to the limitations of observers. All data need to be cleaned and, where possible, checked.

In quantitative analysis, it is often useful to think in terms of categories of variables:

- *Inputs*—elements necessary to attaining outcomes, for example, teachers (in a school system), textbooks, supervisory visits
- *Controls*—factors that affect the outcome but cannot be changed, only controlled, through statistical or by design, for example, sex, age, first language
- *Processes*—indicators of activities or program processes necessary for inputs to lead to outcomes, for example, supervisory visits, teacher evaluations, continuous assessment, teacher training

- *Intermediate Outcomes*—measures of intermediate internal processes, generally consequences of program activities; necessary interim steps to achieving the larger, longer-term outcomes, for example, achievement gains, in a reform aiming ultimately to increase national competitiveness
- *Outcomes*—measures of what it is the reform is trying to maximize, for example, achievement test scores, better attitudes, skills in a certain domain, and so forth, higher levels of human capital
- *Unintended Outcomes*—indicators of unplanned consequences of reform, positive and often negative, side effects, spillovers, spinoffs, for example, increased differences between high and low performers in a rapidly improving education system.

Such a scheme allows for a visual representation of program theory: inputs are applied through program processes to intermediate outcomes, independently of controls, hopefully leading to desired longer-term outcomes as well as unintended consequences. Fleshed out in detail, such a scheme permits tracking of implementation, reporting on achievement of intermediate outcomes, and testing of program theory.

The characteristics of qualitative data are much less well mapped, depending primarily on the understandings and approaches of the researcher to the phenomenon being observed. In contrast, quantitative data are intended to be as standardized as possible—a different researcher using the same procedures should come up with the same results. However, qualitative research gains most of its value from the *particular* insight of the researcher, the particular *relationship* s/he develops with the object of research, what might be called the authenticity of the particular. Qualitative data are not intended to be standard and replicable so much as uniquely true and insightful. Like quantitative data, qualitative data may be collected using a variety of techniques, ranging from multiyear ethnographic studies to short focus group interviews, document review, and short, open-ended questions.

Perhaps to a greater extent than for quantitative researchers, qualitative researchers must go to great lengths to establish the validity and reliability of their measures, and the precise procedures by which research and analysis was carried out. This intent is not to demonstrate the data as independently verifiable and replicable, but as credible, well-documented, and authentic. The detailing of procedures of data collection and analysis helps establish confidence in the credibility of the findings. Qualitative research, to a much greater extent than quantitative research, relies on an iterative process of question posing, data collection, analysis, more data collection and reformulation of questions, analysis, and so forth. (Quantitative approaches tend to a more sequential strategy: formulation of questions and design, then collection of data, followed by analysis, interpretation and reporting, then proposals for next steps). Because of the emergent nature of qualitative research, it is often difficult for researchers to know when they have gathered sufficient data. One guideline is that data are sufficient when most of the new the researcher encounters has been seen before, when she or he has largely exhausted new findings.

Sampling

Rarely is it possible to examine an entire population, even on a limited number of measures. As a result, it is almost always necessary to select some members/sites to be observed, interviewed, tested, and so forth. Not surprisingly, qualitative and quantitative research approach sampling differently. Quantitative research tends to rely on random sampling (also known as probability sampling), which selects subjects according to chance, and thus minimizing systematic bias. Rigorous procedures are used to exclude bias. The idea is to select a sample that represents the entire population, so that results from statistical analysis of sample data can be inferred to the whole. Generalizability is the goal. A simple random sample often uses a sampling frame, a listing of all individuals or units in the population, from which individuals, or cases, are selected using a random selection procedure.

Often in the case of evaluation of large-scale efforts, a random sample is impossible due to time and cost constraints. A simple random sample, for example, is likely to draw one individual from one location, while the next closest individual may be a substantial distance. Collecting data on all such individuals would not be feasible. In such cases, researchers often use a cluster sample, by which larger units such as schools or communities are randomly selected. Then individuals are selected from among the members of those communities or schools.

Another problem with simple random samples is that they are likely to underrepresent small (but often important) subgroups in the population. A sample of 300 that contains two individuals of a certain ethnic group about which there is policy interest is unlikely to be very useful in understanding the impact of an intervention on that ethnic group. Stratified random sampling is used to ensure that data are collected on sufficient numbers for particular subgroups. Thus, for example, a stratified random sample might randomly select members from five strata, each corresponding to an ethnic group of interest. The overall statistics would be weighted to account for the overrepresentation of some groups in the sample.

Qualitative researchers tend to use purposive sampling, by which the researcher selects particular cases for particular reasons. Purposive sampling is useful when one wants to understand unusual, or particular, rather than average cases, if, for example, one wanted to understand the effects of a reform on the most isolated schools in a country. Qualitative researchers use a variety of sampling methods, including snowball sampling, in which one conducts one observation, then asks for the next, and so forth; ideal case sampling, in which the best (or worst) example of a phenomenon is studied to see what makes it so good (or bad). Patton (2002), for example, lists 14 types of purposive sampling. Again, with qualitative research, the purposes are both less codified in general and less aimed at generalizing to others than in understanding the group in front of the researcher.

Participation and Dissemination

As discussed above, the evaluation plan will need to be explicit about participation: Who will participate? What groups will not participate? What aspects of the evaluation will various groups be involved in? How are the roles defined and limited? How much authority can and should be ceded to different groups, and how much should the evaluator or others maintain? What is the timing and manner of input from different groups? How can disagreements be resolved?

A similar set of questions will need answers for dissemination of results. In addition to the report, what materials will be prepared? How will they be distributed and to whom? What other means of dissemination will be used? To what extent is advocacy useful or necessary? What strategies are most appropriate and likely to work? How does dissemination fit into the larger strategy for organizational learning and bringing about change necessary for reform?

In these ways, then, the completed evaluation plan will discuss the methodology, design, sources of data, sampling, instruments, measures of different types, as well as a listing of research questions and a description of how they will be answered, and the basis for confidence in the answers. It may also be useful to organize a pilot phase to test instruments, procedures, and data collection. The evaluation plan will need to discuss logistical details such as the location of sites, timing of data collection, training of assistants, and so forth. To the extent that the evaluation is participatory, opportunities and strategies for participation will have to be structured into the plan. We have also suggested that dissemination, even advocacy, be structured into the planning of evaluation, rather than tacked on or conceptualized at the end, as they often are.

Step 4: Collection, Analysis, and Interpretation of Data

We do not attempt to replicate the work of numerous fine technical books that discuss data collection, analysis, and interpretation. However, we will assert that it is useful for policy makers, advocates, and other stakeholders to bring a sufficient understanding of the language, methods, and conventions of formal research to understand the technical rationale for researchers' conclusions as well as the conclusions themselves. Such an understanding will enable consumers of research to be critical about the findings and ways in which they were reached.

Step 5: Communication of Findings and Steps to Promote Utilization of Results and Organizational Learning

Regardless of the rigor of research, in the context of the reform, evaluation is only as good as its use. The record, as suggested throughout this book, is not good. Utilization surveys suggest that few evaluations are widely read, and relatively little organizational learning results from them. We would suggest two reasons for this state of affairs.

Neither Organizations nor People Learn Much from Reports

Evaluations typically end up as reports, read by a few people, skimmed by a few more, but digested by relatively few, often very few of those in positions to make change and quite probably none of the final "beneficiaries" of the reform/program. A report is useful for bringing together the evaluation and providing a permanent and systematic record of what was found. However, unless it arouses political energy, which is often mobilized in opposition to issues of concern, rather than support, a report is not a very good way of bringing about change. Evidence and argumentation are rarely sufficient to spark organizational change (Porter, 1997; Reimers & McGinn, 1997).

Most people, policy makers included, learn most of what they know and believe through interpersonal relationships, in particular through conversation (Weiss, 1998). Reports alone have little impact unless they are used:

- to confirm strongly-held beliefs;
- to support policies/programs an individual/organization is pre-inclined to support;
- to defend or discredit a program an individual or group is concerned with; or
- to raise a credible threat.

Also, except in unusual cases of great political momentum, incremental changes are more easily implemented than major shifts in organization and philosophy.

Participatory approaches may increase the use of evaluation findings. Research utilization can be increased by involving practitioners in the research process itself (Weiss, 1998), when researchers:

- include potential users in the research process of carrying it out—defining questions, responding to early results, helping interpret data;
- listen to practitioners—soliciting the ideas and opinions of practitioners and listening with respect;
- sustain interaction with practitioners throughout the research proc-

ess and beyond (to include the time when practitioners must apply findings to their organization and context).

It Takes More Than a Correct or Good Idea to Change an Organization

We have asserted that organizations are quite resistant to change. Let us briefly think through some of the barriers to adoption of a new idea. For a change to be worth the political and organizational cost, funding must be secured. The problem solved must assume greater importance than the many other problems for attention. The benefit must be greater than the cost of upsetting those invested in the old ways. The new way must be politically possible to bring about. A careful political strategizing may be useful in bringing about change.

The effort involves three steps:

- raising awareness of the "problems" and the "solutions" (to use Porter and Hick's concepts);
- increasing the value of stakeholders' stake in the problems and solutions, personally, interpersonally, and over time; and
- generating political energy.

Any of these steps can be initiated at any stage. We would argue that these steps are generally better undertaken during the process of evaluation rather than afterwards.

Step 6: New Planning–Implementation–Evaluation Cycle

The final step in reform begins a new cycle of planning, implementation, and evaluation, hopefully informed in substantive, organizational, and political terms by the experiences of reform.

SUMMARY: CONTINUING THE LEARNING CYCLE

This chapter has discussed a common process for evaluation along with a number of considerations and complications of the evaluation process. Two types of evaluation have been considered, formative and summative. Formative evaluation looks at the policy or program during implementation to assess the extent to which it is achieving its planned activities and objectives. Formative evaluation goes beyond project monitoring to include an evaluative component in relation to project objectives. Summative evaluation is carried out at the end of a project, program, or policy, at a point when it is possible to step back and assess effects. Evaluation may be focused on the extent to which a project or policy has attained its objectives, or it may cast a broader look at the wider effects, intended or not. Ideally in theory but unusually in practice, the results of evaluation are used to promote organizational learning and the institutionalization of good practice.

NOTES

1. The theory and practice of evaluation have developed through assessments of programs, projects, and, to a lesser extent, policies. The use of evaluation in the context of a package of programs, projects, and policies is consistent in tone with much of evaluation research, but much less frequently discussed. Throughout this discussion, we use reform, program, and intervention as the focus of evaluation.

2. Guba and Lincoln would likely disagree with this statement. For a robust, compelling, and different approach to evaluation, see their *Fourth Generation Evaluation*, 1989.

3. There are a number of different formulations of the evaluation process, many, though not all, similar to the material synthesized here.

4. Much of the discussion in this section is organized into the broad categories of quantitative and qualitative research. This organization permits discussion of a range of options in a relatively concise way. It runs the risk of portraying the two general approaches as more monolithic and necessarily oppositional than they may be in actuality. In fact, there are many differences within the broad approaches, and many similarities between them.

Conclusion

This book has sought to furnish a framework for teaching and thinking about planning processes in the development of education systems. We have located current thinking about education reform at a transitional phase in a history of approaches to education planning and reform. Over time, the approach to change (or at least the rationale) has shifted from one which predominantly exported metropolitan models of education (though metropolitan approaches remain highly, often less visibly influential), to state-led strategies of reform, to decentralized models of reform, including both market-oriented, "demand-side" strategies as well as bottom-up, community-based approaches to change. Interestingly, parallel to these more recent decentralized approaches has arisen a sectoral approach to education reform, an approach that is much more encompassing in its scope and requirements. In addition, school- and classroom-based research has elaborated a full range of characteristics of "effective schools."

Thus, on the one hand, we have a pretty good idea of the *elements that seem necessary* for high-quality education. Sufficient funding, for an obvious example, is necessary for schools to function effectively. Teachers must be paid well enough to live, there must be textbooks available of sufficient quality, and so forth.[1] On the other hand, we have argued, we know with very little certainty *what is sufficient* to produce system-wide improvements in learning. Provision of textbooks or increases in teacher pay, however necessary, do not seem to be sufficient, in many cases, to lead to improvements in student learning. Moreover, while we know how to produce high-quality learning environments in pilot schools, we don't know how to do so on a system-wide scale. Nor do we know how top-down and bottom-up approaches to change can be synchronized, to bring about and institutionalize needed changes in education systems, to produce high levels of learning, on an ongoing basis, in the multiple and diverse contexts in which change must take place. Instead of useful experimental blends that synthesize the wisdom of different approaches, top-down and bottom-up, for example, we find that the discourse tends to speak to its own adherents.

This book has attempted to inscribe a balance, a middle ground between one-size-fits-all and every case is different. We have attempted to do this in three ways: first, by seeing education reform in terms of a multiple but finite number of patterns. A finite multiplicity of patterns suggests both options and regularities, both of which are justified, we feel, by the data. Secondly, we have emphasized the need to think about education change in the contexts of its implementation and institution-alization as well as that of planning and policy formation. Doing so, we believe, goes a substantial way toward bringing a bottom-up perspective to central initiatives. Finally, we have discussed the policy process not in terms of prescription, but in terms of options, at each "stage," for organizing participation and information. The specification of options serves two purposes. First, it suggests alternate ways in which a given policy process can be carried out. Secondly, it highlights the idea that any given process represents a choice, conscious or not, not a universally correct or necessarily scientific way of doing things.

This is not to suggest that all choices are equally valid and appro-priate for a particular situation, but that validity and appropriateness depend, in substantial part, on who one is and where one stands. Start-ing from such a premise, the empirically appropriate (and democratic) way to proceed is not to privilege the values and wisdom of a particular stance, even one based on the best available science, but to develop the capacity of the range of stakeholders to debate, in an informed way, the merits of different approaches, what our colleagues call "informed dialogue" (Reimers & McGinn, 1997). This too, of course, is a choice.

A substantial number of countries may fail, it appears, to reach the EFA targets for 2015 set at Dakar at the turn of the century, in 2000. Unfortunately, it is beyond the scope of this project to link empirically, even theoretically in any precise way, the assertions of process and context made here with the outcomes described in chapter 4. Given the state of cross-national data, it would be difficult, likely impossible at this point, to demonstrate such a connection systematically. And so we continue, as we have accused others of doing, to propose reform on the basis of belief, not evidence. Still and all, we would argue, these are the best beliefs we've got at hand at present. Further, by describing the arc of possible approaches rather than a single one best way, we, like all potential science, offer the possibility of experimenting the way into truth.

We believe that the trends of increasing expectations for education systems; more constrained finance; and the multiplication of education actors, "partners," stakeholders, and clients will likely continue into the foreseeable future. Under such conditions, none of the existing approaches to education reform really works. Until a new paradigm emerges—and we believe it will emerge in practice not from the pen strokes of academics (though academics may luckily chronicle its emergence and will certainly document it well after the fact)—the best reform is likely to emerge from a context-sensitive picking and choosing from existing practice, aware always of the limitations of past approaches.

We have argued that one cannot plan reform, for the outcome of a reform process cannot be known in advance. However, one can, and we would argue should, *plan for reform.* Our approach suggests that the policies and planning process represent but one part of the reform process:

Reform = Context + Process + Policies & Planning + Implementation + Evaluation + Institutionalization & Organizational Learning

Here, we attempt to sum up.

Education systems being institutions, reform is an institutional process. Made up of groups of people, fraught with politics and political economy, steeped in culture, history, and rules of the game, education systems bring to reform a great deal of what is colloquially referred to among individuals of a certain age as "baggage." Current efforts are understood in light of the history of the system, whether conscious or not. Education systems differ from each other in profound ways, but there are patterns to these differences, many of which can be traced back to colonial models of education exported from metropolitan centers to peripheral locales and, there, internalized. Once a pattern is institutionalized, systems tend to honor that pattern, working to close the error or gap between observation and the internalized ideal. One way of seeing reform is a more or less permanent change in institutionalized patterns, deep change in Fullan's (1999) words. Systems do not change direction on a dime; they are not blank slates. New initiatives are understood in the phenomenological context of the institution, where the intended meaning may vary considerably from its original intent. As we have repeatedly if not correctly claimed, all implementation is local.

Education systems have choices, and *their choices are constrained by history, internal and external context.* Our examination of the history of dominant education systems, the systems established and influenced by the colonial systems, and the current "performance" of education systems suggests to us that systems are neither free to do what they decide nor determined by history and context. Policy decisions seem to make a difference in the performance of countries with similar starting points. Perhaps a finer understanding of context would reveal the factors that would perfectly predict outcomes. Our experience, and belief, suggests otherwise, that most countries, while tightly constrained, have more or less policy space in which to maneuver. At the same time, it would be misleading to assume that any country can adopt any policy whenever it wants—history, politics, institutions, and culture—internally, and the global economy and the ongoing dominance of some countries and their ideas suggests otherwise.

We don't really know how to improve education systems reliably. Our approaches to change are profoundly nonempirical. A review of broad historical approaches to change in education systems suggests that we actually know very little about how to promote reform on a systemic basis. New approaches or paradigms of the reform process tend to arise out of dissatisfaction with the shortcomings of previous paradigms. Community- and school-based approaches to reform, for example, tend to focus on the lack of penetration of centrally initiated approaches into local contexts. In doing so, they have developed a number of locally appropriate models of education. Most, however, have failed to solve the problems of scale and sustainability. Existing approaches to change are profoundly reactive, and generally prescientific, grounded in faith rather than evidence. Existing theoretical approaches to planning and policy tend to deal well with part, but not the whole, of the education problem. Ad hoc approaches to planning and policy are often based, it would seem, on what can sensibly be done, not on what should be done to address the problem in its complexity—the problem of necessary rather than sufficient steps. Not that existing efforts are necessarily ill-intended but they, like all current efforts, are incompletely informed by current theory. We just don't know.

We know enough to start reform (but not to finish it). At the same time, we know a great deal of what needs to be done. Structured as a process of the right kind, reform can acquire added dimensions as it goes, if the reform is able to maintain a focus on original or new energizing goals, maintain its political support, and continue to provide solutions perceived as addressing problems considered worth solving.

Planning and policy-making, we believe, should be contextual. Planning does not always take *context* into account: first of all, planning has tended to focus on the context of planning and policy formulation but not that of implementation or of institutionalization. As a result, perhaps, many "well-planned" initiatives are poorly implemented and/or not sustained. Planning and policy for that matter have often focused on the problems to be addressed, rather than the internal political economy of the context in which the reform is to be implemented and sustained; the external context or political economy, which influences to a greater or lesser extent the internal workings of education; or the context of the intervener, that is, the political economy of the planning and policy process itself and the agency of actors involved. Many attempts to change education systems are based in part on untested assumptions that may or may not be conscious to those who use them. Some assumptions are likely helpful in promoting change. Others are likely to lead the change agent astray. If unexamined, such assumptions tend to live long beyond their usefulness.

Planning and policy-making should result in a good process as well as a good product. The change process is best understood as recursive and indeterminative rather than as a series of sequential stages. In this context, stages models of the change *process*, while useful as a checklist of steps in rational planning, mislead if they focus the planner away from contexts of implementation and institutionalization. Stages models of change tend to lead to front-loaded plans with less attention than we find appropriate for most education change processes to the structuring of participation and evaluation of evidence over time in a legitimate and rigorous manner. The planner, we would argue, should focus as much on developing a good process for the reform as s/he does on developing a good plan. Given the time that reform takes, and the inevitability of politics, ongoing intelligence is as important as initial intelligence in the process of reform.

Planning and policy-making should be organized for implementation and eventual institutionalization. Due to their oft-cited loose coupling, education systems are arguably better planned using backwards rather than or at least in addition to forward mapping. From one perspective, the point of implementation of education reforms is the classroom. From this perspective, everything else in the system supports, or should support, classroom instruction. We have argued that a certain empathy with implementers and sustainers is necessary for effective policy-making and planning.

The best policy-making and planning results in organizational learning. As discussed, organizations tend not to question the assumptions that guide their activity. We have argued that an evaluation perspective serves not only to assess the effects of an intervention but also to assess unintended effects, to check program theory, to test out new program hypotheses, to see error as a possible mistake, or a possible innovation, and to seek ways of uncovering the governing variables and assumptions of an institution.

Volume I has discussed contexts and processes of policy-making for reform. Volume II will discuss options for reform in terms of different goals and by subsector of the system. Some goals are frequently discussed in terms of planning and policy, for example, access, learning, equity. Others appear less commonly, for example, education for social cohesion, education for critical thinking, and education for employment and social engagement, etc. Being socialized by EFA, we speak to the concerns of basic education of course, but we also devote time to subsectors of education less commonly discussed in the same texts—secondary education, nonformal education, early childhood and higher education.

NOTES

1. This reliance on low-cost strategies is understandable, as national treasuries are increasingly stretched by multiple demands, some internal—for example, increasing demand for places and for higher quality at all levels of education; challenges of providing education in an HIV-afflicted population. Other demands are external, such as severe debt burdens or structural adjustment programs that, however necessary they may be, result in cutbacks in education spending. As a result, it is difficult to see whether it is the reform strategies that didn't work, whether reforms were simply funded at levels where they never really had a chance, or whether there hasn't been enough time to reap the results.

References

Adams, D. (1993). Defining educational quality. *Educational Planning 9*, 3–18.

Adams, D. (2000, December). Extending educational planning discourse: A new strategic planning model. *Asia Pacific Education Review.*

Allison, G. (1971). *Essence of decision: Explaining the Cuban missile crisis.* Boston: Little, Brown.

Amano, I. (1990). *Education and examination in modern Japan* (William K. Cummings & Fumiko Cummings, Trans.). Tokyo: University of Tokyo Press.

Archer, M. (1977). *Social origins of educational systems.* Beverly Hills, CA: Sage.

Argyris, C., & Schön, D. (1978). *Organizational learning: A theory of action perspective.* Reading, MA: Addison Wesley.

AusAID. *AusGUIDE.* Retrieved July 30, 2004, from www.ausaid.gov.au/ausguide/ausguidelines/1-3.cfm.

Baker, D., Goesling, B., & Letendre, G. K. (2002). Socioeconomic status, school quality, and national economic development: A cross-national analysis of the "Heyneman-Loxley Effect" on mathematics and science achievement. *Comparative Education Review 46*, 291–312.

Beeby, C. E. (1961). *The quality of education.* Cambridge, MA: Harvard University Press.

Bellah, R. N. (1975). *The broken covenant: American civil religion in time of trial.* New York: Seabury Press.

Benavot, A., & Riddle, P. (1988). The expansion of primary education, 1870–1940: Trends and issues. *Sociology of Education 61*, 191–210.

Bolman, L., & Deal, T. (1997). *Reframing organizations: Artistry, choice, and leadership.* San Francisco: Jossey-Bass.

Bruns, B., Mingat, A., & Rakotomalala, R. (2003). *A chance for every child: Achieving universal primary education by 2015.* Washington, DC: World Bank.

Burns, J. M. (2003). *Transforming leadership: A new pursuit of happiness.* New York: Atlantic Monthly Press.

Byrne, D. (1998). *Complexity theory and the social sciences.* London: Routledge.

Capper, J. (1996). *Testing to learn—learning to test.* Newark, DE: International Reading Association.

Carnoy, M., & J. Samoff, with Burris, M. A., Johnston, A., & Torres, C. A. (1990). *Education and social transition in the Third World.* Princeton, NJ: Princeton University Press.

Chabbott, C. (2003). *Constructing education for development: International organizations and education for all.* London: Routledge-Falmer.

Chapman, D., & Walberg, H. J. (Eds.). (1992). *International perspectives on educational productivity.* Greenwich, CT: JAI Press.

Christensen, P., Dounkoure, A. B., Laugham, P., Moreau, T., Moulton, J., Muskin, J., & Welmond, M. (1997). *Kids, schools, & learning: African success stories, A retrospective study of USAID support to basic education in sub-Saharan Africa* (SD Technical Paper No. 56). Washington, DC: USAID.

Coleman, J. S., Campbell, E. Q., Hobson, C. J., McPartland, J., Mood, A. M., Weinfeld, F. D., & York, R. L. (1966). *Equality of educational opportunity.* Washington, DC: U.S. Government Printing Office.

Colletta, N., & Cullen, M. (2000). *Violent conflict and the transformation of social capital: Lessons from Cambodia, Rwanda, and Somalia.* Washington, DC: World Bank.

Crouch, L., & Healey, H. (1997). *Education reform support. Vol. 1–6* (ABEL Technical Paper No. 1, SD Publication Series, Paper No. 47). Washington, DC: Office of Sustainable Development, Bureau for Africa, U.S. Agency for International Development.

Cuadra, E. (1990). *Indicators of student flow rates in Honduras: An assessment of an alternative methodology* (Bridges Report Series No. 6). Cambridge, MA: Harvard Institute of International Development.

Cuban, L. (1988). A fundamental puzzle of school reform. *Phi Delta Kappan 69,* 341–344.

Cummings, W. K. (2003). *The institutions of education.* Oxford: Symposium Books.

Cummings, W. K., & Altbach, P. G. (Eds.). (1997). *The challenge of East Asian education: Implications for America.* Albany: State University of New York Press.

Cummings, W. K., & Riddell, A. (1992). Alternative policies for the finance, control and delivery of basic education. *International Educational Research 21*, 751–776.

Current Issues in Comparative Education (Vol. 6, No. 2: Participatory Development: A Promise Revisited).

Davis, R. (1980). *Models and methods in systematic planning of education.* Cambridge, MA: Center for Studies in Education and Development, Harvard University.

Eisner, E. (1991). *The enlightened eye: Qualitative inquiry and the enhancement of educational practice.* New York: Macmillan.

Elmore, R. (1982). Backward mapping: implementation research and policy decisions. In W. Williams (Ed.), *Studying implementation: Methodological and administrative issues* (pp. 18–35). Chatham, NJ: Chatham House.

Elmore, R. (1996). Getting to scale with good educational practice. *Harvard Educational Review 66*(1), 1–26.

Evans, D. (Ed). (1994). *Education policy formation in Africa: A comparative study of five countries* (ARTS Technical Paper No. 12). Washington, DC: USAID, Bureau for Africa.

Fergany, N. (1991). *Final report of the labour information system project, general features of employment in the domestic economy.* Cairo: CAPMAS.

Freire, P. (1993). *Pedagogy of the oppressed.* New York: Continuum.

Fullan, M. (1999). *Change forces: The sequel.* London: Falmer.

Fuller, B., & Rubinson, R. (1992). *The political construction of education: The state, school expansion, and economic change.* New York: Praeger.

Glass, D. (1981). *Meta-analysis in social research.* Beverly Hills, CA: Sage.

Glassman, D., & Millogo, M. (2003). *Save the Children US village schools in Mali 1992–2003: A future to quality access?* Paris: Association for the Development of Education in Africa.

Greaney, V., & Kellaghan, T. (1996). *Monitoring the learning outcomes of education systems.* Washington, DC: World Bank.

Grindle, M. S., & Thomas, J. W. (1991). *Public choices and policy change: The political economy of reform in developing countries.* Baltimore: Johns Hopkins University Press.

Guba, E., & Lincoln, Y. (1989). *Fourth generation evaluation.* Newbury Park, CA: Sage.

Guthrie, G. (1990). In defense of traditional teaching. In V. Rust (Ed.), *Teachers and teaching in the developing world* (pp. 219–234). New York: Garland.

Haddad, W. (1979). *Educational and economic effects of promotion and repetition practices.* (Staff Working Paper 319). Washington, DC: World Bank.

Haddad, W., & Demsky, T. (1994). *The dynamics of education policymaking: Case studies of Burkina Faso, Jordan, Peru, and Thailand.* Washington, DC: World Bank.

Heneveld, W., & Craig, H. (1995). *Schools count. World Bank project design and the quality of primary education in sub-Saharan Africa* (World Bank Technical Paper Number 303. Africa Technical Department Series). Washington, DC: World Bank.

Herman, J. L., Morris, L. L., & Fitz-Gibbon, C. T. (1987). *Evaluator's handbook.* Newbury Park, CA: Sage.

Howley, A., Howley, C. Johnson, J., & Williams, J. H. (forthcoming). *Thinking about schools: New theories and innovative practice.* Mahwah, NJ: Lawrence Erlbaum.

IEQ. (2002). *Pathways to quality.* Washington, DC: Improving Educational Quality Project, American Institutes of Research.

IEQ/Malawi. (2003). *Exploring factors that influence teaching and learning: Collection of selected studies using the IEQ/Malawi longitudinal data 1999–2002, Volume 2.* Washington, DC: American Institutes for Research.

Jackson, G. (2003). [Class materials . . . (my docs\gw courses\813 KeySteps)] Washington, DC: George Washington University.

Jackson, G. (2004). *Education reforms: Two centuries of lessons applied to current reform efforts.* [unpublished manuscript]. Washington, DC: George Washington University.

James, E. (1987). The public/private division of responsibility for education: An international comparison. In E. H. Haertel, T. James, & H. M. Levin (Eds.), *Comparing public and private schools* (pp. 95–127). New York: The Falmer Press.

Khaniya, T., & Williams, J. H. (2004). Necessary but not sufficient: Challenges to (implicit) theories of educational change: Reform in Nepal's primary education system. *International Journal of Educational Development 24,* 315–328.

Kingdon, J. W. (1984). *Agendas, alternatives, and public policies.* Ann Arbor: University of Michigan.

Korten, D. C. (1980). Community organization and rural development: A learning process approach. *Public Administration Review,* Sept/Oct, 480–511.

Lamberti, M. (1989). *State, society, and the elementary school in Imperial Germany.* New York: Oxford University Press.

Levin, H. M., & McEwan, P. J. (2001). *Cost-effectiveness analysis: Methods and analysis* (2nd ed.). Thousand Oaks, CA: Sage.

Lewin, K., Little, A. W., & Colclough, C. L. (1982). Adjusting to the 1980's: Taking stock of educational expenditure. *IDRC, Financing Educational Expenditure*. Ottawa: IDRC.

Lipsky, M. (1980). *Street-level bureaucracy: Dilemmas of the individual in public services*. New York: Russell Sage Foundation.

Lockheed, M. E., & Verspoor, A. M. (1991). *Improving primary education in developing countries*. Washington, DC: World Bank.

Maslow, A. (1970). *Motivation and personality* (2nd ed.). New York: Harper & Row.

McMahon, W. M. (1999). *Education and development: Measuring the social benefits*. New York: Oxford University Press.

Mehrota, S., & Buckland, P. (1998). *Managing teacher costs for access and quality* (Staff Working Paper, evaluation, policy and planning series. No. EPP-EVL-98-004). New York: UNICEF.

Meyer, J. W., & Hannan, M. T. (Eds.). (1979). *National development and the world system: Educational, economic, and political change, 1950–1970*. Chicago: University of Chicago Press

Mingat, A. (2001). *Teacher salary issues in African countries*. World Bank Africa Region, Human Development Analysis and Policy Development Support Team. Washington, DC: World Bank.

Ministry of Education (MOE). (1980). *Japan's modern educational system: A history of the first hundred years*. Tokyo: Author.

Moulton, J. K., Mundy, K., Welmond, M., & Williams, J. H. (2002). *Education reforms in sub-Saharan Africa: Paradigm lost?* Westport, CT: Greenwood.

Mueller, H. E. (1984). *Bureaucracy, education and monopoly*. Berkeley: University of California Press.

Nielsen, D., & Somerset, H. C. A. (1992). *Primary teachers in Indonesia: Supply, distribution, and professional development*. Washington, DC: World Bank.

Nielsen, H., & Cummings, W. K. (1997). *The impact of "impact": A study of Dissemination of an Innovation in six countries*. Mimeo.

Patrinos, H. A. & Ariasingam, D. L. (1997). *Decentralization of education: Demand-side financing*. Washington, DC: World Bank.

Patton, M.Q. (2002). *Qualitative research and evaluation methods* (3rd ed). Thousand Oaks, CA: Sage.

Pigozzi, M. J., & Cieutat, V. J. (1988). *Education and human resources sector assessment manual*. Tallahassee, FL: Improving the Efficiency of Educational Systems Project, Florida State University & Washington DC: Office of Education, Bureau for Science and Technology, U.S. Agency for International Development.

Porter, R. with I. Hicks. (1997). Knowledge utilization and the process of policy formation: towards a framework for action. In D. W. Chapman, L. O. Mahlck, & A. E. M. Smulders (Eds.), *From planning to action: Government initiatives for improving school-level practice* (pp. 32–67). Oxford: Pergamon Press.

Prescott-Allen, R. (2001). *The well-being of nations*. Washington, DC: Island Press.

Ravitch, D. (1983). *The troubled crusade: American education, 1945–1980*. New York: Basic Books.

Reimers, F., & McGinn, N. (1997). *Informed dialogue: Using research to shape education policy around the world*. Westport, CT: Praeger.

Reisner, E. H. (1923). *Nationalism and education since 1789: A social and political history of modern education*. New York: Macmillan.

Ringer, F. (1974). *The decline of the German Mandarins*. Cambridge, MA: Harvard University Press.

Rondinelli, D. A. (1993). *Development projects as policy experiments: An adaptive approach to development administration*. London: Routledge.

Selden, W. (1960). *Accreditation: A struggle over standards in higher education*. New York: Harper and Bros.

Senge, P. (1994). *The fifth discipline: The art and practice of the learning organization*. New York: Doubleday/Currency.

Sergiovanni, T. (2003). *Educational governance and administration* (5th ed.). Boston: Allyn and Bacon.

Shaeffer, S. (Ed.), (1992). *Collaborating for educational change: The role of teachers, parents, and the community in school improvement*. Paris: International Institute for Educational Planning.

Stecher, B., & Davis, W. A. (1987). *How to focus an evaluation*. Newbury Park, CA: Sage.

Stufflebeam, D. L., Madaus, G. F., & Kellaghan, T. (Eds.) (2000). *Evaluation models: Viewpoints on educational and human services evaluation* (2nd ed.). Boston: Kluwer.

Tietjen, K. (1999). *Community schools in Mali: A comparative cost study*. Washington DC: USAID.

UNDP. (2002). *Human development report*. New York: Oxford University Press.

UNICEF. (1994). *A survey of access to primary education and acquisition of basic literacy skills in three governorates of Egypt*. Cairo, Egypt: Author.

Warwick, D. (1982). *Bitter pills: Population policies and their implementation in eight developing countries*. Cambridge: Cambridge University Press.

Warwick, D., & Reimers, F. (1995). *Hope or despair?: Learning in Pakistan's primary schools*. Westport, CT: Praeger.

Watkins, K. (2000). *The Oxfam education report*. London: Oxfam.

Weick, K. (1976). Educational organizations as loosely coupled systems. *Administrative Science Quarterly 21*, 1–9.

Weiss, C. H. (1998). *Evaluation research: Methods for assessing program effectiveness* (2nd ed.) Upper Saddle River, NJ: Prentice Hall.

Wheatley, M. (1994). *Leadership and the new science: Learning about organization from an orderly universe*. San Francisco: Berrett-Koehler Publishers.

Wheeler, C., Radenbush, S., & Pasigna, A. (1989). *Policy initiatives to improve primary education in Thailand* (Bridges Report Series No. 5). Cambridge, MA: Harvard Institute of International Development.

Wheeler, D. (1984). *Human resource policies, economic growth, and demographic change in developing countries*. Oxford: Clarendon Press.

Williams, J. H. (1997). The diffusion of the modern school. In N. F. McGinn & W. K. Cummings (Eds.), *International handbook of education and development: Preparing schools, students, and nations for the twenty-first century* (pp. 119–136). London: Garland Press.

Williams, J. H. (2002). School quality and attainment. In C. Talbot, J. Crisp, & D. Cipollone (Eds.), *Learning for a future: Refugee education in developing countries* (pp. 85–108). Geneva: United Nations High Commission for Refugees

Windham, D. (1991, September). Indicators of educational efficiency. *Forum for Advancing Basic Education and Literacy 1*(3).

Wolf, J., with Lang, G., Mount, L. L. B., & VanBelle-Prouty, D. (1999). *Where policy hits the ground: Policy implementation processes in Malawi and Namibia* (Technical Paper No. 95). Washington DC: USAID, Bureau for Africa.

World Bank. (2004). *World development indicators*. Washington, DC: Author.

World Bank. (1993). *East Asian economic miracle*. New York: Oxford University Press.

Index

About the Authors

James H. Williams is assistant professor of international education and international affairs at The George Washington University. An international education specialist focusing on the improvement of education in developing countries and the larger social effects of formal education, Dr. Williams has worked in 18 countries and authored over 40 books, articles, and monographs in the field.

William K. Cummings is professor of international education and international affairs at The George Washington University. As policy advisor to the governments of Indonesia, Sri Lanka, and Ethiopia, Dr. Cummings has examined a wide range of policy issues in education and national development, particularly in East Asia and sub-Saharan Africa. He has worked in over 25 countries and is author of more than 150 books, articles, and monographs.